The Super Allergy Girl™

Gluten-Free, Casein-Free, Nut-Free

Allergy & Celiac

Cookbook

From A Mother Who Knows™

LISA A. LUNDY

The Super Allergy Girl™

Gluten-Free, Casein-Free, Nut-Free

Allergy & Celiac

Cookbook

From A Mother Who Knows™

www.TheSuperAllergyCookbook.com

Important Note to Readers: The author of this book is not a medical physician or medical practitioner. Readers should seek personal medical evaluations and advice from qualified, licensed health care professionals. The author and publisher of this book recommend that you consult with your primary health care provider before implementing dietary changes. Since food allergies can be fatal, and restricted diets can lead to vitamin and mineral deficiencies, it is extremely important that you receive proper individualized advice from your physician before you make changes to your diet. The author and publisher disclaim any liability directly or indirectly arising from the use of this book, any suggestions contained in this book, and from any products mentioned in it. Products mentioned in this book may change formulation and may not be free of allergens in the future. Readers must be vigilant and monitor product labels at all times.

Additionally, the author and publisher make no representation or warranty with respect to the accuracy of information contained on Web sites referenced in this book. The author and publisher have received no financial support from any products or Web sites mentioned herein. The author and publisher disclaim any liability for products mentioned in this book.

Acknowledgements

Book Editors: Diane Gregor, Linda Breitbach, Christine Schaefer

Set-up and Formatting: Randy Garrett

www.TheSuperAllergyCookbook.com

*This book is dedicated to transforming the future
of health care such that people are healthy and well,
and that health care works for all.*

Contents

How This Book Can Help You

This cookbook contains both recipes and information for beginners to advanced cooks. If you are brand new to the gluten-free, dairy-free, tree-nut and peanut-free and egg-free cooking and baking, you are most likely overwhelmed. To be overwhelmed and even frightened by the myriad of complexities is normal. The more you read and the more you practice in the kitchen; the easier it will become.

One way that this cookbook can help you is to give you new and valuable information. I would guess that most readers are not familiar with the history of food allergies even if you have been dealing with food allergies for decades. As a person with anaphylactic tree nut and coconut allergies, I have lived a life of food allergies personally, but I did not have a clue about the history of food allergies until I found references in our local medical library. A Brief History of Food Allergies, which is included in this book on page 21, gives most people room for pause and exploration depending upon their individual state of health.

The topics covered in Part One of this book include:

- The Role of Nutrition in Food Allergies
- Food Allergies in Infants and Children
- A Brief History of Food Allergies
- Special Diets & Celiac Disease
- Avoiding Common Food Allergens
- Special Ingredients & Products
- Technical Know-How for Special Cooking
- Saving Time & Money
- Where to Purchase Pasta, Flours & Other Ingredients
- Rotation Diets & Food Families
- Meal Ideas

Many people with Celiac disease develop additional food issues due to the fact that they are eating rice every single day. Many parents of children with autism who use the gluten-free, casein-free diet as a dietary intervention have also noticed additional food allergies with their children. The section on rotation diets and food families can be informative and helpful to these individuals. Because we as a family use a rotation diet, you will find recipes that are rice-free since we only eat rice every fourth day.

Saving time and money is of interest to many people and I have included ideas on how to do both on page 89. If you are new to allergies or have developed new food allergies since your initial diagnosis, you may find value in the chapter on Avoiding Common Food Allergens, as well as the chapters on Special Ingredients & Products and Technical Know-How for Special Cooking.

The number of gluten-free and dairy-free commercially available products has expanded enormously over the past eight years. This is a big bonus for those of us managing food allergies. Add to that the new food labeling law that went into effect in 2006 and life is really much easier than it was years ago.

Whatever your level of expertise, from beginner to advanced, I am sure you will find value in the information and recipes contained within these pages. One question that comes up frequently is what is my background relative to food allergies and cooking and baking.

My Expertise & Training in Food Allergies

I have a lifetime of personal experience with food allergies starting with myself and my anaphylactic allergy to nuts of any kind and coconut, and continuing with my three food allergic children. By the time I was 18-months old, I was getting allergy shots for allergies to dust, molds, grasses and trees. I had been sickly as an infant, so my father tells me, and the pediatrician directed my parents to an allergist after a long course of antibiotics produced no improvement.

The allergy shots were continued until I reached 18 years of age (nearly 16 years), when my allergist released me from treatment. It was a highly irregular circumstance to have a toddler getting allergy shots back in the early 1960's. Still today, it is highly unusual for a child under the age of five to receive traditional allergy shots. As a child I was also painfully thin – so thin that I was teased by my classmates and given a "tonic" by the family doctor to help increase my weight. Too bad I got over that problem later in life! My shots were, in my humble opinion, very effective. I have not had to take allergy medications since my release from treatment, and I have been very healthy.

What all of this means is that I have a long-standing and quite personal relationship to allergies and not just food allergies. It also means that my children received my allergy genes and were more likely to have allergies.

My first son, Luke, had food allergies from birth which I did not realize until it was time to wean him from breast milk. My second child, Noah, displayed dramatic symptoms from food allergies as an infant and by the time he was six months old I knew that wheat was a problem. Later I would find out that gluten was problematic as was dairy of any kind, eggs, tree-nuts, peanuts, soy, and several other foods. I quickly entered the world of gluten-free, dairy-free, and allergy-free cooking and baking.

Over the years, I have helped many people learn how to cook and bake gluten-free and dairy-free foods. I taught baking classes at a local kitchen store for Celiacs and parents of children with autism. And I have helped train restaurant owners in gluten-free, dairy-free, and allergen-free baking and cooking.

My paternal grandmother, Nan Lundy, taught me to bake wheat bread when I was about twelve or thirteen years old. She was an excellent baker and was known to many for her delicious treats. My grandmother made great bread, sweet rolls, cookies and she was a good teacher. My maternal grandmother, Jo Holcombe, was also an excellent cook, and shared many of her recipes with me over the years. So, I started early with my exposure to baking and cooking. My mother, Jean Holcombe Gottas, who is also a great cook, supported my kitchen adventures by getting me involved with 4-H and the wonderful cooking programs they had available during the same time frame. I began collecting family recipes at this time as it was a natural expression of learning to bake and cook. I collected recipes from family, from co-workers at Peoples National Bank when I worked there, and pretty much everywhere I went.

Some of the recipes included in this cookbook are family favorites that I have converted and altered to meet our allergy needs. Others I invented out of necessity. My role model in the gluten-free world of baking is Bette Hagman who is the author of many cookbooks and a pioneer in this arena.

I met Bette Hagman when I was newly into baking gluten-free. We got acquainted and have become friends over the years. I admire, respect, trust and like her very, very much. I highly recommend her cookbooks however they are not dairy-free, egg-free, nut-free or peanut-free. I admire Bette so much that I had *"Official Member of the Bette Hagman Fan Club"* t-shirts made up, with her permission, of course. So, Bette has been a friend, a support and an inspiration to me for several years. *Author's update: Bette Hagman passed away in 2007 after this book was complete.

My third child, Anne, was really the cause of this cookbook. She is my Super Allergy Girl™. Her list of food allergies includes milk, eggs (whites and yolks), gluten, peanuts, tree nuts, some fruits and vegetables, fish, seafood and many other foods. I was forced to create recipes to meet her expansive food allergies and this cookbook is the result. I've had to learn most of my lessons by making mistakes. I'd love to be able to contribute to you by helping you avoid the same mistakes, and for you to be able to make great foods free of your food allergens. Unfortunately, there will never be a cookbook to meet every single food allergy person's needs because we are all different in our food allergies. I wish you the very best in your efforts to make delicious foods free of the allergens that you need to avoid. I welcome feedback on this book as well as your cooking and baking questions. My goal is to help you be successful in this area.

You can e-mail me at: *Lisa@TheRoosterCrows.com*, or you can go to my website and post a question or comment on my blog. My website is: *www.TheSuperAllergyCookbook.com.* You may also write to me at:

Suite 400-257
3842 Harlem Road
Buffalo, NY 14215.

With Love,
Lisa A. Lundy

August 2007
Revised January 2010 for the 3rd Printing

Important
WARNING for FOOD ALLERGY& CELIAC Consumers
It is extremely important that you read food labels. Food manufacturers have the right to change their food product formulation at any time without notification. A food made gluten-free, egg-free, nut-free or dairy-free today, may not be gluten-free, egg-free, nut-free or dairy-free tomorrow. This warning cannot be emphasized enough. Please read your food labels on an on-going basis to be responsible and avoid serious health problems.

The Role of Nutrition in Food Allergies

It has taken me several years to understand the significant role that nutrition plays in food allergies. Specifically, the role that nutrition plays when you are on what I call a restricted diet like that of a gluten-free, dairy-free diet. Your diet is your source for nutrition and it is nutrition that fuels your health. Your body runs on intricate amino acid chains. This has long been understood by scientists and nutritionists, but not well understood by the average consumer. To quote Robert Cooke, author of <u>Dr. Folkman's War: Angiogenesis and the Struggle to Defeat Cancer</u>:

> "If amino acids are left out, or the wrong ones are put in place, a protein such as an enzyme or growth factor is made incorrectly, or not at all, and the result can be the disaster of a genetic disease, or cancer."[1]

What this quote from Robert Cooke's book refers to is the basic concept that if you do not have the proper nutrition, you will likely end up with either a genetic disease or cancer. All of this underscores the importance of nutrition. When dairy and gluten are removed from your diet that removes important sources of calcium, protein, and other important nutritional elements.

Amino acids are the building blocks of protein. When you have eaten foods that contain amino acids, they ultimately end up in your bloodstream after the digestion process is complete. In the bloodstream the amino acids combine with other amino acids to form specific proteins needed by the body. There are 22 different types of amino acids and the eight to ten that your body cannot make are called "essential amino acids". The remaining amino acids are referred to as non-essential amino acids because your body can make them if you have enough of the other essential amino acids.

---

[1] Robert Cooke, <u>Dr. Folkman's WAR: Angiogenesis and the Struggle to Defeat Cancer,</u> (New York: Random House, 2001), p. 206.

Rather than look at diet from the amino acid perspective, we typically look to the consumption of proteins to determine if enough amino acids are being eaten. A protein is considered a "complete" protein if it contains all of the essential amino acids. A protein that does not contain all of the essential amino acids is considered an "incomplete" protein. The foods that are complete proteins are meats, fish, eggs, poultry, soybeans and dairy products like milk, cheese and yogurt. Right off the bat, you can see that many of the main sources for protein are eliminated in a gluten-free and dairy-free diet. Our family has been forced to eliminate eggs, and fish as well, leaving us with meats, poultry and soy as sources of protein.

The sources of incomplete proteins include dried beans, peas, lentils, seeds, tree nuts, grains, and vegetables. It is possible for you to combine incomplete proteins together to get all of your amino acid needs met. Vegetarian meals typically combine grains and beans such as beans and rice to form complete proteins. Amino acids are only one aspect of nutrition that must be considered in a restricted diet.

Vitamins and minerals must also be considered. The most obvious missing nutrient in a gluten-free and dairy-free diet is calcium since many of the sources for calcium come from dairy products like milk, cheese and yogurt. A cup of skim milk has an estimated 306 mg of calcium in one serving. One cup of spinach (frozen and boiled) has 291 mg of calcium, which is very close. But it takes a real sense of rigor to make sure that you are getting enough calcium on a dairy-free diet. Vitamin D is closely related to calcium and is another nutritional item that could be missing in a restricted diet.

In addition to Vitamin D and calcium, other vitamins and minerals are required for proper health. Minerals are used by the human body to build tissue, help with muscle contractions, and function to help nerve reactions and blood clotting. Minerals also help with regulating the body pH and enzyme processes, release energy from food, and help conduct many other critical body functions. The human body requires about 25 different minerals to be strong and healthy. Our family gets our minerals from the foods that we eat and from nutritional supplements.

Plants are one source of minerals for humans. Plants take up minerals from the soil and when we eat the plants, we then obtain the minerals that the plants contained. Plants cannot make minerals. The minerals must be available in the soil for the plants to take up during the growing season. The soils in the U.S. have been stripped of minerals since the 1930's according to congressional documents. Organic farmers as part of the organic farming process put minerals into the soils for their plants. Therefore, if you are not eating organic fruits and vegetables it is likely that you could become deficient in minerals. Minerals can also be obtained from quality dietary supplements.

Malnutrition is defined in the dictionary as faulty or inadequate nutrition. Malnutrition affects nearly every organ in the body, and restricted diets can, without the proper medical supervision, lead to malnutrition on some level. Malabsorption is another medical condition that often goes hand in hand with malnutrition. Malabsorption is when your body does not absorb nutrients properly. This is why it is extremely important to have a medical doctor or health care provider who is familiar with food and nutrition to oversee your medical care. The mistakes that can result from simply following a restricted diet can be devastating. I know this personally from experience.

My daughter has a serious problem with malnutrition and malabsorption. I know this factually from two consecutive years of specific nutritional blood testing. She doesn't have the emaciated, third world child look, so it was extremely difficult for me to believe that she had malnutrition when the treating specialist told me this three years ago. This specialist knows a great deal about food, nutrition and restricted diets and could tell from my daughter's diet history that she would have to be malnourished, and probably had a malabsorption problem as well.

When I finally agreed to do the nutritional blood testing which I had resisted because our HMO would not financially cover it, I was stunned to see that the specialist was absolutely correct. As I began to give my daughter nutritional supplements to correct her severe malnutrition, I would come to understand that she did indeed also have a malabsorption problem. This meant that my daughter was not absorbing nutrients from her diet and the supplements. I am now in the process of correcting this problem through nutritional IV's (intravenous nutrition) because nutrition given through the blood system bypasses the absorption problem.

Unfortunately, you usually can't tell if someone has malnutrition or malabsorption by looking at them. You can if they have the emaciated look or the distended belly such as that of a third world starving child. But in America, that is not how malnutrition typically presents itself. My daughter looked healthy to us, our pediatrician, and to other people. Other than being small, she did not "look" malnourished.

In the two years since this book was originally printed, 2007 to 2009, the increased visibility of vitamin and mineral deficiencies has been dramatic. According to new research publicized in 2009, at least one in five U.S. children ages 1 to 11 don't get enough vitamin D. Food manufacturers, who typically spend thousands of dollars on consumer marketing research, are now focusing their magazine ads on the nutritional value of their foods. One food company states in their ad: "Did you know that 70% of our kids aren't getting enough calcium?" Even fast food chains are advertising menu items under so many calories. The nutritional consciousness of Americans is on the rise at a record pace, and the food manufacturers are taking notice and making changes.

Adults or children who are not feeling well, or who have other health issues would probably do well to consider looking at their nutritional status. Unfortunately the impact of a lack of nutrition in the human body does not affect people in the same way. Therefore, it would be difficult to say, if you are experiencing "X" symptoms, you probably have nutritional issues. From a mother who knows, trust me when I say that seeking out proper medical advice is well worth the investment. Malnutrition and malabsorption are not problems that you want to further complicate your life.

Since I am not a medical professional and I can't give you medical advice, I can't tell you what to do. I can tell you that our family takes liquid nutritional supplements every day. We eat better now than we ever did before, but based on my nutritional insights, I wouldn't go without the liquid nutritional supplements. They are not invasive, we don't overdo them, and it is the best proactive measure we can take. We take liquid nutritional supplements because I found resources that indicated that many tablets, pills and capsules are not absorbed by the body and end up in your sewer system.

If your physician is not knowledgeable about food and nutrition you can ask for a referral to see a registered dietitian. Registered dietitians study food and nutrition. Some registered dietitians are more familiar with gluten-free diets than others. There is a growing body of physicians who are becoming more educated on the importance of food and nutrition, so you can look for a new primary care physician if you are not satisfied with the one that you have. Your local health food store is a good resource for information and may be able to direct you to support in your community. The Internet is also a good resource for information, organizations and practitioners who are well versed in restricted diets, nutrition, and food. It is a "buyer beware" market for consumers.

You have to become educated enough to distinguish if an Internet source, or any source for that matter, is a reputable one. With the explosive growth in the gluten-free market, many new people are entering the gluten-free and allergy arena. Make sure anyone you are dealing with has science-based information. You can find out more about how to be an educated and savvy consumer on my website in one of the free downloadable tip sheets.

Emergency Planning

For people with special dietary needs I feel that it is critical to have a disaster supplies kit for emergencies. A disaster supplies kit consists of a variety of items that you might need during and after a disaster to stay safe and be more comfortable. For more than six years, we have had such a kit and I would not be without one. Here is a list of what we have assembled for our kit.

- Four bags of groceries including dry mixes for rolls, waffles, & muffins, as well as a limited supply of prepackaged gluten-free foods such as crackers, cereals, and canned foods (and a can opener!)
- Supply of bottled water
- Camping cook stove with propane canisters
- Comprehensive First Aid kit
- Camping tent
- Sleeping bags, blankets and towels
- Paper goods: toilet paper, paper towels, napkins, paper plates
- Personal care products like shampoo, toothpaste and feminine supplies
- Matches in a waterproof container
- Portable, wind-up radio
- Games, cards, or other materials to keep you occupied when there is no TV or electricty
- A large, empty cooler to load food from the freezer in the event of an evacuation
- Cash (ATM's don't work without electricity)
- A large checklist of items to be added that are not stored with our kit for practical reasons
- Extra warm clothes (we live in a cold climate)

The Red Cross is one of the organizations working to prepare consumers for natural and other disasters. You can download several helpful materials from the Red Cross website at *www.redcross.org* including a list of items to include in a disaster supplies kit as well as other ways to be prepared for unexpected events.

Food Allergies in Infants, Toddlers and Young Children

Food allergies in infants, toddlers and young children can be difficult to pinpoint and extremely frustrating to all involved. As a mother who dealt with three infants who had food allergies, I know from personal experience the hardship, heartache, and worry food allergies can cause. I would classify my three children in birth order as being low/mild, high, and severe in their food allergies. It was a struggle for me because I did not have any experience with nursing a baby, and no experience with the symptoms of food allergies in babies. I learned from each one of my children with the help of other mothers, the La Leche League, and by doing medical research on the subject.

My first son had a diaper rash that would not go away until I changed my diet. I had no idea as a first time mom that what I ate could impact my baby. The minute I took dairy, onions, garlic and tomatoes out of my diet I saw a dramatic improvement in his evening crying and the diaper rash disappeared. He would later get diarrhea from milk-based formulas when I tried to wean him from breast milk. My second son was much more dramatic. He screamed for hours on end (six hours was the worst of it) if I ate a meal that was high in wheat or gluten and dairy or soy. These were all foods that he would later be reactive to when he was weaned and eating table foods. He would also have either diarrhea or become constipated, and on a few occasions he had a tiny amount of blood in his stool from foods that were bothersome during the time he was breastfed.

My daughter proved to be even more challenging with her food issues as a nursing baby. But by the time I had my daughter, I was at least wise to the idea that if you tried to manage your diet you could at least figure out what bothered your baby. It was an amazing adventure. If you are nursing, use an elimination diet to restrict your foods so you can detect which foods may be offending your baby. Then, add the foods back in one at a time eating a fairly large quantity when you re-introduce them into your diet. Over time, you will be able to pinpoint problem foods.

It is my personal experience that many food allergy babies are misdiagnosed with acid reflux or GERD (Gastro Esophageal Reflux Disease). Some of the symptoms of food allergies and acid reflux or GERD are the same, so it is easy to understand why this might be the case. In the hundreds of people that I have interviewed over the past ten years, many parents encountered the problem of their child's food allergies being misdiagnosed or not diagnosed at all. The parents of a baby with "colic" are worn out and exhausted and find no relief until friends, family members or a co-worker miraculously suggest changing to a new formula or changing the mother's diet. Poof! Overnight their baby's colic disappears with a more suitable formula.

Overall, there is a lack of recognition of the symptoms of food allergies in infants in the medical community. Symptoms of food allergies in infants are varied and can include, but are not limited to:[2],[3],[4],[5]

- Colic (sharp intestinal pains and gas)
- Vomiting – mild, severe or projectile
- Diarrhea
- Runny nose
- Wheezy bronchitis or wheezing
- Eczema
- Watery or runny eyes
- Headache
- Hives
- Rashes on the face and upper body
- Watery stools that can be green, mucousy, or bloody
- Redness around the anus
- Stuffy nose
- Diaper rash

[2] Marvin S. Eigler, M.D. and Sally Wendkos Olds, The Complete Book of Breastfeeding, Rev. ed. (New York: Bantam Books, 1972, 1987), p. 88.

[3] Arlene Eisenberg, Heidi E. Murkoff and Sandee E. Hathaway, B.S.N., What To Expect The First Year, (New York: Workman Publishing Company, 1989, 1996), p. 232.

[4] Kathleen Huggins, R.N., M.S., The Nursing Mother's Companion, Fourth ed., (Boston, MA: The Harvard Common Press, 1999), p.

[5] Doris Rapp, M.D., Is This Your Child?, (New York: Quill/William Morrow, 1991), p. 103.

- Uneasy or poor sleeping
- Irritable or unhappy – restless or needs a lot of attention
- Repeated ear infections
- Constipation
- Excessive drooling
- Screaming or prolonged crying
- Extreme perspiration
- Anaphylactic shock

Symptoms for GERD can include: spitting up or vomiting, nausea, heartburn, coughing, laryngitis, respiratory problems like wheezing, asthma, or pneumonia, arching of the back, irritability, refusal to feed, and poor growth[6]. With my second son, I did not know that food allergies in an infant and acid reflux/GERD had similar if not the same symptoms. So when my pediatrician recommended an over-the-counter antacid product, Zantac, I used it. But when my pediatrician recommended Propulcid®, a prescription medication, for my son, I did not use it. My girlfriend who just happens to be a Registered Pharmacist (R.Ph.) used her position to obtain medical documentation from the pharmaceutical manufacturer. Propulcid® was known to cause cardiac arrest according to the manufacturer's data she received. Propulcid® was eventually removed from the U.S. market by the Food and Drug Administration (FDA) because of the number of deaths that it caused.

So what can parents do? If you are using a commercially made formula, you can discuss with your pediatrician changing formulas. There are some infants who do not tolerate commercially made formulas due to their food allergies. If you had an infant who was allergic to milk (and the milk components casein and whey), soy, corn, coconut oil, sunflower oil and safflower oil, then you would effectively eliminate nearly every

---

[6] National Digestive Diseases Information Clearing House (NDDIC) website: A service of the National Institute of Diabetes and Digestive and Kidney Diseases (NIDDK), part of the National Institute of Health (NIH): http://digestive.niddk.nih.gov/ddiseases/pubs/gerd/

formula including the hypoallergenic ones. This makes a strong case for breastfeeding infants. If you are breastfeeding a baby who has food allergies, you have other options.

Before I leave the subject of infant formulas, I must mention the controversy about soy infant formulas and soy as a food source. Soy as a food source did not enter the American diet until after the 1920's because it was considered to be an industrial product, not a food. Soy has been used on farms to clean up the soil because it will uptake from the ground unwanted particles, which end up in the soy plant. There are organizations and individuals who have evidence to support the negative impact of soy on infants and humans. To be more educated, visit the Internet and plug "soy controversy" in your search engine. That will give you both sides of this issue.

If you are breastfeeding your baby you can experiment with your diet to bring relief to yourself and your baby. One of the largest organizations that provides on-going critical support to breast-feeding mothers is the La Leche League International (*www.lalecheleague.org*). Founded in 1956, this organization has local support groups, online resources and a great deal of support to offer nursing moms. In terms of books, Kathleen Huggins' book The Nursing Mother's Companion is one of my favorite nursing books because Ms. Huggins digs in and provides excellent advice about how to alter your diet to reduce the symptoms in your baby. Additionally, many areas have nursing stores where you can get lactation help either free or for a fee. My personal experience with three food allergy babies is that babies are unique in how food affects them. It would be so much easier for all of us if babies reacted the same!

Symptoms for food allergies in toddlers and children takes the previously mentioned list *and adds a few more*:

- Emotional meltdowns (could also be caused by disciplinary issues)
- Inattention
- Bedwetting or bladder/bowel problems
- Nightmares

- Hyperactivity
- Allergy shiners (dark or red circles under the eyes)
- Bright cheeks or flushed look
- Redness around the ears
- Aggression or meanness
- Bad breath or "chemical smelling breath"
- Unhappy disposition
- Whiny or clingy disposition
- Tiredness
- Limiting foods (only eating a few select food items)
- Food cravings
- Stomach aches

If you suspect that your toddler or young child has food allergies, there are a number of things that you can do. If your child experiences any immediate reactions to foods, see your pediatrician or physician right away as your child could have a potentially life-threatening allergy. The life-threatening food allergies, also known as IgE allergies, can strike at any time and without warning or history. The condition of having an extreme allergic reaction is called anaphylaxis. Because anaphylaxis can cause death in minutes, prompt action is required. Frequently the symptoms for a life-threatening food allergy (anaphylaxis) are hives or itchy skin, a tightening or closing of the throat, swelling of the lips, tongue or throat, headache, nausea, vomiting, abdominal cramps, wheezing, coughing, hoarseness, shortness of breath, a sense of impending doom, or a loss of consciousness[7]. These symptoms may appear within a few seconds or up to 2 hours after eating a food or being exposed to a food.

If your child or anyone has the above listed symptoms of immediate food allergies or anaphylaxis, I would recommend that you not only see your pediatrician or doctor, but that you request a prescription for an EpiPen 2-Pak®. Get the prescription filled and carry the EpiPen® with you at all times. Food allergies can be

[7] "Anaphylaxis Extreme Allergic Emergency", a brochure available at physician and allergist offices: DEY Manufactured for DEY, Napa, California, 94558, USA by Meridian Medical Technologies, Inc. Columbia, MD 21046, USA. #03-500-01 (BRS) March 2003, page3. www.epipen.com.

fatal. This is not something to take lightly. If you are not sure if you are dealing with anaphylaxis, please seek medical help from your physician. Doctors can help you better determine if the situation you are concerned about is anaphylaxis or something less serious.

Should your infant or child have a food allergy that could result in anaphylaxis, this calls for rigor and vigilance on your part as the parent. You absolutely cannot depend on other people to remember your child's food allergies. As an adult who has lived an entire lifetime being anaphylactically allergic to tree nuts, I can say with authority and certainly that other people will not be as dependable as you need them to be. It is not that the people in your life are bad, or irresponsible, it is simply a matter that is easily overlooked.

I have personally ordered menu items in a restaurant and made myself very clear about my allergy to tree nuts, and I have _still_ been served meals that contained nuts! So in the area of anaphylaxis and children, you as parents need to take control and not assume that other relatives, school personnel, or other school parents will remember or comply with your child's food allergies.

On the other hand, if you are not dealing with an immediate or anaphylactic food reaction, you may find it difficult to pinpoint what food is causing a symptom. Ah, I wish I could give you a magic pill to make this detective work easier. Keeping a food log of what your child eats, the quantity of the food, time of day and the environment that the food is consumed in is one place to start. I know it is a pain in the neck. I know it is bothersome. With that said, however, many parents have been able to pinpoint foods that are problematic. And some parents have done that in a very short time.

My second child had the sweetest temperament and disposition in the world. _Unless_ you gave him a touch of gluten or dairy in which case he became a totally different child. At the time that I was struggling to understand how food could impact an infant and then later a toddler so much, I would have no idea that physicians from over 2,000 years ago knew that there was a link between food and behavior, and food and illness. Since we are specifically considering the impact of food allergies on children, one physician worth noting is Dr. Ben F. Feingold.

In the mid-1960's, using an allergy diet designed by Dr. Lockey of the Mayo Clinic, Dr. Feingold began studying the impact of foods and food additives on behavior and learning abilities.[8] The Feingold Organization is alive and well today and has many resources available to help parents struggling with behavioral problems, learning problems, and other diagnoses. More information is available on their website at: *www.feingold.org*.

An elimination diet is another way to try to narrow the focus of which foods are causing what symptoms. An elimination diet is a process by which you remove as many foods as possible until you have a clear baseline, and then gradually, over time add the foods back into your child's diet. This is not an easy process either. Many parents are reluctant to remove gluten, dairy or XYZ food from their children's diet because they think it will be too hard. Some parents think that their child will suffer. It is really quite the reverse. When a child feels better, doesn't wet the bed, can sleep through the night, or improves with some other symptom, it is worth the dietary effort.

I understand that it is difficult for some parents to comprehend that the food that their child is eating could be causing inattention, hyperactivity, or bedwetting for example. I completely understand that. Had I not experienced this myself, I would be in the same boat of disbelief. There are organizations, books, and medical studies to support this point of view.

My two older sons simply cannot tolerate dairy and gluten and a few additives like food coloring and MSG. They have different reactions, but none of the reactions are pleasant or make them happy. Will gluten or dairy send them to the emergency room like it would their younger sister? No. But will they pay for eating any gluten or dairy? Yes. At least I am privy to this significant

---

[8] Feingold website: www.feingold.org ; Dr. Feingold's Biography.

information. I can choose if I am going to let the boys have foods that bother them, and then all of us will suffer the consequences of bedwetting, inattention, hyperactivity, meltdowns, rashes and bowel problems. With issues like that, I do not make it a habit of allowing gluten or dairy.

In summary, foods can negatively impact newborn infants, toddlers and children. If you look for support and try to figure out what foods are bothering your child, you will most likely be successful. If you have a "high maintenance" child, then you have substantial and serious benefits to gain by altering your child's diet. Looking at foods as a possible source for the previously listed symptoms is non-invasive, inexpensive, safe, and proven. While food elimination is not the easiest route, it can produce the most phenomenal results.

A Brief History of Food Allergies

It is relevant, pertinent, and quite important to provide a brief review of the history of food allergy. This chapter is included to give you power in the form of information so that you can begin to explore your relationship to food as it relates to your health and wellness. For more than two thousand years there has been medical recognition that food can cause illnesses, diseases and health concerns for some people. Hippocrates was a Greek physician who is considered to be the *Father of Medicine* according the Merriam Webster Dictionary. Over two thousand years ago Hippocrates[9] wrote about the negative effects that food could have on different people:

> "For cheese does not prove equally injurious to all men, for there are some who can take it to satiety, without being hurt by it in the least, but, on the contrary, it is wonderful what strength it imparts to those it agrees with; but there are some who do not bear it well, their constitutions are different, they differ in this respect, that what in their body is incompatible with cheese, is roused and put in commotion by such a thing; and those in whose bodies such a humor happens to prevail in greater quantity and intensity, are likely to suffer the more from it. But if the thing had been pernicious to the whole nature of man, it would have hurt all."

What this quotation from Hippocrates means to you as a consumer is that since the beginning of medicine there has been a significant acknowledgment that food can cause health problems. This is not the society that we live in today. For the most part, this knowledge base, which is rich with substantial scientific research, has all but disappeared from our culture. For that reason, I believe that it is important for consumers to have an understanding of the history of food allergies as it has evolved over time. Historically, physicians were recognized for being able

---

[9] Adams, Francis. *The Genuine Works of Hippocrates*. Baltimore: Williams, 1939.

to treat their patients' illnesses by diet manipulation. That means that throughout history, doctors treated illness by changing a patient's diet. An example of this written approximately 200 years ago and credited to Matthew Baillie[10] is as such:

> "To judge of the true skill and merit of a physician requires a competent knowledge of the science of medicine itself; but to gain the good opinion of the patient or his friends, there is perhaps no method so ready as to show expertness in the regulation of the diet of the sick. Discretion and judgment will, of course, be required; the rules should not be unnecessarily severe or rigid, otherwise they will not be followed; but the prudent physician will prescribe such laws as though not the best are yet the best that will be obeyed."

What Dr. Baillie is addressing in the above quotation is that doctors of that time would recommend changes in a patient's diet to help relieve symptoms of illness and that the dietary changes would have to be such that they were not so complicated that the patient would follow the recommended changes.

Moving into the early 1900's there is a plethora of medical writings that support the fact that foods are a problem for some individuals and can cause a whole host of medical illnesses and diseases. One of the physicians who made substantial contributions to the area of food allergies was Dr. Francis Hare of Brisbane, Australia. In 1905 Dr. Hare wrote a two-volume 1,000 page book titled *The Food Factor in Disease*[11] which was a result of his observation in 1889 that migraine headache incidentally was relieved when the patient was put on a special diet that largely excluded fats, carbohydrates, and saccharine alcoholic drinks. Dr. Francis Hare sought to explain that a whole host of diseases were related to food allergies including migraine, asthma, gout, nervousness, epilepsy, mania, dyspepsia, biliousness,

---

[10] MacMichael, William. *The Gold-Headed Cane*. New York: Hoeber, 1926. p. 223.

[11] Hare, Francis. *The Food Factor in Disease*. London: Longmans, Vol. I, II, 1905.

---

headache, bronchitis, eczema, hypertension, gastrointestinal disturbances and other degenerative diseases.

But Dr. Hare was only one of many physicians that were discovering what Hippocrates had written over two thousand years before. **In 1906, Dr. Clemens Von Pirquet[12] suggested the use of the word "allergy" to describe an inappropriate reaction to food or other substances not typically harmful or bothersome.** A physician in England, Dr. Alfred Schofield, wrote in 1908 about successfully treating a boy who suffered from angioedema and asthma because of an allergy to eggs.[13]   Dr. Keston, Dr. Walters, and Dr. Hopkins confirmed this egg desensitization.[14]   Thus, a hundred years ago physicians were successfully treating patients with food allergies.

New York physician Oscar Schloss reported a similar experience as that of Dr. Schofield in 1912.[15] In 1917, the *Journal of Urology* published an article by Dr. Longcope and Dr. Rachemann describing six patients who reacted to foods with urticaria and renal insufficiency.[16] The *Archives of Internal Medicine, Journal of the American Medical Association, and Annals of Clinical Medicine* would all publish medical articles on the relationship between food and medical illnesses by Dr. W. W. Duke from 1921 to 1923.[17,18,19]

A major contributor to the study and advancement of food allergies was Dr. Albert Rowe who in 1931 published a book called

---

[12] von Pirquet, C. Allergie. *Munch Med Wochenschr* 52:1457, 1906.

[13] Schofield, Alfred T. *A Case of Egg Poisoning.* London: *Lancet*, 1908, p. 716.

[14] Keston, B, Walters, I & H, Gardner J. Oral Desensitization to common foods. *J Allergy* 6:431, 1935.

[15] Schloss, Oscar M. A Case of Allergy to Common Foods. *Am J Dis Child*, 3:341, 1912.

[16] Longcope, W.T., and Rachemann, F.M. Severe renal insufficiency associated with attacks of urticaria in hypersensitive individuals. *Journal of Urology* 1:351, 1917.

[17] Duke, W. W. Food allergy as a cause of abdominal pain. *Arch Int Med 28*:151, 1921.

[18] Duke, W. W. Food allergy as a cause of bladder pain. *Ann Clin Med 1*:117, 1922.

[19] Duke, W. W. Meniere's syndrome caused by allergies. *JAMA 81*:2179, 1923.

Food Allergy: Its Manifestations, Diagnosis, and Treatment.[20] Dr. Rowe documented that food allergies can cause a wide range of symptoms affecting any part of the body, and that allergies can show up at any age. Forty-one years later, Dr. Rowe and his son co-authored a follow-up book on food allergies titled *Food Allergy: It's Manifestations and Control and the Elimination Diets – A Compendium.*[21]

Dr. Warren T. Vaughan began studying food allergies in 1932. Dr. Vaughan studied an entire village of 508 people who lived in and around Clover, Virginia in 1934. Of the population that he studied, ten percent had allergies severe enough to require medical attention and another 50 percent had minor allergies, which meant that 60 percent of the population studied, had some degree of allergy. Dr. Vaughan took his survey one step further and looked at the possible causes for the allergies. Of the 60 percent with major and minor allergies that were able to attribute symptoms to definite causes, "62.6 percent reacted to foods, 23 percent to inhalants, and 14.4 percent to contact allergies."[22]

In 1941, Dr. Vaughan published a book called *Strange Malady*[23] in which he presents the multiple manifestations of food allergy and the interplay of food reactions with other environmental exposures and concealed excitants. In *Strange Malady* Dr. Vaughan states three key points: **food allergies or sensitivities are the most common form of human allergy; a person can become sensitized to any food; and it is unusual to be allergic to just one food.** Several years later in 1948 Dr. Vaughan published a book called *Practice of Allergy*[24] further adding to the knowledge of food allergy that already existed.

---

[20] Rowe, Albert H. *Food Allergy: Its Manifestations, Diagnosis, and Treatment.* Philadelphia: Lea & Febiger 1931.

[21] Rowe, Albert H., and Rowe, A. Jr. *Food Allergy It's Manifestations and Control and the Elimination Diets – A Compendium.* Springfield: Thomas, 1972.

[22] Vaughan, Warren T. *Practice of Allergy.* St. Louis: Mosby, 1948.

[23] Vaughan, Warren T. *Strange Malady.* New York: Doubleday, 1941.

[24] Vaughan, Warren T. *Practice of Allergy.* St. Louis: Mosby, 1948.

Also making additional substantial contributions to books published on the topic of food allergies and allergies in general was a Dr. Arthur Coca. Dr. Coca authored *Familial Nonreaginic Food Allergy* in three editions, which were published in 1942,[25] 1945, [26] and 1953.[27] One of Dr. Coca's significant observations was that exposure to food allergens resulted in a change in the pulse of the human body. *The Pulse Test* was published as a tool for the layman in 1956.[28]

The Pulse Test outlines the direct relationship between food allergies and backaches, headaches, epilepsy, diabetes, ulcers, hemorrhoids, obesity, hives, fatigue, migraine, high blood pressure, depression, and even multiple sclerosis with the most fascinating case histories and references to successfully treated patients. (We purchased a used copy of *The Pulse Test* on-line and were extremely pleased with the information contained in this easy-to-read book written by Dr. Coca.)

Dr. Arthur Coca was not just any other allergist who discovered that food allergies had a significant relationship to illness, diseases, and health and well-being. Dr. Coca had more accomplishments than most medical physicians ever accrue. Dr. Coca was the founder and first editor of the *Journal of Immunology*, which is still the foremost medical publication in its field. He also served on the editorial boards of the *Journal of Allergy,* the *Journal of Investigative Dermatology*, and the *Journal of Applied Nutrition*. He taught at Cornell, the University of Pennsylvania and Post-Graduate studies at Columbia University. He was also Honorary President of the American Association of Immunologists. And he was a member of many other medical organizations such as the American Association for Cancer Research, the American Society for the Study of Allergy, and the Society for Experimental Biology and Medicine. Dr. Coca and the other pioneers in allergy were no ordinary physicians; they had

---

[25] Coca, Arthur F. *Familial Non-Reaginic Food Allergy* 1st edition, Springfield: Thomas, 1942.

[26] Coca, Arthur F. *Familiar Non-Reaginic Food Allergy* 2nd edition. Springfield: Thomas, 1945.

[27] Coca, Arthur F. *Familiar Non-Reaginic Food Allergy* 3rd edition. Springfield, Thomas, 1953.

[28] Coca, Arthur F. *The Pulse Test*. New York: Arco 1956.

more credentials than most physicians had at the time, or have now currently.

Yet another major contributor to the field of food allergies was a physician by the name of Dr. Herbert Rinkel who did work beginning in the 1930's. *Food Allergy,* published in 1951 by Dr. Rinkel, Dr. Theron G. Randolph, and Dr. Zeller, was a comprehensive book covering the nature and cyclic concept of food allergy, the deliberate feeding test and the rotary diet.[29]

According to Dr. Lawrence D. Dickey [30], "Dr. Rinkel's last major contribution had to do with the symptom-provoking and relieving food test. It was presented at the First International Congress on Food and Digestive Allergy in 1963[31] nine days after his death. Dr. Rinkel's presentation was delivered by Dr. Dor Brown. This presentation speaks to the worldwide recognition that exists for Dr. Rinkel and his co-authors' work. It also speaks to the global recognition that food allergies are a significant problem.

Dr. Rinkel's observations of reactions to two closely spaced feedings after at least 4½ days of avoidance of that particular food can be traced back to Hippocrates who wrote over two thousand years ago:

> "Such persons, provided they take dinner when it is not their wont, immediately become heavy and inactive, both in body and mind, and are weighed down with yawning, slumbering, and thirst: and if they take supper in addition, they are seized with flatulence, tormina, and diarrhea, and to many this has been the commencement of a serious disease, when they have merely taken twice a day the same food which they have been in the custom of taking once."...

---

[29] Rinkel, H.J, Randolph, T.G., and Zeller, M. *Food Allergy.* Springfield: Thomas, 1951.

[30] Dickey, Lawrence D., The food factor in disease: its history & documentation. *Clinical Ecology.* Vol. 1, No. 2, pgs 67-68. Fall/Winter 1982-83.

[31] Rinkel H.J., Lee CH, Brown, D Jr. Willoughby JW, and Williams JM. The Diagnosis of food allergy. *Arch Otolaryng* 79:71:, 1964.

Hippocrates also wrote:

> "...if a patient fast for the first two or three days and take food of a heavy nature on the forth and fifth, he will be much injured."[32]

This reference from Hippocrates and later Dr. Rinkel and other notable physicians provides the foundation for rotation diets. Rotation diets are a concept where you do not eat the same foods every day, but rather you have a system for eating specific foods every four or so days. This cookbook provides detailed information on rotation diets and instruction on how to set up your own rotation diet.

An internationally known and renowned allergist who made remarkable contributions to the field was a Dr. Theron G. Randolph. While Dr. Randolph did not begin in private allergy practice until 1939, his interest in allergy was clearly evident when he attended a national allergy meeting during his senior year of medical school in 1933. During that same time he also attended a national meeting of the American Association of Immunologists, and heard the presidential address of Dr. Arthur F. Coca, a man with whom Dr. Randolph would later become friends. Dr. Randolph was the third person trained through a fellowship offered by the Harvard Medical School and Massachusetts General Hospital.

Dr. Randoph's bibliography of published articles and presentations is both extensive and diverse. Throughout the course of his career, Dr. Randolph published and presented over 393 articles, books, or presentations.[33] He was known around the world, speaking at meetings such as the 1st and 3rd International Congress of Social Psychiatry, the First International Congress on Food and Digestive Allergy in Vichy, France, and 3rd World Congress of Psychiatry to name a few. Dr. Randolph was also

---

[32] Adams, Francis. *The Genuine Works of Hippocrates.* Baltimore: Williams, 1939.

[33] Randolph, Theron G. *Environmental Medicine-Beginnings & Bibliographies of Clinical Ecology.* 1987. Clinical Ecology Publications, Fort Colins, CO. Pgs 349-357.

called upon to provide his testimony to the United States Government on several different aspects of allergy during the course of his brilliant career - one that incorporated relationships with Dr. Coca, Dr. Rowe, and Dr. Rinkel.

Depending on how you enter Theron Randolph, M.D.'s name into a World Wide Web search engine, you will get a range of hits from 74,000 to 122,000 or more. If you spend the time to look up many of these hits, you will eventually encounter pages that are in foreign languages. Dr. Theron Randolph was an internationally known pioneer in the field of allergy. The importance and significance of Dr. Randolph's work has been recognized by Harvard where Dr. Randolph's medical papers and writings are archived in one of their many medical libraries. This underlines the stature and credibility of a leader who dedicated his life to understanding the root causes of allergies.

To put the medical research of the early 1900's into perspective relative to life at that time, things were very, very different. At the turn of the century there were no cars zooming around the United States, as that would come later. Henry Ford founded the Ford Motor Company in 1903 with the first Model "T" being produced in 1908. The Manhattan Bridge would not be completed until 1910. The Holland Tunnel and Lincoln Tunnel, which connect New York State and New Jersey for automobile transportation, would not be completed until 1927 and 1937 respectively. A refrigeration process for meat cargo was not developed until 1934, which meant that you had to obtain your meat from a place close to where you lived.

In these early days of medicine and allergy, there were no computers, no short wave radio, no televisions, and no mass transportation systems. But there was also no pollution from automobiles, trains and airplanes; no preservatives or mass-produced foods; and few chemicals and pesticides. There was no plastic. Life was radically different in the early days of the 1900's. A physician would make an observation in his medical practice, from which he or she would develop a theory or hypothesis. The physicians of the time would then test their theories out with their patients. Physicians practiced independently prior to the advances of the railways, automobiles and airplanes. Yet, for over two thousand years physicians independently came up with the same conclusions all over the world: food allergies can cause illness, disease and poor health.

There was also a recognition that people react differently to foods, and that a food, which is a problem for one person, may not be a problem for another person. In the past, physicians were judged by their ability to treat their sick patients through diet manipulation. The vast majority of the current medical profession knows very little about food allergy symptoms, the ways that foods can negatively impact an individual's health and the diseases related to food allergies. It is certainly less expensive, not to mention less invasive, to rule out food allergies in the course of helping a patient who is experiencing health concerns. However this is not routinely done in the present medical establishment in the United States.

Most allergists only test for IgE (immediate and more serious) allergies, which accounts for only 5-10% of food allergies. Most people with serious and immediate reactions already know that they have a problem with food and they usually know the source. It has been stated that IgE mediated food allergies will present within one hour of food ingestion. Delayed food allergies account for 90-95% of food allergies. This is the one area of allergy that is sadly lacking in terms of the availability of treatment options, recognition of prevalence, and acknowledgement of the wide variety of illnesses and diseases that are due to delayed allergies. It is medically documented that delayed food allergies are the most difficult to pinpoint because of their cyclic nature and because of a medical phenomenon called "masking".

Some delayed food reactions will not appear for several hours while others will appear after two or more days. Therefore without a complete elimination diet or medical testing, it is nearly impossible for a patient to discern if a reaction experienced from food was from that day or day's prior. Elimination diets are difficult for patients to do and are impacted by noncompliance. Deliberate food tests or challenges are extremely time and labor intensive and have other issues as well. It was because of this exact issue that more precise and comprehensive testing, known as intradermal neutralization testing, came into existence.

A relatively recent study demonstrated that 93% of 88 children with severe, frequent migraine recovered on a special diet.[34] Another article reviews 40 children with severe eczema that had not responded to conventional treatment, yet 100% of these 40 children improved on a hypoallergenic diet.[35]   These medical conditions have been historically proven to be related to food allergy, but today it is as if the authors of such recent studies have "discovered" some new phenomenon.

The list of physical illnesses, diseases and health related problems that can be explained primarily by this type of allergy includes asthma, hay fever, itchy skin, headaches, fatigue, nausea, vomiting, hives, stomach pain, irrational behavior, edema (swelling), hyperactivity, muscle pain, joint pain, reflux esophagitis or acid reflux, back pain, acne, phlebitis, arthritis, anxiety, mood swings, dizziness or tingling sensations, diarrhea or persistent bowel problems, bad breath, constant congestion, irritating twitches, eczema, depression, inability to concentrate, and behavioral and emotional problems.   While there is no question that currently there is no mainstream conversation about the importance and impact of food allergies on health, illness and disease, that fact does not erase over two thousand years of medical literature, research, and proof that food allergies can be a serious problem to many people.

As the saying goes, when we forget history we are destined to repeat it.   When individuals recognize that foods can affect how they feel, they begin to have the power to explore what foods could be problematic for themselves or their family.   Many organizations have recognized that special diets can bring relief from health issues.   Some of the special diets recommended by consumer groups are covered in this cookbook under the Special Diets

[34] Egger J, Carter CM, Wilson J, Turner MW & Soothill JF. Is migraine food allergy? A double-blind controlled trial of olioantigenic diet treatment. *Lancet* 2:865-869. 1983.

[35] Hathaway MJ, Warner JO. Compliance problems in the dietary management of eczema. *Arch Dis Childhood* 58:463, 1983.

section. There is much more that could be written about the history of food allergy as it is an expansive field of knowledge. I do believe that this is a sufficient history for most consumers to come to understand that for centuries, physicians around the world have written extensively about how food can negatively impact health and wellness in human beings.

The information in this chapter came from a medical paper that I wrote a few years ago when I was pursuing health insurance coverage for one of my children. I ran across bits and pieces of the history of food allergy in a variety of medical papers from our local medical library. Several of the medical papers had a paragraph or a few sentences that I found to be amazing. I then pieced together the history of food allergy based on the various references. If I had more time, money or interest, I'm sure a whole book could be written on the subject. For people like myself, this is enough data and background to point to the conclusion that food can indeed affect your health and wellness.

Special Diets & Celiac Disease

There are many, many different kinds of special diets in the world. Many people think of a diet as a way to lose weight. The special diets that I will outline in this chapter are not intended for weight loss, but rather to relieve symptoms, behaviors or feelings. I have included a brief discussion of some of the more common special diets. Celiac Disease is covered in more detail at the conclusion of the Special Diet material. More information is available on the Internet on each of these special diets:

- Allergen Restricted Diet
- Candida or Yeast-free Diet
- Celiac or Gluten-free Diet
- Elimination Diet
- Feingold Diet
- Gluten-Free & Casein-Free Diet (GFCF Diet)
- Ketogenic Diet
- Low Oxalate Diet
- Raw Foods Diet
- Vegan Diet

Allergen Restricted Diet - just as the name implies someone on an allergen restricted diet is using a diet of foods free from the ingredients that they are highly allergic to or that produce symptoms that are unpleasant. Someone who is mildly allergic to milk, but gets a physical symptom of daily diarrhea, may use a milk-free diet to avoid daily diarrhea. All of these diets are done individually according to that person's reactions to foods, preservatives, or other additives.

Some one who reacts to sulphites or MSG, for example, will restrict foods that are known to contain sulphites or MSG. What is critical for people on allergen restricted diets is to get proper medical guidance from a licensed medical doctor so that you do not become malnourished in the process of avoiding food allergens. This is one of the mistakes that I made with Anne. While I spoke to many Registered Dieticians, none of them were competent to advise me on what should be done to make sure that Anne received the proper nutrients while she was on her allergen restricted diet.

Candida or Yeast-Free Diet - You commonly think of yeast as an ingredient in breads and other baked goods. Foods associated with yeast (or fungus) sometimes use a fermentation, aging, or pickling process. Cheeses, alcohols, vinegars, salad dressings, mayonnaise, ketchup, mustard, chocolate, coffee and tea are also sources of yeast. Many other additives or foods processed with chemicals are typically associated with yeast including citric acid, enzymes, added B vitamins, stabilizers, anti-oxidants, and flavorings.

An individual who has a Candida or yeast problem, often referred to as Candida overgrowth, may have a wide variety of health symptoms including but not limited to: chronic depression, extreme fatigue, severe PMS or Premenstrual Syndrome, dizziness, weakness, inability to concentrate, headaches, migraine, sinusitis, asthma, colitis, endometriosis, hypoglycemia, constipation, conjunctivitis and arthritis.

If you know or suspect that you have a yeast overgrowth problem or Candida, one book that would be extremely worthwhile is _The Yeast Connection_ by William Crook, M.D. This is considered a classic book on the subject, and if you have this problem, it would be to your benefit to become educated as you have access to huge relief with your symptoms by changing your diet, and in many cases by using a pharmaceutical drug to help kill off the yeast.

Some physicians still tell patients to eat yogurt after they finish a course of antibiotics. The reason they tell patients that is to replace the good bacteria or "flora" that an antibiotic kills. Consumers who can't tolerate milk, yogurt, or dairy can still get the benefits of the components of yogurt, which is acidophilus through commercially available dietary supplements. Our family uses a gluten-free, dairy-free acidophilus capsule that we open up and use in a vitamin shake. So going dairy-free doesn't have to remove your access to acidophilus. Read your supplement label carefully to make sure that your supplement is free of any allergens.

Foods that do not normally contain yeast (or fungus) include fresh vegetables, beans, meats, chicken, fish, some nuts and glass bottled water. People on a yeast-free or Candida diet normally avoid carbohydrates that contain sugar or yeast (sugar feeds the yeast), sweets, and fresh fruits because of the sugar content in addition to the previously mentioned yeast-containing foods. In this book, I have included several recipes that are free of sugar, yeast, and other problematic ingredients.

The health condition of yeast overgrowth or Candida can be extremely debilitating, however there are proven techniques to help a person with this problem improve dramatically. This issue is more common than people realize. If you have had on-going health problems that have not been resolved, this may be one area for you to investigate.

Celiac or Gluten-free Diet - More specific information about Celiac Disease is available at the end of this chapter as this is an overview. The Celiac diet is a gluten-free diet. Gluten is found naturally in specific grains like wheat, barley, rye, kamut, spelt and a few other grains. Gluten is found in many commercially made products like salad dressings, sauces, mayonnaise, gravies, and products made from flours like breads, crackers, cookies, cakes, and other baked goods.

A person who has been placed on the Celiac or gluten-free diet has to be willing to read food labels and ask questions to adhere to the gluten-free diet. This is not optional. Gluten is also found in personal care products, some paper products (like envelope glue), some band-aids, and in many other products. Once a person on the Celiac or gluten-free diet becomes educated, they still have to read labels and check for gluten because food manufacturers can and do change their food formulations every so often. A product that is gluten-free today may or may not be gluten-free tomorrow.

The good news is that since 2000 there has been an explosion in the array of gluten-free products available. There are more manufacturers offering a wider variety of products. All of the recipes in this book are suitable for people with Celiac disease or who are on the gluten-free diet.

Elimination Diet - Occasionally you may hear someone say that they are on an Elimination Diet. This type of diet is typically recommended to someone who has health issues and a practitioner or dietician is trying to help the patient determine if the health issue is related to their diet. In an Elimination Diet, typically the patient will remove most or many foods from their diet to see if their health issue improves. Then, as directed by their dietician or health care practitioner, the patient will add individual foods back in over time. This can also be quite difficult and annoying. But it can be helpful in discovering the cause and in relieving symptoms.

Feingold Diet (salicylate) - Before I give you an idea of what the Feingold Diet is, I would like to discuss the symptoms and behaviors that the Feingold Diet has been known to address which includes: marked hyperactivity, impulsive actions, compulsive actions, emotional concerns, destructive behaviors, poor self-control, disruptive behaviors, aggression, depression, nervousness, mood swings, low tolerance for frustration, irritability, overreaction to touch, pain, sound or lights, low self-esteem, impatience, inability to follow directions or listen, poor muscle coordination, seizures, tics, eye muscle disorder, dyslexia and reading problems, speech difficulties and disorders, difficulty writing or drawing, auditory or visual memory problems, difficulty in comprehension and short term memory, difficulties in reasoning, ear infections, asthma, bedwetting (enuresis), daytime wetting, stomach aches, headaches, migraines, hives, rashes, eczema, leg aches, constipation, diarrhea, congestion, nightmares and bad dreams, difficulty falling asleep, restless or erratic sleep, and suicidal thoughts.

The Feingold Diet was named after Ben F. Feingold, M.D., a physician who was Chief of Allergy at Kaiser-Permanente Medical Center in San Francisco, California in the 1960's. The Feingold Diet eliminates artificial coloring, artificial flavoring, Aspartame (Nutrasweet, an artificial sweetener), and artificial preservatives

BHA, BHT, and TBHQ, and foods that containing salicylate (pronounced Suh-LIH-Suh-Late). Salicylate is a group of chemicals related to aspirin. The Feingold Program incorporates the Feingold Diet but also eliminates fragrances and non-food items, which contain the chemicals previously listed.

Since 1976, there has been in existence a parent support group for families using the Feingold Diet. The Feingold Association of the United States is an outstanding organization which has excellent resources on their website which can be found at: *www.feingold.org*. This wonderful organization has medical documentation available on their website which supports this therapy. I would highly recommend parents consider this non-invasive therapy as a method of addressing symptoms listed above. The Feingold Association of the United States can be reached at: 554 East Main Street, Suite 301, Riverhead, NY 11901, FAX (631) 369-2988. They have program materials available for purchase, which guides consumers through the Feingold Program for $69.00. One book on the subject is *Why Can't My Child Behave?* By Jane Hersey, Director of the Feingold Association.

Gluten-Free & Casein-Free (GFCF) Diet - The Gluten-Free Casein-Free Diet, which is also referred to as the GFCF diet is one in which foods containing gluten and casein (dairy) are removed from the diet. The GFCF diet has become increasingly popular in the last few years as a non-invasive therapy or intervention for autism spectrum disorders.

Decades before the GFCF diet was applied to autism, it was used with some schizophrenia patients and it was referred to as the milk-free and grain-free diet. There are many highly scientific articles on the Internet about gluten molecules crossing the blood-brain barrier, and the opiate-effect of casein and gluten in some individuals. All of the recipes in this cookbook are suitable for individuals on the GFCF diet. I have written more extensively about the gluten-free diet in the Celiac Disease section of this chapter.

Ketogenic Diet - The Ketogenic Diet is a rigid metabolic diet used as a therapy for epilepsy patients or people who have seizures. The exact reason why the Ketogenic Diet works is at this point not known. With this diet, meals are high in fat and low in carbohydrates and protein to produce a high blood concentration of incompletely burned fat molecules called ketone bodies. This diet is one which absolutely requires medical supervision and should not be done without approval and on-going medical support.

The Ketogenic Diet, which was developed and implemented at the Mayo Clinic and Johns Hopkins University medical schools, has produced marked improvements in seizure patients. This diet is often used with patients who have a lot of seizures and who do not respond to medication or surgery. Patients are usually on the Ketogenic Diet for two years, after which many patients remain seizure-free and no longer require anticonvulsant drugs or the diet. More information on the Ketogenic Diet can be found on the Internet or from your medical doctor.

Low Oxalate Diet - You can find information on the Internet about the Low Oxalate diet to help prevent kidney stones. However, I have included the Low Oxalate diet topic because it is a relatively new diet being used to treat children with autism and other disorders. Oxalates and the acid form oxalic acid are organic acids that come primarily from three sources: your diet, from molds (fungus) like Aspergillus, Penicillium and possibly Candida, and from your metabolism. A researcher named Susan Owens discovered that the use of a diet low in oxalates markedly reduced symptoms in children with autism and Pervasive Developmental Disorder (PDD).

Oxalates in the urine are much higher in individuals with autism than in normal children according to information put out by The Great Plains Laboratory, Inc. located in Lenexa, Kansas. The Great Pains Laboratory does a great deal of testing and lab work in the area of autism. Susan Owens reports a wide range of cognitive, behavioral and symptom improvements in children with autism. For more information on low oxalates as it relates to autism, search the Internet or contact The Great Plains Laboratory, Inc. and ask for the information flyer titled "Oxalates Control Is a Major New Factor in Autism Therapy" by William Shaw, PhD, Laboratory Director. The e-mail address for The Great Plains Laboratory is: *gpl4u@aol.com*, phone: (913) 341-8949, address: 11813 West 77th Street, Lenexa, KS 66214. Here is a list of some of the foods containing 7 or more mg oxalate per serving. Foods with an asterisk (*) have an extremely high amount of oxalates in them. A complete list of oxalates in foods can be found on the Internet at:

http://patienteducation.upmc.com/Pdf/LowOxalateDiet.pdf

Foods with 7 or more mg Oxalate Per Serving		
Starches	**Vegetables**	**Nuts, Seeds**
Fig cookies	Beans, green	Almonds
Fruit cake	Beans, baked in tomato sauce	Cashews
Graham crackers	Beets (tops, roots, greens)	Green beans, waxed and dried
Grits, white corn	Celery	Peanut butter*
Kamut (contains gluten)	Chives	Peanuts*
Marmalade	Collards	Pecans*
Soybean crackers*	Dandelion	Sesame seeds
Wheat germ* (contains gluten)	Eggplant	Sunflower seeds
	Escarole	Soy protein*
Fruits or juices	Kale	Tofu (soybean curd)*
Blackberries	Leeks*	Walnuts
Blueberries	Mustard greens	
Red currants	Okra*	**Condiments**
Dewberries	Parsley	Cinnamon, ground
Figs, dried	Parsnips	Parsley, raw*
Grapes, purple	Peppers, green	Pepper, >1 tsp/day*
Gooseberries	Pokeweed*	Ginger
Kiwi	Rutabagas	Soy sauce
Lemon peel*	Sorrel	
Lime peel*	Spinach*	**Miscellaneous**
Orange peel	Summer squash	Beer
Raspberries	Sweet potatoes*	Cocoa
Rhubarb*	Swiss chard*	Chocolate*
Strawberries	Tomato soup	Coffee, instant*
Tangerines	Vegetable soup	Tea*
	Watercress	
Dairy	Yams	
Chocolate milk		

* Extremely high oxalate content.

Raw Foods Diet - The Raw Foods Diet is not a weight loss diet, but rather a way of living for some individuals in the U.S. and around the world. Individuals who adhere to the Raw Foods Diet usually only eat raw foods. They don't cook or bake their foods. Individuals on the Raw Foods Diet typically eat tree nuts, peanuts, and coconut in addition to the raw fruits and vegetables. The rationale behind the Raw Foods Diet is that it is more in line with how our ancestors ate in days gone by. Raw foods contain helpful enzymes that are destroyed during the cooking and baking process. I would highly recommend seeking expert medical advice before considering the raw foods diet if you have food allergies or other health issues as there may be additional concerns. Given my children's food allergies, they would never be able to get enough protein, vitamins and minerals from a Raw Foods Diet.

Vegan Diet - The Vegan Diet contains no animal foods or dairy products. Individuals who use a Vegan diet often are referred to as vegans. It is common for *vegetarians* to eat eggs and dairy, however the Vegan Diet eliminates both eggs and dairy products thus distinguishing it from the vegetarian diet.

Celiac Disease

This subject is near and dear to my heart personally. My second son was very young when we first began to suspect that he might have Celiac disease, so I have been in the Celiac disease conversation for more than ten years. Celiac disease is an autoimmune disorder in which foods that contain gluten destroy the villi in the small intestine. Celiac is one of the most treatable diseases on the planet, because if you catch it early and alter your diet to remove gluten, your body has the opportunity to repair itself. Every single recipe in this book is absolutely gluten-free. We are a gluten-free household and we know what life is like to be gluten-free (and dairy-free, and egg-free, and nut-free, etc.).

Gluten is found in wheat, barley, rye, spelt, kamut and other grains which means that gluten is most often found in breads, crackers, and other starches made with flour. Gluten is also found in other food products, which we will get into later. There are around 256 symptoms for Celiac disease, which make it confusing to lay people. More important than the 300 signs, symptoms and associated conditions is the fact that 60% of children with Celiac disease and 41% of adults with Celiac disease will never have any symptoms (or be asymptomatic). The value in getting diagnosed early is that you avoid other serious health complications, like osteoporosis, infertility, neurological conditions and even cancer.

The statistical prevalence of Celiac disease in the U.S. in average healthy people is 1 out of 133 people which makes Celiac disease much more common than Alzheimer's disease, Cystic Fibrosis, Hemophilia, Parkinson's, Autism, Rheumatoid arthritis, Lupus, Multiple Sclerosis, and Crohn's disease. The interest and awareness of the gluten-free diet and celiac disease has exploded in the last two years since this book was originally printed.

Because 60% of the children and 41% of adults with Celiac will not have symptoms, it means that there are a lot of people who have the disease who simply don't know it. The earlier a child is diagnosed with Celiac disease the better they fair in avoiding the development of an autoimmune condition. If a 20 year old is diagnosed with Celiac disease, they then have a 34% chance of developing an autoimmune condition. The incidence of autoimmune diseases in the general U.S. population is 3.5% to give you a comparison.

Many children and adults with Celiac disease do have symptoms and yet they still do not get diagnosed. According to a Facts and Figures sheet by the University of Chicago Celiac Disease Center, it takes an average of **11 years** for a person with celiac symptoms to be diagnosed. That typically means a consumer experiencing symptoms going from doctor to doctor to doctor looking for an explanation and relief of their symptoms. So what are some of the general or typical symptoms for Celiac disease? Before I even list one, it is important to drill into your head that 60% of children will not have any symptoms and 41% of adults also will not have any symptoms.

People with Celiac disease may have <u>only one</u> symptom if they have any. The most common symptoms include: anemia, stress, nervous condition, depression, irritable bowel, stomach ulcer, edema, gallstones, food allergy, colitis, diarrhea, fatigue, abdominal pain, constipation, weight loss, weakness, malnutrition, and bloating. More recent research (A. Vojdani, et al, 2008) reports that organs well beyond the intestinal system can be affected by gluten sensitivity including the heart, thyroid, bone, joints, brain cerebellum and the neuronal synapses, which are involved in the regulation of the neurotransmitter release. A. Vojdani, et al also point out that gluten sensitivity has been associated with the following neurological disorders: cerebellar ataxia (ataxia is the loss of muscle control), epilepsy, myoclonic ataxia, chronic neuropathies and dementia. He also suggests that the variability of neurologic disorders that occur in gluten sensitivity is broader than previously reported and includes "softer" and more common neurologic disorders such as chronic headache, developmental delay (autism), hypotonia, and learning disorders or ADHD.

The chance of being diagnosed with Celiac disease if you have any of the symptoms is 1 in 56. The emphasis is on early detection and getting the individual on a gluten-free diet to avoid the development of additional health problems which can occur after the intestinal villi are destroyed and other health issues set in.

There are many conditions or diseases associated with Celiac disease which include: diabetes (insulin dependent, 6%), thyroiditis, Sjogren syndrome and other connective tissue diseases, primary biliary cirrhosis, Down's syndrome, Turner syndrome and Williams syndrome.

Celiac disease is inherited and therefore the risk increases if one of your relatives has it. If you have a first-degree relative who has Celiac disease, which would mean your parent, child or sibling, you have a 1 in 22 chance of developing it too. If you have a second-degree relative who has Celiac disease, which would mean your aunt, uncle, or cousin, you have a 1 in 29 chance of having it. It has been my experience that many relatives of people diagnosed with Celiac disease do not want to get tested. They don't want to know if they could have it. That would constitute avoidance and possible denial, which is sad because Celiac disease is a very manageable disease.

What these consumers don't understand is that if they do have Celiac disease and don't get diagnosed earlier than later, they are at a much higher risk for developing serious health problems including cancer. The small intestine is where your vitamins and minerals and other nutrients are absorbed. If the villi in your small intestine are destroyed and you are not absorbing vitamins, minerals, and other nutrients, you are at risk for a whole host of medical issues.

Testing for celiac disease most often begins with blood testing. If the blood tests show elevated levels sufficient to merit a biopsy, then that will be ordered. There are 275 papers on Atypical celiac disease, 239 papers on silent celiac disease, and 179 papers on latent celiac disease – a sum total of 693 papers – all published in PubMed, a service of the U.S. National Library of Medicine and the National Institutes of Health. The most recent research calls for a redefinition of celiac disease and has some startling findings.

One finding by Alberto Rubio-Tapia, et al (Gastroenterology 2009) indicates that during 45 years of follow-up, undiagnosed celiac disease was associated with a nearly 4-fold increased risk of death. That same study reported that the prevalence of undiagnosed celiac disease seems to have increased dramatically during the same period.

Many consumers diagnosed with Celiac resort to eating large quantities of rice and rice-based products. I know that is a common mistake as I made it with my son, Noah. Noah could not tolerate any gluten as an infant displaying such symptoms as projectile vomiting when given just a small amount of it. We used rice as a mainstay in Noah's diet and by the time Noah was just two years old, he could not tolerate rice at all. It was a painful day to realize that rice was now the problem. Had I known more about food allergies and the development of additional food allergies when he was born we could have avoided this problem completely. My friend, Linda Breitbach, spent four years in China eating rice every day. She became allergic to rice as well. It is important for people with Celiac disease to vary the foods that they eat or they stand a very good chance of developing additional food problems.

The last time I checked, the organizations who work to promote Celiac awareness and education knew that over 40% of people with Celiac disease were also lactose intolerant. And a high percentage of people with Celiac also had issues with one or more other foods like soy and canola. The Celiac community has begun to recognize the incidence of additional food allergies with Celiacs. But it needs to move to the next level. Individuals with Celiac disease would do very well to incorporate a rotation diet so that they avoid becoming allergic to rice, corn, potatoes, or other foods common to their diet.

A rotation diet is not that difficult. Mostly we avoid doing a rotation diet because it is foreign to us and it "seems like" a lot of work. In a separate chapter I have provided the foundation for anyone to develop their own rotation diet. This is the one thing that is proven to prevent the development of new food allergies. Many people from the Celiac support group that I knew well would complain of gastrointestinal issues. Food allergies can show up with the same symptoms as gluten contaminations. I hope over time that the Celiac communities will adopt and promote the rotation diet as a way of preventing further hardships for their members. After all, it is a real tragedy to have Celiac disease and then become allergic to rice because most of the commercially made gluten-free products contain rice. Trust me on this one. It is not a road you want to go down!

There are three major universities in the U.S. which have really made it a point to have Celiac programs, invest in research and development, and promote awareness. The three universities are The University of Chicago, The University of Maryland, and Columbia University in New York City. In recent years, the University of Chicago's Celiac Disease Program was upgraded to be a Celiac Disease Center. The Mayo Clinic is also doing more in the area of celiac disease than they were ten years ago. These are great places to get information and support. They are leading edge when it comes to Celiac disease information.

There are many support groups available in the United States and Canada. Celiac Sprue Association USA, Gluten Intolerance Group of America, Celiac Disease Foundation, American Celiac Society Dietary Support Coalition and the Canadian Celiac Association to name just a few. You can find a great deal of information using the Internet as well. In addition to the support groups, many grocery stores are now carrying gluten-free foods and products. In Buffalo, New York, Wegmans has done an amazing job of increasing their supply of gluten-free foods and baking ingredients. The number of gluten-free food manufacturers has also increased dramatically in the last seven years.

Eventually we in America will get to the place that Europe has been for years and we will have gluten-free hamburger buns in almost every restaurant. McDonald's in Europe has gluten-free hamburger buns available. Celiac disease is really one of the best health problems you could have. If everyone woke up tomorrow and had to go stand in line for the disease of their selection, if everyone knew about Celiac disease, it would have the longest line. In the scheme of health related problems, I'd take Celiac disease any day.

Avoiding Common Food Allergies

The top 8 food allergens account for approximately 90% of all food allergies. They are also the foods most likely to cause a severe or life-threatening allergic reaction known as anaphylaxis.

Top 8 Food Allergens in the United States:

- Milk
- Wheat
- Eggs
- Tree nuts
- Peanuts
- Fish
- Shellfish
- Soy

Every recipe in this cookbook is free of milk, wheat, eggs, tree nuts, peanuts, coconut, and gluten. If you are avoiding soy you should be forewarned that some recipes and products used in this cookbook contain soy. The soy ingredients used in recipes contained herein are typically in the form of non-dairy soy based cream cheese and sour cream substitutes, soy sauce, Bragg™ Liquid Aminos, or a soy preservative in a packaged cereal recipe ingredient.

Avoiding Wheat and Gluten

If you are only allergic to wheat, you have additional flours and food choices that are not allowed if you have a problem with gluten. Gluten is found in foods containing wheat, barley, rye, spelt, kamut, semolina, durum, graham, and triticale. All of the recipes in this cookbook are wheat-free AND gluten-free. Gluten has the effect of holding foods together. When you bake with gluten-free flours you need to add either xanthan gum or guar gum as a binder to hold the baked good together otherwise it will fall part more often than not.

Gluten is found in many, many food products and therefore you must learn to read labels carefully. One approach is to assume a food contains gluten unless you read the label. Crackers, breads, pasta, sauces, salad dressings, potato chips, croutons, processed lunch meats, soy sauces, gravies, candy, soups, stuffing, and some drugs and medications are just a few of the foods that often contain gluten.

Naturally Free of Gluten	NOT ALLOWED (contains gluten)
Alcoholic beverages (DISTILLED only)	Ales
Amaranth	Barley
Arrowroot	Beer (unless specifically made gluten-free)
Buckwheat	Bulgur
Beans	Durum
Bean flours	Einkorn
Corn	Graham
Garfava flour	Kamut
Millet & millet flour	Lagers
Potatoes & potato flour	Malt or malt flavoring
Rice and rice flour, rice products	Malt vinegar
Quinoa and quinoa flour	Rye
Sorghum	Semolina
Tapioca	Spelt
Teff	Triticale
Vinegars (distilled)	Wheat
Wines	

Fresh fruits and fresh vegetables do not contain gluten. Commercially available fruits and vegetables may or may not contain gluten. You will have to read the labels. Gluten is a pervasive ingredient that is common to many, many foods. Thanks to a new labeling law, foods containing gluten are now being labeled as such more than in the past. The reason that you need to train yourself to read labels regularly if you have food allergies, Celiac disease, or are on the Gluten-free – milk-free diet, is because food manufacturers sometimes change their food formulation. A product that is gluten-free today may or may not be gluten-free tomorrow.

Avoiding Milk and Milk Proteins

Avoiding all milk and milk proteins can be tricky business. It would be great if any item that came from milk would just say that. There are many names for foods that contain either milk or milk proteins. The following is not a complete list, but it should be helpful in getting you started. If you are in doubt about whether or not a product contains any milk or milk proteins get in touch with the company who makes the product.

The following items may contain milk:

Ammonium caseinate
Artificial butter flavor (some)
Butter solids or butter fat
Calcium caseinate
Caramel color (some)
Caramel flavoring (some)
Casein
Caseinate
Curds
Delactosed whey
Demineralized whey
Dried milk
High protein flour (some)
Hydrolyzed casein
Hydrolyzed vegetable protein
Lacalbumin
Lactabum
Lactabum phosphate
Lactate
Lactate starter

Lactoferrin
Lactoglobulin
Lactose
Lactulose
Magnesium caseinate
Milk derivative
Milk fat
Opta (fat replacer)
Potassium caseinate
Rennet
Sherbet (some)
Sodium steatoyal (not always)
Solids
Sour cream solids
Sour milk solids
Sour solids
Whey
Whey and casein hydrolsates
Whey protein concentrate

Other products that sometimes contains milk:

Drugs (frequently)
Grout for your tub
Household paint (some)

School glue or craft glue
Cosmetics
Some pet foods

If you are on a milk-free diet, there are many substitutes for milk that are completely milk-free. Some of the milk substitutes are: rice milk, Vance's DariFree™ potato milk, soy milk, and all of the milks that originate from seeds, tree nuts and coconuts. You can make your own milk from rice, any grain, or seeds by soaking the rice, grain, or seeds in pure water. Then puree them in the blender with water, a pinch of salt and any sweetener if desired. It is very simple and straightforward. There are non-dairy imitation cheeses made from rice and soy. There is Tofutti Brand non-dairy sour cream and non-dairy cream cheese.

There has been a dramatic increase in food allergies, and in the awareness that there are therapeutic dietary interventions that can improve health, and in some cases behavioral symptoms, as with the gluten-free and casein-free diet used with children who have autism. What that means is that there has been a corresponding increase in the number and variety of non-dairy products available to consumers. That is all good news to milk allergy consumers. As with all food allergies, make sure to read the labels and educate yourself as to the various names that mean milk or milk derived.

Avoiding Corn

At the present time, corn is _not_ considered to be one of the top 8 allergens. Corn allergies are, however, on the rise and one of the reasons for this could be the fact that corn in one form or another is present in a high percentage of the foods that we consume in the U.S. Corn as a food ingredient is not always listed on a food label as "corn". Avoiding corn is on the same page as avoiding gluten. It can be in foods and products under many, many names including but not limited to: maltodextrin, sucrose, fructose, and dextrose. Only a few of the recipes in this cookbook contain corn. We have one day that we use corn in our foods as we limit the amount of corn as much as possible. Corn is in many infant formulas, lunchmeats, jams, jellies, salad dressings, baking powder, powdered sugar, and foods and products too numerous to list. It is extremely difficult to avoid corn, and I do speak from experience as we have had problems with corn in the past.

Raw fruits and vegetables and fresh meats do not contain corn. Many individuals with corn allergies learn to bake their own foods to avoid the corn added to processed foods. If you are lucky enough to be able to eat corn, it might be beneficial to reduce your corn intake so as to prevent developing this food allergy. It is an extremely difficult food to avoid in our society when it comes to ready-made foods.

If you are avoiding corn, you may be interested in knowing about a product called *Lyle's Golden Syrup* which is cane sugar syrup made in London. This product looks very similar to corn syrup except it is a bit darker in color. It works very well in place of corn syrup. We were able to find it at our local Wegmans grocery store. I found it easy to work with and I would give it high marks. It's not as cheap as corn syrup, but then when you use corn; it's a blessing to have *Lyle's Golden Syrup*.

Avoiding Soy

Soy is one of the top 8 allergens and it is a very difficult food to avoid because it is added to many foods as a preservative in the form of soy lecithin. There are many consumers in the U.S. who avoid soy not because of allergies but because of the controversy surrounding soy. Soy is one of the crops that farmers plant to uptake contaminates from the soil. That is because soy as a plant is good at cleansing the soil. It does mean, however, that the contaminates from the soil end up in the soy plant. And that is the reason that some consumers in the U.S. avoid soy. Perhaps that little fact will make your soy allergy seem not so bad.

Soy, like gluten, wheat, milk and corn, is found in one form or another in a wide variety of foods in our society. If you are new to soy and soy products, tofu is made from soy. Consumers who are highly allergic to soy will have to watch for Tocopherol or vitamin E on food products because the source for the vitamin E or Tocopherol is often soy. Soy is often cheaper than other plant sources for vitamin E.

Many consumers end up making their own foods because of their soy allergies. The soy used in this cookbook is in the form of a few products used in some of the recipes. Tofutti Brand non-dairy sour cream and Tofutti Brand non-dairy cream cheese are made from soy and are used in a few recipes. Two other soy products that we use are the Bragg™ Liquid Aminos (or soy sauce) and tofu. If you are allergic to soy, you can skip the Bragg™ Liquid Aminos in most of the recipes and it will not make that big of a difference. If you can eat soy, but can't get the Bragg™ Liquid Aminos, you can substitute soy sauce. Minor amounts of soy are in some cereal products as a preservative. Therefore, if you are avoiding soy, please read your products and ingredient labels carefully.

Avoiding Eggs

Avoiding eggs is just plain difficult. Eggs in baked goods function to provide either moisture, leavening, or they act as a binder. It is difficult to get a good texture if you are baking without eggs, in my opinion, which is why I have written this cookbook. You can have moist, delicious tasting baked goods without eggs; it just takes a bit of finesse. All of the recipes in this cookbook are free of eggs. If you are allergic to eggs, you need to be careful. Products like Egg Beaters contain eggs. If you are not sure whether or not a product contains eggs, read the label or call the company. Many of the "egg substitutes" contain egg whites.

Like many of the other top 8 allergens, eggs can be found in unexpected places like candy, frostings, and other sauces and dressings that you would not associate with eggs. With the new food labeling law, however, food manufacturers should now be labeling any products that contain egg. This is to your benefit and a dramatic improvement over the past.

If you can tolerate eggs, you can use them in place of the Ener-G Egg Replacer™. In this cookbook if a recipe calls for 3 teaspoons or more of Ener-G Egg Replacer™ then you know you can substitute one or more eggs. The maximum number of eggs you would substitute if you can tolerate eggs is two. If you can eat eggs, simply eliminate the Ener-G Egg Replacer™ and about 3 tablespoons of water. Some recipes state how many eggs you can use.

We have lots of baked goods and rolls that have a great texture and are egg-free. You can even have French toast without eggs. If you can tolerate soy, you can make an egg-free quiche. If you can tolerate soy, you can even make some "mock" scrambled eggs using tofu. Since eggs are in the top 8 allergens, foods are now being labeled with eggs as an ingredient which makes life much easier for the food allergy consumer.

For me as an experienced baker prior to entering the gluten-free and dairy-free baking world, baking without eggs was an extremely difficult transition. Almost all of my recipes call for the dry powdered non-egg Ener-G Egg Replacer™. However, if for some reason you cannot use the Ener-G Egg Replacer™, I am providing alternative substitutions for eggs in baking. Now, I am not promising or representing that the following egg substitutions will work in my recipes. You will have to try them. But as a reference and resource here are all of the egg substitutions that should work.

Egg Substitutes:

For each egg, substitute one of the following:

As Binders:
- ½ large mashed banana
- ¼ cup applesauce or puréed prunes
- 1 tablespoon ground flaxseed mixed with 3 tablespoons water
- 1½ tablespoons water, 1½ tablespoons oil, and 1 teaspoon baking powder
- Combine one packet of unflavored gelatin with one cup boiling water (3 tablespoons of this mixture equal one egg)

As Leavening:
- 1 teaspoon baking powder, 1 tablespoon water, and 1 tablespoon vinegar (add vinegar separately at the end for rising)
- Dissolve 1 teaspoon yeast in ¼ cup warm water

Egg Substitutes: - As Leavening: (continued)

- 1 tablespoon of arrowroot powder mixed with 3 tablespoons water
- 1 tablespoon cornstarch mixed with 3 tablespoons water

For Whipping:

- ¼ teaspoon xanthan gum with about ¼ cup of water. Let stand. It thickens, and can be whipped like an egg white.

You can also try a ground flax seed and water mixture as an egg substitute in a ratio of 1 to 3. For example, to make the equivalent of 3 eggs, use ¼ cup flax seed (finely ground) and ¾ cup water blended very well. Use this mixture within 24 hours. The approximate ratio for one egg is 2½ tablespoons flax seed and ¼ cup water.

For use in sweet baking:

Try substituting 1 banana or ¼ cup applesauce for each egg called for in a sweet, baked recipe. These will flavor the recipe; however, so consider if banana or apple will taste good in it.

Cross Contamination, Dining Out and School Issues

Cross Contamination - Cross contamination occurs when you use a toaster for gluten bread and then put in a slice of gluten-free bread and the gluten-free bread picks up some gluten crumbs on it. Another example is that you fry eggs in a frying pan and it is not completely cleaned out leaving some residual egg in the pan which can be picked up the next time the pan is used. Yet another example is using a knife in jelly and placing it back in the container with some crumbs on the knife. The jelly is now contaminated with crumbs of whatever kind of bread was spread.

How serious the issue of cross contamination is depends in part upon how serious the food allergy or health issue is. If you become anaphylactic to trace amounts of egg, then a pan that is not completely cleaned out could be fatal to you. You will thus begin to develop policies and procedures for your home that fit your individual health needs.

My daughter is anaphylactic (IgE) to milk, eggs, and a few other foods like peanuts. We therefore find it simpler and easier to keep these foods out of the house. Other families choose to take other paths. Cross contamination can be handled in some cases by having two toasters, or special separate pans. For me, this is a lot of work, but it works for some people. If you have repeated visits to the emergency room for anaphylaxis, then I would suggest that you re-consider. If you have the proper set-up at home, emergency room visits for food anaphylaxis are simply not necessary.

There are families unwilling to remove foods from their home, or to refrain from taking the proper procedures when dining out, who end up in the emergency room repeatedly. This is definitely not necessary, and in fact, could be deadly.

Dining Out - If you have food needs that a restaurant cannot meet, you should feel comfortable bringing your own food while dining out with family and friends. Restaurants do not want to lose all of their business because of one individual. In other words, ten family members are going out to dinner. One child has severe food allergies, which the restaurant cannot meet. Either no one goes out to dinner, or you take the special food for the one child and the restaurant gets the benefit of 9 lunches or dinners purchased which is better than none.

Right now, I just happen to have a child which no restaurant in the country could feed. On the rare occasion that we have taken her out to a restaurant, we have brought her entire meal already cooked and in food containers. The restaurant simply has to then warm it up and serve it. My daughter requires organic foods or her eye will swell shut for starters. She is on the gluten-free, dairy-free (GFCF), egg-free, nut-free, peanut-free, and coconut-free diet with no preservatives or additives at all due to her allergies. There are many fruits and vegetables she cannot eat, and she is on a strict rotation for her foods. And I have to say it has been a challenge.

I have worked with restaurants in the past, and it would be rare that a restaurant would rather lose all of your business, than have you bring your food along and be safe. If you are that sensitive, restaurants don't want you eating their food and having a reaction for which they could be liable. Some consumers are uncomfortable bringing their own food. To you I say, either get over it, or have one of your assertive friends or relatives handle it for you. If that doesn't work, just invite people to your home and entertain there.

School Issues - There are many school issues of safety and concern for the parents of celiac children or food allergic children or children on the GFCF or other special diets. Parents can improve the compliance of the special diet by developing and honing a great relationship with the school administration and your child's teacher. If your child is anaphylactic to any foods, you will need to be responsible and make sure safeguards are in place to protect your child. It would not be prudent to assume that your child's school "gets it". School guidelines for managing students with food allergies can be found on the FAAN (Food Allergy & Anaphylaxis Network) at *www.foodallergy.org*.

Special Ingredients, Products & Preservatives

Allergy-Free Baking

How easy or hard allergy-free baking will be for you will depend on you! If you believe that you will be successful at it, you will. If you expect to be a failure, I can promise you that you will indeed fail. As Franklin Delano Roosevelt (F.D.R.) said, "The only thing we have to fear – is fear itself." If you expect to never have a failure, you will be disappointed, and let me explain why. Allergy-free baked goods that are defined as gluten-free, dairy-free, egg-free, tree-nut-free, peanut-free and coconut-free are the most sensitive baked goods. What I mean by that is baked goods containing gluten and dairy or gluten and eggs or any combination are much more forgiving. What that means is that if your true or actual oven temperature is off from the temperatures recommended in a recipe, your baked good may not turn out well. If you are a "light" measurer when it comes to measuring flour, your baked goods may well flop. But the good news here is that I'm going to give you the best tips on how to avoid failures and what to avoid. The bottom line, however, is that you will be successful if you are determined to be successful.

Flours

There are many gluten-free flours. This is an overview of the gluten-free flours. You will see in my recipes that I typically use at least two different kinds of gluten-free flours for each recipe. This is done in order to achieve the best texture in the final baked good. If you alter any of the recipes to use only one kind of flour you will most likely get a poor result. My experience is that gluten-free flours are best used in combinations. Flours that contain gluten or wheat are to be avoided for gluten-free diets.

The following flours contain gluten:

Spelt flour, Kamut flour, Durum flour, Bulgur flour, Einkorn flour, Semolina flour. In prepackaged or baked gluten-free foods these may be labeled as spelt, kamut, durum, bulgur, einkorn, or semolina and should be avoided completely.

The following flours are all wheat-free and gluten-free. These flours are made from grains, beans, roots or plants that are ground into flour.

Amaranth Flour - We have found amaranth flour to be a real bonus for the gluten-free baking. Amaranth as a grain and as a flour has a stronger flavor and taste than the bland flours of tapioca, potato or rice. Amaranth is probably best combined with other flours. We have recipes that combine amaranth with other flours. This is important for Celiacs and others on the gluten-free diet so that they do not become allergic to rice and other commonly used gluten-free flours.

Arrowroot Flour - This flour has a particular smell to it which I do not like. Therefore, I do not use it in baking. Arrowroot is white in color, and functions like tapioca or cornstarch in baking. You can use arrowroot flour or arrowroot starch measure for measure in recipes that call for cornstarch.

Corn Flour - Corn flour is much heavier than cornstarch or some of the other gluten-free flours. There are only a few recipes in this book that use corn flour or corn.

Cornstarch - Cornstarch works very well as gluten-free baking flour. There are just a few recipes in this book that use cornstarch or corn and you can substitute other flours for the corn flour or cornstarch.

Garbanzo Bean Flour - Garbanzo bean or chickpea flour can be substituted in the recipes in this book that call for garfava flour. It is heavier than some gluten-free flours and I find it best when used in combination with other flours. One advantage of garbanzo bean flour is that it comes from the bean family and not the grasses or grain family which is good if you are using a rotation diet or if you are minimizing the quantity of grains you eat.

Garfava Flour - Garfava flour is a combination of ground garbanzo beans and fava beans. I have found this to be a fantastic flour for gluten-free baking, and as such I have several recipes that use this flour in combination with tapioca flour. It is heavier than some of the gluten-free flours and is more nutritious. This is a good flour to use because it does not come from the grasses or grain family, a plus for rotation diets.

Millet Flour - As a grain, millet looks like birdseed and is in fact often found in birdseed. But don't let that deter you from trying this wonderful flour. It is heavier than many of the gluten-free flours and for that reason we use it in combination with rice flour to produce a good texture in baked goods.

Potato Starch - A few recipes contain potato starch, which is distinctly different from potato flour. When I was new to gluten-free baking I purchased potato flour, but I never ended up using it, and have never ordered it again. Potato starch is extremely light and very white. It looks just like cornstarch or tapioca flour. We stopped using potato starch when we got into the rotation diet because we'd rather eat potatoes than have potatoes in our baked goods. Only a few recipes contain potato starch.

Quinoa Flour - Quinoa flour works well when used in combination with other flours. It is a heavier flour with a stronger taste than many of the bland gluten-free flours. One advantage to quinoa flour is that it does not come from the grasses or grain family like many of the other gluten-free flours although people refer to quinoa as a 'grain'. Quinoa comes from the beet family, which is also called the goosefoot family.

Rice Flour –Rice flour has a slightly gritty consistency compared to some gluten-free flours. The advantage of rice outside of the fact that it is widely available is the fact that it is bland and goes well with most flavors. It does not have a strong taste or smell that you have to try to overcome. We have drastically cut down on the amount of rice flour that we use in baking which would be something that I would advise anyone on the gluten-free or GFCF diet. So many gluten-free products are made with rice; it would be advisable to reduce your rice consumption so as not to develop a rice allergy.

Sorghum Flour - The sorghum grain makes a heavier flour than some of the gluten-free flours. It is not as easy to find in local stores, and it has a stronger taste than some of the bland flours. It is just a tad on the sweet side and is often sold as "sweet sorghum flour". We use this flour in combination with other flours.

Soy Flour - Soy flour is made from ground soybeans. There are no recipes in this book that use soy flour. Because soy is found in so many products and because soy itself can be controversial (hormone effect on children, and that it uptakes contamination from the soil), we limit the amount of soy that we use in our home to as little as possible.

Sweet Rice Flour - This is a sweeter version of rice flour that can be used in small quantities in some baked goods. I purchased sweet rice flour once and didn't use it. There are no recipes in this book that contain sweet rice flour.

Tapioca Flour - Tapioca flour comes from the Spurge Family of plants (*Euphorbiaceae*) and is a great gluten-free flour to work with. It is extremely light and airy and has no taste or flavor to it. We use it on two rotation days to cut the taste of stronger flavored gluten-free flours.

Teff Flour - The teff flour is very dark and in my opinion has a pretty strong flavor. You will not find any recipes in this book using Teff flour. It is gluten-free flour that I did not feel had enough advantages to merit the investment of time and money for experimentation. It is a flour that adults may find pleasing, but many children used to wheat products may reject easily.

Buckwheat Flour - Buckwheat flour alone is gluten-free. You must be careful, however, in the purchase of any flour, mix or food containing buckwheat because it is frequently combined with wheat, so read your package label carefully. As a flour it is heavy and has a very distinctive flavor that many people do not like at all. For that reason, I have not included any recipes containing buckwheat flour in this book.

Sweeteners

Until I entered the Celiac and allergy baking arena, I was used to ordinary white and brown sugar for sweetening, and every once in a while a recipe would call for corn syrup. There are quite a few ingredients that you can use to sweeten your baked goods and for cooking besides sugar and corn syrup. I do not eat a large amount of sweet foods. While I have several recipes for desserts or sweet treats, I use them infrequently. I rotate our sweeteners because two of my children have a past history of becoming allergic to foods that they ate frequently or in large quantities.

The sweeteners that I use are white sugar (also called cane sugar), beet sugar which is derived from the beet plant but looks and works just like white sugar, as well as honey, and maple syrup. There are many more sweeteners available. A conversion chart is provided in the event that you cannot use the sweetener called for in a given recipe. Sweeteners are often classified into two categories: natural sweeteners and highly refined sweeteners.

Artificial Sweeteners: Artificial sweeteners are not natural in any regard; however they have become an accepted part of American society. By artificial sweetener I mean those sugar substitutes that come in the yellow, pink and blue packets that contain zero calories. In addition to being listed under this Sweeteners section, I have also included artificial sweeteners under the Preservatives and Problem Ingredients section (see page 71). There are five artificial sugars approved for use in the United States, which are saccharin, aspartame, sucralose, neotame, and acesulfame potassium. Artificial sweeteners are chemical compounds made by man and there has been controversy surrounding artificial sweeteners for decades.

What we can notice in the last twenty or so years that the term "artificial sweeteners" has been dropped in favor of "sugar substitute". How would you feel about eating artificial rice, or potatoes? It is not natural and somehow unappealing. These artificial sweeteners have not been around very long and consumers would be well advised to question the breakdown of these man-made chemicals in the human body. There is a wide range of educational books and other materials available on the Internet about the negative impact of artificial sweeteners on the human body. As a rule, individuals committed to health and well being completely avoid artificial sugar use. If you are looking for a zero calorie natural sweetener, see the listing for Stevia in this section.

Natural Sweeteners are found in nature like honey, maple syrup, date sugar, and fruit juice, or they are made from natural (unprocessed) foods like rice syrup and sorghum syrup or sweetener. The advantage of natural sweeteners is that because they are unrefined or only lightly refined they have more nutrient value. They are also digested more slowly so they don't have the same negative impact on your body as refined sugars. Please note that some rice syrups contain gluten or barley malt, so please check the labels on your sweeteners to make sure that no wheat, or gluten is used in the manufacture of that product.

Highly Refined Sweeteners are highly processed and therefore contain no nutritional value. Many foods in the American diet use highly refined sweeteners. White sugar, brown sugar, turbinado or raw sugar, and corn syrup are examples of highly refined sweeteners.

Agave Nectar or Syrup is a sweetener that is derived from the agave plant. It can be used in place of sugar or honey, and is often used by vegans and raw foodists. It is reported to be sweeter than sugar by 1.4 to 1.6 times. It has a lower glycemic index; however it is primarily comprised of fructose and glucose.

Stevia comes from the leaves of the stevia plant (*Stevia rebaudiana Bertoni*) and is a natural sweetener. Stevia can be purchased in the U.S. in health food stores and through the Internet. It provides 250 to 300 times the sweetness of sugar although it can have a slight bitter aftertaste.

Sugar Substitutions – Equivalent to One Cup of Sugar		
Sweetener	**Amount to Equal 1 cup of Sugar**	**Reduce Liquid in Recipe by:**
Agave Nectar or Syrup	⅔ cup	¼ to ⅓ cup
Brown Rice Syrup*	1 to 1¼ cups	¼ cup
Date Sugar	1 to 1¼ cups	¼ cup
Fruit Sweeteners	1 cup	¼ cup
Honey	½ cup	¼ cup
Maple Syrup	⅓ to ½ cup	¼ cup
Molasses	½ cup	None
Stevia	1 teaspoon	None
Sucanat	1 cup	None
Turbinado	1 cup	None

*Sometimes made with gluten or wheat, so check the package label before you purchase it.

Rice

Rice is a staple in the diets of people who are avoiding wheat and gluten. Rice is typically an ingredient in gluten-free commercially available foods and mixes. Many people on the gluten-free and wheat-free diets consume a large amount of rice and typically eat rice on a daily basis. This can result in the individual becoming allergic to rice. We experienced this with our second child who ate a very high amount of rice in his first two years. By the age of two, Noah could not tolerate any amount of rice. And Noah is by far not the only person who developed a problem with rice because of eating a large amount on a daily basis. This cookbook contains many rice-free recipes for this very reason.

While rice is delightful, it is extremely unpleasant to be on the gluten-free diet and not be able to eat rice. Being allergic or intolerant to rice eliminates most of the foods that you can purchase leaving the option of making your own foods. With this warning firmly established, you are free to choose to eat rice all of the time. There are many varieties of rice and once you know how to properly cook rice, it will come out perfect every time.

Some of the rice varieties available in the U.S. include white rice, brown rice, sushi rice, sweet rice, wild rice, basmati rice, Japonica rice and Wehani rice. Wild rice is not actually rice, but rather the seed of an aquatic grass which is related more closely to corn than to rice itself. Wild rice is substantially more nutritious than rice containing twice the protein, four times as much phosphorus, eight times as much thiamin and twenty times as much riboflavin as other rice varieties.

Our favorite is basmati rice, which has an aromatic smell when it is cooked. It is often used in Indian cooking because of its appealing smell and delicious taste. Brown rice has more fiber, B-vitamins, calcium, phosphorus, iron, vitamin E, protein, and linoleic acid than regular white rice making it the best choice nutritionally if you are eating any rice. When cooked, brown rice has a tendency to be moist and kind of sticky which is why it is often used in sushi, rice puddings, and for croquettes.

Long-grain rice works well in pilafs, stuffing, salads, casseroles and fried rice because the rice kernels are light and fluffy when cooked. The most important aspect of rice is that it is cooked properly. Most rice sold comes with instructions for how much water to use and how long it should be cooked. In my cooking classes, the issue of how to cook rice is a frequent question.

In cooking rice it is important to get the water to rice ratio correct as well as the cooking time. Brown rice and the longer grain rices require substantially longer cooking times. The next aspect that is important and required to get a batch of rice to turn out right is not to keep stirring the rice. For best results, rinse your rice first and pick out any blemished rice or stones. Then place the rice and water in a saucepan over high heat until the water and rice come to a boil. You may add a bit of oil and salt if desired. Once the rice has come to a boil, immediately turn down the heat to low, cover the pan and cook for the indicated time. When the cooking time is complete, remove from heat and allow to sit for 5 minutes.

If your rice is too moist, you can remove the cover and cook over low heat to allow some of the water to evaporate. Rice can burn easily, so watch it closely. I have found that when I follow the manufacturer's directions with the water to rice ratio, and the other directions I have provided here, I always get a perfect pan of rice. If you happen to buy rice that does not have instructions, here are some water to rice ratios that may be helpful. One cup of dry rice kernels will yield about 3 cups of cooked rice.

Water to Rice Ratios and Cooking Times			
Rice Variety	**Water**	**Cooking Time**	**Yield**
1 cup White Basmati	1 ¾ cups	15 minutes	3 cups
1 cup Brown Basmati	2 cups	30 to 35 minutes	3 cups
1 cup Brown	2 ½ cups	30 to 45 minutes	3 cups
1 cup White (enriched)	2 cups	15 minutes	3 cups
1 cup Wild	2 ½ cups	45 minutes	3 cups

Oils and Fats

There seems to be a fair amount of confusion about oils and fats in general. I know that as I have moved away from solid fats in the form of margarine, lard, and other hydrogenated solid shortening in favor of liquid oils, I have been unsure what "expeller pressed" or "cold pressed" meant on a bottle of oil. Also, with all of the hype about "trans-fat" it seemed like a good reason to provide some specific information about oils and fats.

First of all, fat (in the diet) is required by the human body to absorb the fat-soluble vitamins A, D, E, K, and carotenoids. Vegetable oils, that is, oils that are derived from vegetables, are one of the few sources of two essential fatty acids: linoleic (omega-6) and linoleic acid (omega-3). These two essential fatty acids are important to good health. So the question becomes where do fats and oils come from, and which have the most health benefits?

Fats are classified as saturated, monounsaturated, and polyunsaturated. Notice that all three classifications contain the word "saturated" in them. Saturation refers to the carbon-hydrogen makeup of the oil or fat in question. In general, the more hydrogen, the greater the degree of saturation and solidity of the oil.

Saturates include foods such as coconut oil, butter, lard, meat, full fat milk, cheese, , palm kernel oil, cottonseed oil, deep fried fast foods, and some commercially baked foods. Saturates are solid at room temperature.

Monounsaturated Fats include canola oil, olive oil, peanut oil, avocado, and tree nut oils. Monounsaturated fats are usually liquid at room temperature; however, they become either semi-solid or solid when refrigerated.

Polyunsaturated Fats include flax oil, hemp oil, pumpkin seed oil, safflower oil, sunflower oil, corn and soybean oils, walnuts and oily fish. Polyunsaturated fats do not become solids even if you refrigerate them. These fats are rich in linoleic (omega-6) fatty acids.

Trans-fatty Acid refers to the hydrogenation process that destroys nutrients and transforms fat into trans-fatty acids. Hydrogenation is the chemical process that uses heavy metals, hydrogen gas and extremely high temperatures to transform liquid oil into a solid or partially solid form. Margarine and shortening are products that have been hydrogenated. Other sources of hydrogenated or partially hydrogenated oils are packaged snacks like cookies, crackers, chips and baked goods.

When purchasing liquid oils, there are a few terms that will be helpful for you to understand since these terms affect the quality, flavor, and nutritional content of the oil. The first term to understand is the extraction process. Extraction refers to how the oil is removed from the plant. The common methods for extraction are expeller pressing, cold pressing, vacuum extraction, and solvent extraction.

Expeller Pressed - A process that uses mechanical pressure instead of chemicals to extract oil from the source. In expeller pressing the temperature can reach as high as 185°F due to the friction of the pressing mechanism.

Cold Pressed - This term is sometimes used for expeller pressed oils in which the temperature is below 120°F. Cold pressed is a term that you see on some olive oils, and in that case, it refers to the first pressing of the olives.

Vacuum Extraction - This refers to a relatively new process that extracts oils in a non-oxygen and light-free environment with temperatures as low as 70°F.

Solvent Extraction - Oils that are extracted chemically with petroleum solvents. The solvent extraction process destroys the oil's nutritional value.

In cooking, one additional point that is helpful to understand is the impact that refining has on your frying or sautéing. Oils that are refined can withstand a higher temperature for frying or sautéing. The unrefined oils will have what is called a lower "smoke-point" or the point at which the oil smokes. You can purchase organic oils that are naturally refined instead of exposed to chemicals and you may find them more suitable to your sautéing and frying.

Special Allergy Ingredients

There are now more special allergy ingredients available to consumers than ever before. The following are some of our favorites. Many other special allergy products are eliminated from our household because of the "may contain trace amounts" of milk, egg, nuts, etc. If you are not IgE or seriously allergic to foods, you will have a much wider range of specialty foods available to you.

Nu-World™ Amaranth Cereal Snaps **(Original Flavor)** – These are a surprise item on the list because we don't eat them plain! However, they do fit with our need to have different foods, and these little cereal snaps work well for a granola cereal or snack food. See the Feel Good Granola recipe on page 157. Made by Nu-World Foods, these Amaranth Cereal Snaps are made in more appealing flavors if you plan on eating them as cereal. The ingredients are whole grain amaranth flour and tapioca flour. This is not a food that most children or adults will jump and down about, however they are an option for many people on a limited diet due to allergies. Look for them on-line at *www.nuworldfoods.com.*

Barkat™ Organic Porridge Flakes – My two sons just love this product! Made from rice flakes, millet flakes, and agar-agar, this product is a perfect match for our rice food day. This product is labeled to be free from gluten, eggs, milk, nuts, soy and yeast. The company who makes it is Gluten-Free Foods Limited out of the United Kingdom whose website is *www.glutenfree-foods.co.uk* or at your favorite gluten-free retailer.

Bragg™ Liquid Aminos - Distributed by BRAGG Live Food Products, Box 7, Santa Barbara, CA 93102. The ingredients of Bragg™ Liquid Aminos are vegetable protein from soybeans and purified water. I've used it in some of the recipes in the recipe section of this book. It contains 16 amino acids, and I really find it to be a delightful product. If you are IgE allergic to soy by blood test or skin test, I would not recommend it. If you are less allergic to soy (non-IgE), you could try it and see if you can tolerate it.

DariFree™ - which is distributed by Vance's Foods, Inc., is a potato based non-dairy milk alternative. DariFree™ is vitamin fortified, and contains as much calcium as milk. DariFree™ is free of gluten, casein, fat, soy, rice, MSG, protein and cholesterol. Best of all, it tastes great! DariFree™ is available at *www.vancesfoods.com* or by contacting their Customer Service at 800-497-4834. The Kosher and Parve symbols are also on the DariFree™ label. DariFree™ is one of the best allergy products on the market. DariFree™ comes in a dry-mix formula, which makes for a longer shelf life, and takes up very little storage space especially if you are traveling. One can of DariFree™ yields six liquid quarts. DariFree™ makes delicious ice cream, which is included in the recipe section of this book. We use DariFree™ as a milk substitute on our potato/beef food rotation day as well as baking on that same day. This is a superior allergy product that I can't say enough good things about!

Ener-G Foods, Inc. Egg-Replacer™ - There is not one lick of egg in this dry powdered Egg Replacer™. Made by Ener-G Foods, Inc., 1-800-331-5222, PO BOX 84487, Seattle, WA 98124-5787, *www.ener-g.com*, this dry powder contains: potato starch, tapioca flour, leavening (calcium lactate, calcium carbonate, and citric acid), cellulose gum, carbohydrate gum and NO DAIRY. The calcium lactate is NOT from dairy. It contains NO lactose and no sulphites. We love this product as it is flexible and easy to use. Many of the recipes contained in this book use the Ener-G Egg Replacer™ dry powder.

Enjoy Life™ Semi-Sweet Chocolate Chips - These gluten-free, dairy-free chocolate chips are also free of soy!! Made by Enjoy Life Natural Brands, LLC, 1-888-50-ENJOY, 3810 N. River Road, Schiller Park, IL 60176, *www.enjoylifenb.com*. The ingredients in these amazing chocolate chips are evaporated cane juice, chocolate liquor, and non-dairy cocoa butter. And if that is not enough, they are made in a dedicated gluten-free and nut-free facility and are routinely batch tested for casein. Unless you are allergic to chocolate, there is no need to miss the joy of chocolate chips! Thank you so much to Enjoy Life™ Natural Brands for an outstanding product!

Food Coloring (Natural) – Long before I published this cookbook, I had stopped using artificial food coloring in favor of the natural food coloring that my health food store sold. Typically natural food coloring is made from the richly colored plants like blueberries, beets, and turmeric. My friend, Jane Hersey of The Feingold Association, shared with me this resource for natural food colorings. The Squirrel's Nest has been providing natural alternatives for food coloring since 1980. You can purchase products from their website, *www.squirrels-nest.com*, or by contacting them by mail: Nancy Kemble, The Squirrel's Nest, 1 N. Broad Street, Middletown, DE 19709. Their phone number is (302) 378-1033.

Glutano™ Ice Cream Cones - The product is labeled that it may contain trace amounts of milk and egg, so it may not be appropriate for your household. The ice cream cones are made from maize flour (corn), sugar, maize starch (corn), emulsifier soy lecithin (soy), soy oil and salt. If you can tolerate the ingredients and it poses no risk, these are a delightful treat to go with the non-dairy ice cream recipes in this cookbook.

Guar Gum - I never use guar gum in my gluten-free baking because it bothers my second son with his food allergies. Guar gum is used in very small quantities in commercial products like ice creams and salad dressings for its binding properties. If you are used to using guar gum in your gluten-free baking, you could substitute guar gum for the xanthan gum listed. I have found many people to be sensitive to guar gum, so I never use it in my baking or recipes. Guar gum is frequently used in commercially made gluten-free baked goods because it is much cheaper than xanthan gum.

Lyle's™ Golden Syrup – This is cane sugar syrup and it is a great substitute for corn syrup in baking and cooking. We used this product when we had problems with corn. The label indicates that it can be used in most recipes in equal amounts to other liquid sweeteners like honey, corn syrup, and molasses. For free recipe information you can contact the company at: Tate & Lyle Sugars, Thames Refinery, Silvertown, London E 16 2EW, UK. We found it at our local Wegmans grocery store. It may be difficult to find, but if you can't eat corn, this may be a product worth considering.

Perky's™ Nutty Flax – This whole grain crunchy cereal is made from whole sorghum flour, ground flax seed, honey, raisin juice concentrate, and salt. We think it tastes great! In addition to being a good stand-alone cereal, it works very well for the granola recipes that I have included in this cookbook. The product is labeled that it is made in a nut-free facility; however the facility does manufacture products containing gluten and soy. Perky's™ also makes a great Nutty Rice cereal.

Suzanne's™ Ricemellow Crème – This is an excellent substitute for marshmallow crème if you can tolerate the ingredients used in standard marshmallow fluff (like the eggs). It looks just like marshmallow crème when you first open it, and then it looks a bit less like it over time. It is made from brown rice syrup, soy protein, natural gums and natural flavors. It is labeled gluten-free, non-dairy, and vegan, no animal products, no GMO's, no fat, no cholesterol, no refined sweeteners, no corn sweeteners, no cane sweeteners, no *added* salt, no preservatives, and no artificial additives. We use it for making our Marshmallow Cups recipe on page 338.

Xanthan Gum - Xanthan gum is used in gluten-free baking to act as a binder. Most people are not allergic to xanthan gum and it is used in very, very, very small quantities in gluten-free baked goods. If you can't find xanthan gum at your health food store or other specialty store, you will definitely be able to find it on-line. If you spill xanthan gum on your kitchen counter it will feel very gummy. The ratio varies with different flours and recipes but one rule of thumb is to use from ¾ teaspoon to 1 teaspoon per cup of flour.

Preservatives and Problem Ingredients

Consumers have been concerned about additives to their foods for more than one hundred years as evidenced by written literature.[36] Processed foods today contain many chemicals, that are added to preserve food (extend shelf life and prevent spoilage), add color, enhance flavor and to kill insects, fungi, or bacteria. Chemicals in foods fall into several categories: preservatives, pesticides, growth hormones, antibiotics, artificial sugar, and other additives (like coloring). The United States Food and Drug Administration (FDA.) has allowed a wide variety of food additives to enter our food supply. Other countries have stricter rules governing the additives permitted in their food supply. There are several U.S. consumer organizations questioning the safety and long-term health effects of the chemicals we use in our foods. Many health practitioners, nutritionists, naturalists, and other health-minded consumers avoid preservatives, additives and other chemical additives.

On a topic that itself could fill a whole book, I will hit the high points on some of the chemicals added to foods. A good rule of thumb is that if you don't know what an ingredient is, or how to pronounce its name, it is more than likely a chemical food additive. A wealth of information is available on the World Wide Web on this topic and the specific listings that follow.

Antibiotics - Low concentrations of antibiotics have been added to animal feed for more than forty years as a vehicle to promote animal growth and to prevent and treat disease in farm animals. Long-term, low-dose use of antibiotics in farm animals lends itself to the development of antibiotic resistant bacteria in said animals.[37] What consumers need to understand is that the antibiotic resistant bacteria from these farm animals can enter

---

[36] Harvey Washington Wiley, M.D., Ph.D., <u>Foods and Their Adulteration: Origin, Manufacture, and Composition of Food Products; Infants' and Invalids' Foods; Detection of Common Adulterations</u> (Philadelphia: P. Blakiston's Son & Co., 1917).

[37] American Society for Microbiology Web site: June 19, 2002 – Preservation of Antibiotics for Human Treatment Act of 2002.

the human intestine when we eat this food. The use of antibiotics in farm animals has another impact on the food chain. Manure containing these antibiotics, when used to fertilize the soil where plants are growing can then contaminate the crops grown.[38] Consumers eating the crops which have absorbed the antibiotics from the soil, get yet another dose of drugs. None of these results are positive for individual consumers, and the primary reason for the use of antibiotics in feeds has to do with increasing profits.

Artificial Colors - Over fifty years ago, food coloring in processed foods was done naturally by adding beets or beet juice to produce a red or pink color, turmeric to add yellow, blueberries to provide a blue color, and so on. You can still color your homemade foods this way or with natural food coloring supplies sold in health food stores. Commercially prepared foods however, are often colored with chemicals. Children today are bombarded with artificial coloring in drinks, crackers, candy, fruit snacks and even applesauce! The question of whether artificial colors are safe or not depends upon who you ask and more importantly who you believe. A Yale University study found that chemical colorings could lead to hyperactivity in young rats given certain conditions.[39] It seems to me that we could probably chart the addition and increase of chemical coloring to our foods and the increase in learning and behavioral issues in the U.S.

Chemical or artificial coloring is added to foods to help make up for the loss of color experienced in packaged foods due to shelf life, light and air exposure, moisture and temperature fluctuations. It is also added to make foods more appealing and fun. Chemical colors fall under the certified colors known as FD&C colors and must be listed on an ingredient label by name. Natural ingredients like annatto extract, beet juice, beta carotene and caramel color do not have to be listed on a food label, however, they will be labeled as "artificial color" even though they are naturally derived. This is because the FDA considers every color

---

[38] University of Minnesota study published in the July-August 2007 issue of the Journal of Environmental Quality. This study was funded by the U.S. Department of Agriculture.

[39] Shaywitz, Bennett A., Pediatric Neurology, Yale University School of Medicine, Neurobehavioral Toxicology, Vol. 1:41-47.

added to a food an artificial color even if it comes from a natural plant or animal source.

Artificial Sugars - Sugar substitute is the new name given to the chemical compounds that were formerly called artificial sugars or artificial sweeteners. These chemicals add no nutrition to the foods containing them, and they bring with them plenty of controversy. There are five artificial sweeteners approved by the F.D.A. for use in food and beverages: saccharin (Sweet and Low®, Sweet Twin®, Sweet 'N Low®, and Necta Sweet®), aspartame (Nutrasweet®, Equal®, and Sugar Twin®), sucralose (Splenda®), acesulfame K (acesulfame K, acesulfame potassium, Ace-K, or Sunett®) and neotame. When you think of artificial sweeteners you can think of those little pink, blue and yellow packets of sweeteners that restaurants routinely make available.

The controversy stems over whether or not these chemicals are safe for human consumption. While the issue of safety has not been on the news or media reports, there are books, web sites, and even film documentaries dedicated to educating consumers to the dangers of artificial sweeteners. A variety of consumer advocacy non-profit organizations also feel that there are serious concerns about the negative effects of these chemicals in the human body. Because of increasing consumer awareness and alarm, some food manufacturers are now using the generic name of the chemical sugar instead of the brand name. In other words, consumers recognize the names like Splenda®, Nutrasweet®, and Sweet'N Low® and have a negative association with the brand name. Most of us do not however recognize the generic name of sucralose, aspartame, or saccharin. If your food or beverage promotes low-calorie or zero calories, it is extremely likely that it contains an artificial sugar.

Benzoates - Benzoates refers to a preservative that is both tasteless and odorless. The chemical name for benzoates is Benaene Carboxylic Acid. They are used to extend the shelf life of foods like sauces, margarines, jams, soft drinks, fruit juices, cider, pickles, milk-shake syrups, ketchup, baked goods, cheeses and some pharmaceutical products. Benzoates have been linked to health issues like allergies, asthma, skin reactions, hyperactivity, gastric irritation, migraine headaches, and uticaria. Other names for benzoates are: benzoic acid, calcium benzoate, methylparaben, methyl-p-hydroxy-benzoate, potassium benzoate, propylparaben, propyl-p-hydroxy-benzoate, and sodium benzoate.

BHA - BHA is a chemical preservative found in some meats and packaged foods in the U.S. BHA stands for butylated hydroxyanisole. It is typically used to keep fats from becoming rancid and is found in baked goods, snack foods, meats, butter, chewing gum, instant potatoes, and beer. BHA is also found in some pharmaceutical products and cosmetics.

BHT - BHT is a chemical preservative that is often found in the same products that use BHA. BHT is an abbreviation for butylated hydroxytoluene, which functions to prevent oxidative rancidity of fats. It serves to protect (preserve) food odor, color and flavor, and is added directly to shortening, some cereals and other foods that contain fats and oils.

Growth Hormones - Growth hormones are given to animals to help them become larger faster, or in the case of cows, to produce more milk. Recombinant Bovine Growth Hormone (rBGH), which is also referred to as BGH, BST, and rBST, is banned in Europe and Canada. The Recombinant Bovine Growth Hormone has been used in the U.S. since 1994. Disturbing information on growth hormones can be found on the World Wide Web, or in an excellent film documentary called "The Corporation", which features a segment on growth hormones.

Imitation Vanilla or Flavoring – Long before I published this cookbook in 2007, I had stopped purchasing imitation vanilla and foods that contained imitation anything because they are made from chemicals. It is best to avoid foods that contain imitation ingredients.

Nitrates & Nitrites - Nitrates and nitrites are found in most red meats and fish products. They function to keep meat from turning brown, and to prevent toxic bacteria that causes food poisoning from developing. Nitrates are added to some canned foods to prevent spoilage (botulism). Because nitrates have been found to foster the development of cancer in many animals, the use of nitrates is highly restricted in other countries. Nitrates can cause reactions in children and adults, but especially in children. You can purchase meats that are free of nitrates and nitrites from the grocery store, Internet, or through local farmers.

MSG - MSG stands for monosodium glutamate, which is a chemical preservative that is more common in the U.S. food supply than many people realize. MSG is a salt of the amino acid glutamic acid (glutamate). Monosodium glutamate is added to foods to "kick-up" the flavor because it is cheaper to use a chemical than real food ingredients. Foods that usually contain MSG include fried chicken, flavored snack chips, canned and instant soups, canned tuna, and fresh turkey just to get started. MSG has been known to affect many body functions like blood pressure, brain function, digestive system, endocrine system, allergic response, hearing, heart rate, hypoglycemia, lungs, nervous system, thyroid function, vision, pancreas, and the hypothalamus function.

Individuals who react to monosodium glutamate should watch for the following names on their food labels as these are indicators for MSG: monosodium glutamate, glutamate, monopotassium glutamate, yeast extract, hydrolyzed protein, glutamic acid, calcium caseinate, sodium caseinate, yeast food, yeast nutrient, natrium glutamate, textured protein, hydrolyzed corn gluten, autolyzed yeast, and gelatin.

It is easy to find out information about MSG. There are several organizations dedicated to getting out truthful and helpful information to consumers who have issues with monosodium glutamate. More information is readily available on the Internet.

Parabens - Parabens are esters of p-hydroxybenzoic acid, which is a chemical derived from petroleum processing. Parabens are found in meats, pickled products, jams, beverages, cheeses, and margarines.

Pesticides – Pesticides are any mixture or substance that is used to prevent, destroy, repel or reduce any insects, fungi, microorganisms such as bacteria and viruses, unwanted weeds or other plants, and mice or other animals. In the U.S., pesticides used on food include: insecticides for insects, rodenticides for rodents, herbicides for weed control, fungicides to control mold and fungus, and antimicrobials to control bacteria. The danger of pesticides for infants and young children is higher than that for adults for several reasons.

The United States Environmental Progection Agency has this to say about the impact of pesticides on young children:[40]

> "Pesticides may harm a developing child by blocking the absorption of important food nutrients necessary for normal healthy growth. Another way pesticides may cause harm is if a child's excretory system is not fully developed, the body may not fully remove pesticides. Also, there are "critical periods" in human development when exposure to a toxin can permanently alter the way an individual's biological system operates."

The *Environmental Working Group*, a non-profit organization whose mission is to use the power of public information to protect public health and the environment, listed this statement on their website about pesticides on your food:[41]

> "There is growing consensus in the scientific community that small doses of pesticides and other chemicals can adversely affect people, especially during vulnerable periods of fetal development and childhood when exposures can have long lasting effects. Because the toxic effects of pesticides are worrisome, not well understood, or in some cases completely unstudied, shoppers are wise to minimize exposure to pesticides whenever possible."

---

[40] From: www.epa.gov/pesticides/food/pest.htm

[41] From: www.foodnews.org a Project of the Environmental Working Group.

Sulphites - Sulphites refer to sulphur dioxide and other sulphite compounds, which are chemical compounds used to preserve some aspect of the food. They can be found in soups, canned vegetables, biscuits, fruit juices, jams, sauces, dried fruits, French fries, instant coffee, vinegar, coconut syrup, lemon juice, wine and other foods. In foods, sulphites can cause a bleaching effect or prevent browning in dried fruits and vegetables, fruit juices and some alcoholic drinks. Sulphites have been known to cause asthma and hyperactivity and other health issues. Sulphites can be listed as follows: calcium hydrogen sulphite, calcium sulphite, potassium bisulphite, potassium sulphite, sodium bisulphate, sodium metabisulphite, sodium sulphite, and sulphur dioxide.

TBHQ - TBHQ is found in many commercially processed foods, including foods served at restaurants; however finding straight-forward factual information about TBHQ is not as easy. TBHQ stands for tertiary butylhydroquinone, and it functions in foods as an antioxidant, which means it is a chemical preservative. One Internet item stated that death has been reported from ingestion of just 5 grams. Nausea, vomiting, tinitis, clouding of the eye lens, delirium and collapse have been associated with just one gram of TBHQ.

Tocopherol - Tocopherol, or vitamin E is often added to foods as a preservative. It merits mention here because the tocopherols (vitamin E) used in preserving foods often comes from soybean oil. Therefore individuals who are highly IgE allergic to soy would do well to understand this preservative and where it is used. Tocopherols or vitamin E can come from many other food sources other than soy including palm oil, sunflower oil, corn, olive oil, tree nuts, wheat germ, seabuckthorn berries, and kiwi fruit.

A Special Word About Fragrances and Health

Consumers with allergies, asthma, respiratory issues and health problems would benefit from information about the impact of fragrances on health. We think of fragrances as perfume. However, fragrances are found in a wealth of products beyond perfumes including shampoo, conditioner, soap, laundry products, and household cleaning products.

The Environmental Health Coalition of Western Massachusetts (EHCWM) is one of many outstanding organizations working to educate consumers about the negative health effects of fragrances. The EHCWM has put together a great educational brochure called *The Hidden Dangers of Fragrances*, which is a must read for allergy sufferers especially those with asthma, respiratory issues (including Reactive Airway Disease), and for the parents of children with allergies and behavioral and learning issues.

The Hidden Dangers of Fragrances brochure covers the impact on health from fragrances, the toxic chemicals contained in fragrances and other products, what to avoid, better products to use, and resources. You can obtain a copy of this valuable brochure for a one dollar donation by sending a self-addressed, stamped envelope to the: Environmental Health Coalition of Western Massachusetts, PO BOX 187, Northampton, MA 01061-0187 with a note requesting a copy of *The Hidden Dangers of Fragrances*. Make checks payable to EHCWM. The EHCWM also has a brochure on healthy homes. You can receive both brochures for a two dollar donation and a self-addressed, stamped envelope.

Technical Know-How for Special Cooking

Storing Flours & Supplies

Many years ago it seems that there was a lot of controversy about whether to store your gluten-free flours in your kitchen cabinets, in your freezer, or in your refrigerator. Except for ground flax meal, I have stored all of my flours in my kitchen cabinets without any problems. It's been over 7 years and I have not had flour go rancid or get moldy. I will say, however, that I keep all of my flours in an airtight container. The airtight containers that we purchased years ago are called Clickclack® and they have held up remarkably well with constant use. I believe that the Clickclack® containers cost a little bit more than the competitive models offered years ago, but that investment has paid off. If you are worried about storing your flours in the cabinets or you live in a high-humidity or high moisture area of the country, by all means feel free to store your flours in your fridge or your freezer.

Cookware

I recommend cooking and baking in glass, stainless steel, enamel, and cast iron. I do not recommend cooking in non-stick coated pans or aluminum unless you cannot possibly avoid it. If you didn't happen to catch one of the major TV network's exposé of non-stick coating, I'd watch for re-runs. Non-stick coatings at higher temperatures are known to off-gas chemicals that can kill pet birds. It was a stunning news piece, and suffices to say you can look on-line for more information about the toxic gases and chemicals related to non-stick coatings. As an educated consumer you can choose what works for you. My recommendations for glass, stainless steel, enamel or cast iron are for health and safety reasons. It is my experience that people with multiple food allergies are more sensitive than a non-allergic person, and may do well to avoid complications caused by sources other than food.

Special Baking Pans

Over the years we have invested in a number of special baking pans to make our baking easier and to produce more attractive results. While these baking pans do not always meet the ideals that I like to subscribe to in terms of the materials that they are made of, they are very helpful in baking. You can purchase these kinds of specialty pans in a specialized kitchen or gourmet store and on-line. Here is a listing of the special baking pans we use:

Breadstick Pan   French Loaf Pan
Cheesecake Pan   Hamburger Roll Pan
Hot Dog Roll Pan   Mini-Bundt Pans
Mini-Donut Pans   Mini-Muffin Pans

Tools for an Allergy Equipped Kitchen

There are many, many tools that you can have for your allergy kitchen. They are not all absolute or required. Here is a list of my favorite items for an allergy-free kitchen. Following the list I'll provide a little bit more information on each as needed.

- Blender
- Cake Tester
- Dehydrator (with temperature controls)
- Dough Scraper (plastic, not metal)
- Extra Freezer
- Extra measuring Cups & Measuring Spoons
- Food Processor
- Garlic Press
- Ice Cream Maker
- Joy of Cooking, Cookbook
- Juicer
- Mesh Strainers
- Toaster
- Waffle Iron

Blender - A heavy duty blender is a great tool to have for mixing green smoothies, or making non-dairy milk shakes. Blenders are also useful for puréeing soups. If the motor is not heavy duty, you will burn out the motor in short order.

Cake Tester - This is a thin metal wire that is very long which is used to test cakes and breads for doneness. I feel strongly that this is an absolute for gluten-free bread baking. I actually advocate making rolls instead as discussed in the breads and rolls section under recipes.

Dehydrator - The kind of dehydrator I am referring to has different temperature controls which can be set. The reason that I am including a dehydrator in the allergy-free kitchen, besides the fact that you can dehydrate organic herbs, and organic fruits and vegetables when they are in season, is the fact that you can make great crackers with them. The crackers can be made from whole grains (gluten-free, of course), and raw vegetables. I have included some recipes for these simple crackers or crisp breads in this book. The crackers or crisp breads are appropriate for yeast-free diets as well as GFCF, Celiac, and allergy-free diets. You can easily modify the recipes that I've included because the dehydrated crackers are very forgiving. Investing in this appliance will save you lots of money too.

Dough Scraper - While dough scrapers can be made out of metal, I recommend a plastic one because you will use this with plastic bags and you may end up poking too many holes in your plastic bags with a metal dough scraper. We received our plastic dough scraper free from Bob's Red Mill as a promotion many years ago. You can however easily find plastic dough scrapers on the Internet. They sell for as little as $0.50 to a few dollars.

Extra Freezer - The reason that I recommend an extra freezer is because you can save money on special allergy, GFCF and gluten-free diets by baking from scratch and freezing the extra. You can also save money by purchasing organic, antibiotic-free meats from organic farmers. When you purchase meat in this way you are actually buying ½ of a pig, or ¼ of a cow, so you will need an extra freezer. This is one significant way to save money. Organic beef (free of preservatives, hormones, and antibiotics) can run $15.99 to $32.00 per pound in a grocery store. The organic beef (free of preservative, hormones, and antibiotics) we purchase from local farmers costs about $4.00 a pound.

Extra Measuring Cups & Spoons - I have at least four sets of measuring spoons and 3 sets of metal measuring cups for dry ingredients and three glass measuring cups for liquids I have acquired over time. This helps to make baking very fast and expedient. When I get out the ingredients to make, say rolls, I place the appropriate measuring cup or spoon on top of each ingredient. Then making the recipe just zips along. The added bonus with this method is there is no "double-dipping" or using the same teaspoon measure for multiple ingredients.

Food Processor - This is an item that you can add when you have the money or the resources. It is also a great item that you can sometimes pick up at yard sales or from the thrift section of the newspaper. You can save a great deal of time chopping, dicing, or shredding vegetables if you have a food processor. A food processor can also be used for purées that are too thick for the blender. This is a valuable tool for most allergy-free kitchens.

Garlic Press - This device is fast and easy and is sold in many stores because they have become so popular. You place the clove of garlic in the opening in the press, place the press on top of the garlic and squeeze hard. This process separates the garlic "guts" from the skin of the garlic. It also releases all of the good garlic juices. Pressing garlic will result in approximately 10 times the potency, so if a recipe calls for chopped garlic and you put it through a press, you should use less garlic than the recipe calls for. In the recipes in this book, when I call for minced garlic, I mean garlic put through a garlic press so you will not need to use less garlic. It is important for you to know this with other recipes.

Joy of Cooking Cookbook - The Joy of Cooking is an absolutely wonderful reference book. While the Joy of Cooking does not have very many gluten-free, GFCF or other allergen recipes, it does contain a great deal of helpful information about fruits, vegetables, cooking techniques, meats, and many other subjects relevant to cooking and baking. I consider it to be my dictionary or encyclopedia for cooking, baking and foods in general.

Juicer -People who are into health or nutrition often have juicers. The reason that I am recommending a juicer is because you can make delicious non-dairy, non-gluten, sugar-free, yeast-free, ice cream from frozen bananas if you have a heavy-duty juicer. You can also use your juicer to make crackers or crisp breads using the by-products of juicing mixed with whole grains. These crackers are "baked" using the previously mentioned dehydrator and are simple and great for even the most restricted diets.

Ice Cream Maker -I recommend this because you can save money by making your own non-dairy ice cream using organic supplies. I have included recipes in this book for non-dairy ice creams. They are easy to make and taste delicious.

Mesh or Wire Strainers - The mesh or wire strainers come in different diameters and vary greatly in the size of the mesh or wire. I use these a great deal for washing and rinsing organic berries, fruits, and draining things like frozen spinach. All whole grains and dried beans should be rinsed well and drained before use, so the mesh or wire strainers are very helpful for that.

Toaster - Everyone knows what a toaster is and what it does. A toaster oven would suffice instead of a toaster, but you can easily get along with just a toaster.

Waffle Iron - This is a must because of the fabulous waffles that you can make! Waffles can be made in advance and tucked in the freezer for a fast and healthy breakfast or snack.

10 Allergy Baking Rules for Success

1) Do NOT substitute in the beginning. This may seem harsh or unreasonable, but in the beginning when you are new to gluten-free and dairy-free, etc. cooking, this will help you be more successful. The more successes you get under your belt in the beginning, the better you will feel. I have found even with my own recipes that I cannot just substitute one flour for another and produce the same result. I found this with my chocolate cake recipe when I tried to make it with different flours to fit our rotation food days. The same recipe that I have used successfully for over 7 years came out terrible when I changed the flour mix. This does not mean that you won't ever be able to substitute ingredients. I am merely suggesting in the beginning when you are working to get your confidence level up that you avoid making substitutions unless the recipe specifically states that you can substitute.

2) Get an oven thermometer. Buy the kind of oven thermometer that hangs from the rack inside and leave it there. Check it often in the beginning to test if your oven is reading at the set temperature. I discovered the critical significance of oven temperatures in gluten-free, dairy-free, egg-free baking quite by accident. One day the chocolate chip cookie recipe that I had made repeatedly suddenly turned out like flat pancakes. This puzzled me since I had used the recipe so many times in the past with perfect results. What I learned was that even though my oven was _set_ at 350°, it may not _be_ at 350°. Trust me on this, it is rare to have an oven that is actually functioning at the exact temperature that it is set for, and in allergy baking this can mean the difference between a flop and a perfectly baked food.

3) Use a full cup of flour. First I'll address how to get a full cup of flour and then I'll give you an idea of where this originated and why it is so important. The first way to get a full cup of flour is by sifting the flour into the measuring cup. The second way to get a full cup of flour is by frequently tapping the side of the measuring cup after you have put flour into it to cause settling. You will then see the flour settles down to be less than one cup of flour and you will add more flour. Seems like a lot of work, doesn't it? Yes, I agree.

So I've invented what I call the fast and easy method to get a full cup of flour which I call the "heaping mound process". In this method, you fill your measuring cup with flour until it is mounded on the top and simply cannot hold any more because it rolls off. This then counts for a full cup of flour. It makes no difference to me how you get your full cup of flour, but for the success of my cookbook recipes you must use a full cup of flour. Now let me explain why this is so important and where the roots of a full cup of flour came from.

This is critical because if you don't use a full cup of flour you will have too much liquid in the recipe for the flour-to-liquid ratio and you will most likely end up with a flop. My estimates are that in a recipe that calls for 3 cups of flour, not using a full cup of flour will put you off by anywhere from ¼ to ½ cup of flour depending upon how light your cup of flour is. That can really make a difference.

The idea of a full cup of flour comes from the fact that most allergy bakers will, once they gain confidence and experience, want to convert their old family favorites to allergy-free recipes. And most of the old recipes contain gluten which is heavier than typical gluten-free flours. Therefore, keeping the flour-to-liquid and fat/oil ratios the same makes converting recipes much simpler. For more information on converting your old recipes, see the section called *Now that You've Had Successes* on page 87.

4) Get a cake testing tool. This is another recommendation for beginners. A cake tester is usually a very long, firm toothpick-thin wire that is used for checking to see if a cake is baked all the way through. Cake testers can be purchased at better baking stores or in the Wilton section of craft and hobby stores like Jo-Ann Fabric and Michaels. This is especially useful when baking breads. If the tool appears to have batter on it, your baked goods are not done. When using it to check bread, if it is gummy or has too much pull to it, your bread is not done.

5) Proof your yeast separately. This is a rule that I will stand by in the face of all of the bakers who say it is not necessary. First of all, it is how I learned to bake bread when I was 12 years old from my grandmother, Nan Lundy. Secondly, it is the only way to know if your yeast is any good. In the beginning, until you've had lots and lots of successes, I strongly advise you to proof your yeast separately. Proofing your yeast separately means that you will place the yeast in a separate container of warm water (or other liquid) with a teaspoon of sugar (or other sweetener) added and stir well.

When you are proofing yeast, the temperature of the water is absolutely critical because water that is too hot will kill the yeast, rendering it incapable of rising. Water that is too cool will not activate the yeast. For that reason, your water or liquid temperature should be between 110° to 115°. I strongly recommend that in the beginning you actually measure the temperature of your water. You will know that your yeast has proofed when it gets a little foam on top much like the head on a draft beer. It is now ready to use. This generally takes about five minutes. If you wait too long, the yeast will continue to make foam and the head will get larger and larger until the yeast is over proofed. So gather all your ingredients and get to the part of the recipe where you combine the dry ingredients and liquid ingredients and THEN proof your yeast.

6) Never use all the liquid given in a recipe unless you really need it. Now why in the world would a cookbook call for a variation in the amount of liquid in the recipe? The variation in the amount of liquid accounts for the variation in how people measure flour. And to be very candid, I myself will measure flour differently on different days. Meaning that over time, I will require more or less liquid in a recipe depending upon how I have measured it that day. I have even measured out two batches of my roll recipes when I am doubling up on my baking and have found that one batch will require more liquid than the other. So, to be on the safe side, don't put all the liquid in that a recipe calls for until you see that it is actually needed to make the appropriate batter consistency.

7) Start with a "proven" recipe. With this cookbook, you are starting with a proven recipe. This is most important in the beginning when you are getting your confidence and skill level up. After you've had success and are moving forward, you can then turn to unproven recipes. Unproven recipes can be found lots of places like the Internet. Don't get me wrong. The Internet is a great place to get recipes, but you have to have some allergy-free baking savvy or you can waste a lot of time, money and energy. If you know someone who can bake allergy-free foods well, this would be a great place to get a proven recipe.

8) Watch the TV cooking shows. This recommendation may upset some readers because you feel sorry for yourself for all the ingredients that you can't have. I only recommend this to novice allergy bakers and cooks so that you can learn some of the basics of cooking. You can watch chicken being sautéed with oil, lemon juice and some herbs and you will learn about sautéing. If you are not experienced in the kitchen in either baking or cooking, then this would be very helpful to you. If it bothers you too much to see the hosts using eggs, gluten, dairy and all of the other foods that you can't have, then skip this recommendation.

9) Find support in your community. If you live in a larger community, you can look to see if there is a Celiac support group in your area. CSA, USA, which stands for the Celiac Sprue Association operating in the USA, has chapters in many of the larger cities. Another place you could look to for support in your community is the autism parent support groups. Many parents of children with autism have found the gluten-free, casein-free diet to be of significant value in improving the quality of their children's lives. I was very, very fortunate to have met Katrina Cheavacci, a mother from Buffalo, who invited me to a newly formed gluten-free, casein-free parent support group in the Buffalo community. Founded by Kathy Doody and her friend, Michelle, this GFCF group has helped many parents.

As a parent of two normal children without developmental delays or autism I was welcomed into the group. And what a blessed education all of my friends from the GFCF group have given me. I am so thankful to know as much as I know about autism. If you live in a more remote area or smaller town, you can find support on-line in a variety of chat sites, support groups and blogs.

10) Have a copy of the <u>Joy of Cooking</u> in your kitchen. The <u>Joy of Cooking</u> is what I like to refer to as a cooking encyclopedia as opposed to an actual cookbook. It is 850 pages, not including the index, of a great deal of technical information. Yes, many or most of the recipes contain gluten, dairy, eggs, nuts, peanuts and coconut, but I'm not recommending it for the recipes. I'm recommending it because it is a good resource for information. I don't think any kitchen should be without one.

Now That You've Had Successes

We can talk about converting recipes after you've had successes. To convert a standard recipe that calls for gluten, you will need to substitute equal amounts of flour and add xanthan gum. The xanthan gum ratio to flour is anywhere from ¾ teaspoon per cup of flour to 1 teaspoon per cup of flour. Converting recipes can be very tricky business if you are eliminating gluten and dairy and eggs all at the same time. So the best advice is to write down what you try out and when all else fails, try, try again.

It took me many, many failed attempts to get a delicious gluten-free, dairy-free, egg-free lemon poppy seed muffin. But with each attempt, I found some improvement until eventually I came up with a recipe that pleased our family. For most of the recipes in this cookbook I have used Ener-G Egg Replacer™ as the ingredient to replace eggs. In the appendix you can find other egg substitutes which will alter how any of my recipes will turn out. I am providing the egg substitutes list to help you see that there are other alternatives for egg substitutes. In making up the recipes in this cookbook, my daughter Anne could not tolerate most of the egg substitutes listed in the appendix, however the Ener-G Egg Replacer™ works well for her.

Now that you've had successes, you can forego proofing your yeast separately if you want to! I still proof my yeast separately, but I do that because the gluten-free ingredients (and organic as well) are too expensive to chance failure on bad yeast. You can also forego the cake tester, but keep the oven thermometer, please!

Saving Time and Money

Saving Time by Baking & Freezing

Whether you are single and baking for one or a busy parent cooking for a family, baking and cooking and freezing is a great way to save time, money and energy. The majority of the recipes contained in this cookbook freeze well. If you are single, or the only person in your family on a special diet, by all means baking rolls and freezing them will make your life easier. You can also bake double batches of selected foods and save more time. Once you have the ingredients out and the pans and measuring cups dirty anyway, it doesn't take that much longer to make a second batch. I use this time saving method whenever possible. On our amaranth days I will make a double batch of amaranth chocolate chip waffles so I will not have to make waffles again for two or more weeks.

Saving Time with Fast Meals

If you are not popping a meal out of a freezer for speed, the other way to have fast meals and to save time is to utilize recipes that are fairly quick to make or use a slow cooker. Stir-frys are a fast meal and can be made even faster if you have prepared the vegetables in advance or use frozen bagged vegetables. Making a pasta dish with vegetables or an added meat for protein is also a quick meal.

Saving Money on Special Diets

There are many ways to save money when you are on a special diet. We use all of the methods that I am going to share here and have been using these techniques for about seven years.

Buying Wholesale - Believe it or not, you can purchase many foods wholesale. What this means is that you are purchasing foods directly from a distributor who sells foods to grocery stores. When you are on a special diet, you will need to contact the wholesalers who service your area and carry the specialty items that you need. I started purchasing through a distributor when my second son was just a year old. The reason that I started was not to save money. It was because at that time the gluten-free diet was not as mainstream and popular as it has since become.

I could not find enough gluten-free pasta for my son in the local grocery and health food stores. I had purchased every last package of gluten-free animal shaped pasta that could be found. Desperate for more gluten-free pasta, I talked to a very helpful Wegmans employee who gave me the name of their distributor of the gluten-free pasta. I called the distributor and they shipped me two cases at the retail price.

I was so happy to have the pasta that I didn't care that I was paying the retail price, which I would have paid at the supermarket anyway. Later, I would realize that if I placed a $400 minimum order, I could save money because I would get the wholesale price. That was equal to saving a dollar per package on the gluten-free pasta, and more on higher priced items. I then organized a wholesale co-op with other consumers from the gluten-free, casein-free diet support group in my area and we would place a group order with the distributor. We then all enjoyed the cost savings.

The catch with purchasing wholesale is that you typically need to order a case of each item and have your money "invested" in a single product that may take you months to use. If the wholesaler or distributor sells a product as a unit product, then you can purchase just one unit. But for the most part, the products are sold in cases the exceptions being vitamins, and some other specialty items. In organizing wholesale orders, I would try to find other people in the group who wanted to split a case of a given food. I would send out an e-mail to the group stating that an individual was looking for people to split cases of the following products. And often, I would find others in the group who were interested in taking a half of a case of that product. The negative to buying in this fashion is that someone has to do the work of setting up the account, being responsible for payment, getting and distributing pricing and product information, drawing up one larger group order, and placing the order.

The other major drawback to ordering directly from a distributor is that they treat you as a store. What that means is that they expect that you will be home to accept your order whenever the truck arrives. Consumers who are working full or part time don't typically have that luxury so accepting the delivery of your order will have to fall on the shoulders of someone who can be home when the truck arrives. Some wholesalers are more flexible than others. The distributor that I set my account up with would let me know within one to two days which day the truck would be arriving. Therefore, I only had to be home two days instead of five. After I established a working relationship with the truck driver, he would call me and give me a heads up just before he was arriving. Other groups who have set up wholesale accounts have made arrangements with their distributors to always get delivery on a certain day of the week with a range of delivery time such as between 8:00 AM and noon, or after 1:00 PM.

There are other issues in arranging such a program. One is having the people who placed their orders come and pick up their foods. Another issue is when the distributor delivers the wrong item and because it wasn't one of your items, you don't recognize that it was the wrong product. Then it becomes an issue of whether or not it can be returned, and if so how. Or considering who could buy the item. If you have one very committed individual or a team of people, this is a great way to save money. You need to go into it with your eyes wide open and are prepared for the problems that can come up.

There are several wholesalers or distributors across the country. One of the best ways of finding out which of them service your area is to ask the store where you buy such products. The local grocery or health food store will usually share such information. Once you know which distributors or wholesalers sell in your geographic area, you can contact the wholesaler directly and see what their minimum requirements are for orders.

Some distributors require that you order every two months or every month. If that is the case, you can often set up an arrangement through your local health food retailer or health food co-op. The distributor that I originally set up my account with later lowered their minimum order to $300.00. And this distributor has no requirements that you order every month or two. It is a smaller regional distributor that handles a great deal of the specialty products so they are more flexible than larger distributors.

Buying Groups - The GFCF diet support group that I belong to approached our local cooperative food store and was able to set up a special buying group through one of the larger distributors. Because the cooperative food store was purchasing every month, we as a buying group did not have to meet that requirement. Our cooperative food store allowed us to purchase the price books, which contained all of the products available. We then had one woman in the group who coordinated all of the orders and placed one large order with the cooperative food store. This resulted in great savings.

Buying Products by the Case - Often if you order a full case directly from the manufacturer or from some retailers, you will get a discount. Some offer 10% discounts and others offer much greater savings. It all depends on what you are buying, and where you are buying it.

Organic Farmers or CSA's -One way that we have saved money on organic produce is to buy a share from a local organic farmer or CSA. CSA stands for Community Supported Agriculture. Typically in organic farming or a CSA, you purchase a particular size share. It might be a small share, a half share or a full share for a specified dollar amount. For your money, you receive a share of the crops that are grown during the season.

Baking from Scratch -In today's age of processed fast foods, it is sometimes less expensive to buy pre-made foods. This is usually not the case for people requiring special diets. The gluten-free, GFCF and allergy foods are not cheap, nor are the dry baking mixes that you can purchase. For people who have the luxury of time, which not everyone has, baking your gluten-free, GFCF or other allergy foods from scratch is the most economical option.

You can purchase flours and other ingredients to make your own mix and save money. What I typically do when I have a recipe that I like, is make up a dry mix of it, label it and put it in the pantry for the next time I need that recipe. Here is what that looks like in practice. We use the Garfava Roll and Danish Mix on our rotation Day 1 which means that every fourth day I have a need for Garfava Rolls or the Garfava Roll Mix which is also the base for the Donut Store Style Coffee Roll recipe. If I have rolls in the freezer, then I may or may not have to bake more rolls. Most often I do need to bake rolls on Day 1 of our rotation diet.

If I'm in a hurry, I'll grab a Garfava Roll and Danish Mix from my pantry. If I'm not, I'll make it up from scratch. If I know that my pantry is empty of the Garfava Roll and Danish Mixes, then the next time I make Garfava rolls I will make up one or two extra mixes. I get out two or three mixing bowls and place them on the counter. Then in each mixing bowl I place all of the dry ingredients that the Garfava Roll and Danish recipe calls for. I will set aside one mixing bowl to add the liquids to that day. I then take a quart size plastic bag and write on it with permanent marker "Garfava Roll and Danish Mix (garfava/tapioca)". I then place the dry ingredients into this plastic bag and seal it tightly. This now constitutes a dry mix ready to go the next time I need to make Garfava Rolls, Danish, a Pizza crust or bread sticks for Day 1 of our rotation diet.

What I typically do is then label a paper bag with "Garfava Roll and Danish Mix" on one side so that it has extra protection and is easy to distinguish. If your plastic bag is not properly sealed and you grab it, some of the flour may come flying out. You really don't need to place your mix in a paper bag, but I've had enough accidents that I still employ this added safety measure.

Hunger in America

Food is a necessity for human beings. Many of us take food for granted until we develop a food issue or implement a dietary intervention. In America, however there are more than 35 million Americans who don't take food for granted because they are hungry, lack food, or are at risk of being hungry. Millions of children are included in the population that lacks food as are senior citizens, disabled, mentally ill, working poor, victims of disaster, and some newly unemployed. I mention this to you, my readers, as a mother and as an individual committed to raising the level of consciousness about food problems which includes hunger. You may be one person who could help eliminate hunger in our great nation or the world (see page 132). If you are volunteering at your local soup kitchen or food pantry, you are very aware of the serious issues of hunger. For most readers, however, this issue is invisible because it is not something we see covered on the daily news.

If you have enough food and resources that you can contribute to help those in need of food, I hope that you will do so. You can volunteer to help and give your time and energy, or you can contribute financially. There are several organizations working to help feed the hungry in the U.S. Two such organizations that you could contact are:

America's Second Harvest   *www.secondharvest.org*
35 W. Wacker Dr., #2000
Chicago, IL 60601
1-800-771-2303

Bread for the World   *www.bread.org*
50 F Street, NW, Suite 500
Washington, DC 20001
(202) 639-9400
1-800-82-BREAD

Where to Purchase Pasta, Flours & Other Ingredients

I'm including this section because the options available for where to purchase pasta, flours, and other special ingredients are dependent upon where you live and your access to the Internet. We purchase our foods and special ingredients from several different stores, the Internet, a local organic farmer and from two food cooperatives. Over the years I have learned that individuals living in more rural areas either have to travel to larger cities to have access to gluten-free and dairy-free items, use the Internet for purchases, or make arrangements to purchase their products from a local wholesaler. If you live in a rural area, the Internet may be your salvation for finding special products.

Here is an overview of places that may be available for you to use to purchase gluten-free pasta, flours, and other special ingredients followed by more detailed information on the individual options:

- Grocery stores
- Health food stores
- Cooperative food stores
- Organic farms or CSA's (Community Supported Agriculture)
- Wholesaler or distributor
- Buying group or club
- Internet sites

Grocery Stores - Larger grocery stores are recognizing that gluten-free and dairy-free as well as organic and other specialty items are a profitable business. Wegmans, a grocery store chain based in Rochester, New York, has realized that meeting the needs of allergy consumers, organic shoppers, and gluten-free consumers is adding to their bottom line. Grocery stores are only an option for your shopping if they (a) carry what you need or want, or (b) are willing to order product in for you if they don't normally carry it.

If your grocery store does not carry a gluten-free, dairy-free, or other specialty food item, ask them to consider it. What you can even do is offer to purchase part of a case if the store will order it in for you. Of course you would only do this with food items that you consume in large enough quantities to merit ordering a half case, or a full case.

Health Food Stores - Health food stores are usually one of your best bets. Many health food stores are willing to order in specialty products for you if you are willing to purchase a case of the product. Some health food stores will start to carry a particular brand or item if you convince them that they will sell the product. Health food stores vary widely in how customer oriented they are, what products they carry, and how helpful they are.

Local Cooperative Food Stores - Not all geographic areas have a local cooperative food store which is also sometimes called a food co-op for short. A local cooperative food store is owned by the members who shop at the co-op. Most food cooperative stores have a membership fee and once you pay that fee, you are a lifetime member. Typically, local cooperative food stores have more organic foods, and usually some specialty products like gluten-free pasta and flours. You may live in an area that has a local food cooperative and you aren't aware of it yet. Sometimes you can find out about local food cooperatives from your health food store, or from people who are into health or organic foods.

Organic Farms (CSA's) - Organic farms, which are also referred to as Community Supported Agriculture (CSA), are a fantastic place to purchase fresh, organic fruits and vegetables. Many of the organic farms have programs where you purchase a "share" of the fruit for the summer or a "share" of the seasonal vegetables. In many instances, you can purchase different sized shares depending upon how many people are in your family. To find the organic farms in your area, look on the Internet and ask around.

Our organic farm brings the fruits and vegetables to a convenient location not too far from where we live. Once a week we go to the distribution site to collect our share of the fruits and vegetables.

We have been purchasing foods from an organic farm for several years now, and we find it to be a wonderful program for many reasons. It is economic, convenient, guaranteed to be fresh, and it is ecologically sustainable.

Wholesaler or Distributor - One frequently overlooked or unknown place to purchase gluten-free and specialty foods is through a wholesaler or distributor. A wholesaler or distributor is a business that sells foods and other products directly to a grocery or health food store. Some distributors will not sell to consumers unless you have an account. Other distributors, typically the smaller regional distributors, will sell directly to consumers *at retail prices.*

I have directed some rural consumers where the retail shopping options are limited to a regional wholesale or distributor because at least they can get the products that way. Wholesalers or distributors usually only sell products by the case. To find out which distributors or wholesalers service your area, ask your local grocery or health food store where they get their foods.

Using a wholesaler or distributor offers the opportunity to save some money if you are willing to get organized. I have discussed this in more detail in the chapter called Saving Time and Money on page 89.

Buying Groups or Clubs - Some savvy shoppers have organized their own buying clubs or groups, which purchase directly from wholesalers or distributors. Often, they are interested in having new members join. To find one in your area, you will probably have to ask around, as they may not advertise. You can also start your own buying group or club. Additional information on this subject is contained in the chapter titled Saving Time and Money on page 89.

Internet - While many consumers are not comfortable with shopping and using their credit cards over the Internet, this is one of the best ways to find a large variety of gluten-free, dairy-free, and specialty allergy ingredients where you don't have to agree to purchase a case of food!

If you are adverse or opposed to ordering on-line, you can purchase "disposable" credit cards from some of the major retailers and use this as payment instead of a credit card.

We use a combination of all of the outlets listed above. When you are brand new to the gluten-free, dairy-free and allergy shopping, it takes a while to figure out what is available in your area. If you live in a very rural or remote area, you will be more limited in your options. With the Internet, however, people living in very rural areas have access to a much wider range of gluten-free and dairy-free options than might otherwise be possible.

Important

WARNING for FOOD ALLERGY& CELIAC Consumers

It is extremely important that you read food labels. Food manufacturers have the right to change their food product formulation at any time without notification. A food made gluten-free, egg-free, nut-free or dairy-free today, may not be gluten-free, egg-free, nut-free or dairy-free tomorrow. This warning cannot be emphasized enough. Please read your food labels on an on-going basis to be responsible and avoid serious health problems.

Rotation Diets & Food Families

Rotation and Rotary Diets

My second child, Noah, became allergic to rice by age two because it was the primary food that he ate. He consumed a great deal of it for 18 months, and by the time he was two years old, foods containing rice would produce the same gastrointestinal symptoms as if Noah had eaten gluten. I was devastated once I realized it was rice that had become the new problem in Noah's diet. And my son is not the only person who has become allergic to rice as a result of eating it on a daily basis. Our family friend, Linda Breitbach, became allergic to rice after eating it every day for four years while living in China. And Linda was not a person who had food allergies or problems with foods.

Rice is a major ingredient in most commercially available gluten-free and wheat-free foods. Rice is a major ingredient in baking mixes and even in recipes. An allergy to rice can produce physical reactions that are unpleasant at best. It is painful to be on the gluten-free diet and not be able to eat rice! Trust me when I say that if you can avoid this problem it is well worth it. I include this section on Rotation and Rotary diets as a tool to help you avoid developing new food allergies.

A rotation diet and a rotary diet are both a type of plan or format for eating your foods such that you are not eating the same foods every day or eating too much of a food on a given day. Rotary diets involve eating one food per meal and rotating the foods until you run out of foods in which case you start over. This type of diet is hard for many consumers to adhere to because it is very different to how we are used to eating. In a rotary diet, for example on day one, we could pick one of our foods, say potatoes, and eat that for breakfast. That is the only food that we would eat for breakfast. Then, we would have a different food for lunch, say beef, and we would only eat beef for lunch.

We would follow the same pattern until we have finished eating for the day. A rotation diet is different from a rotary diet in that you set up your rotation days of different foods and you eat from the foods available for the day. Typically rotation diets are done for four or more days. The wider your array of foods, the longer and wider your rotation diet can be.

In the "olden" days, some of your grandmothers or great-grandmothers followed a weekly meal plan that was some variation of the following:

> Sunday-Dinner = Pot Roast (Beef)
> Monday Dinner = Chicken
> Tuesday Dinner = Pork Roast or Loin
> Wednesday Dinner = Turkey
> Thursday Dinner = Pasta
> Friday Dinner = Fish
> Saturday Dinner = Lamb chops or Venison

What your grandmother and great-grandmother did was cook a big meal for dinner with just enough for lunch the next day. So the family ate a beef pot roast on Sunday night for dinner and also for lunch on Monday. But Monday night's dinner was a different meal. Thus from dinner one day to lunch the next day constituted a 24 hour period. Thus, this was the norm up until the 1950's and early 1960's when more mothers began to work and less time was spent devoted to meal preparation and planning. This was a rotation diet. Many if not most families stopped doing this in the 1950's and 1960's.

In the days before refrigerated rail cars and refrigerated trucking, people ate the foods that were grown locally and the foods that were in season. During the spring, summer and fall they ate fruits and vegetables that were perishable. During the winter months, people ate pumpkins, squash, potatoes, beets, turnips and other root vegetables that would keep in their root cellars. This was another form of a rotation diet. They would eat a food for a period of a few months, and then not again for months and months. Most people abandoned this philosophy and way of life with the introduction of modern conveniences like the grocery store!

I'll be perfectly frank and say that I resisted the finer points of the rotation diet until it was proven to me that is was a necessity. So, I don't fault anyone who resists doing a rotation diet. However, there is a huge payoff for those individuals who are willing to stay the course and stick with a rotation diet; these are the patients who will get better faster. What I have provided here is a 4 day rotation diet. This particular rotation diet includes no fish, shellfish, or seafood of any kind. If you can have fish, shellfish, or any seafood, you could add that. This 4 day rotation also does not include every fruit or vegetable that is available such as grapefruits, kiwis, cherries, plums, lettuce, zucchini, asparagus, and greens like collards, arugula and Swiss chard to name a few.

This 4 day rotation diet is based on plant families which are identified in parentheses. To help you, a list of foods and their plant families follows the 4 day rotation diet along with more directions on how to calculate your own rotation diet.

4 Day Rotation Diet

Day 1: Potato & Beef

Oil:	Olive (Olive Family)
Sweetener:	Cane Sugar (Grain family)
Flours:	Garfava (Legume family)
	Tapioca (Spurge Family)
Juice:	Apple (Apple Family)
	Pear (Apple Family)
Milk Substitution:	DariFree™ (Nightshade Family)
Spices or Flavorings:	Cinnamon (Laurel Family)
	Paprika & Peppers (Nightshade or Potato Family)
Fruit:	Apples & Pears (Apple Family)
Vegetables:	Green Beans (Legume Family)
	Peas (Legume Family)
	Peppers (Nightshade or Potato Family)
	Potatoes (Nightshade or Potato Family)
	Tomatoes (Nightshade or Potato Family)
Protein:	Beef (Bovid or Bovine Family)
Ice Cream:	Potato Based (Nightshade or Potato Family)
Vitamin & Mineral Supplement:	
	IntraMAX®
Other:	Cod Liver Oil (Contains Fish)

Day 2: Turkey & Rice

Oil:	Safflower (Composite Family)
Sweetener:	Honey
Flours:	Millet (Grain Family)
	Rice (Grain Family)
Juice:	Grape (Grape Family)
	Cranberry (Heath Family)
	Blueberry (Heath Family)
Milk Substitution:	Rice (Grain Family)
Spices & Flavorings:	Onion & Garlic (Lily Family)
	Worcestershire Sauce
Fruits:	Grapes (Grape Family)
	Cranberry (Heath Family)
	Blueberry (Heath Family)
Vegetables:	Carrots & Celery (Parsley Family)
	Cabbage (Mustard Family)
Protein:	Turkey (Turkey Family)
Ice Cream:	Rice (Grain Family)
Vitamin & Mineral Supplement:	
	Mother Natures Miracle®
Other:	Flax Oil

Day 3: Chicken & Amaranth

Oil:	Sesame (Sesame Family)
Sweetener:	Beet Sugar (Goosefoot or Beet Family)
Flours:	Amaranth (Goosefoot or Beet Family)
	Quinoa (Goosefoot or Beet Family)
	Tapioca (Spurge Family)
Juice:	Peach (Plum Family)
	Pineapple (Pineapple Family)
Milk Substitution:	Soy (Legume Family)
Spices or Flavorings:	Chocolate (Chocolate Family)
	Peppermint (Mint Family)
Fruits:	Peaches (Plum Family)
	Watermelon (Melon or Gourd Family)
	Pineapple (Pineapple Family)
Vegetables:	Spinach (Goosefoot or Beet Family)
	Beets (Goosefoot or Beet Family)
	Pumpkin (Melon or Gourd Family)
	Squash (Melon or Gourd Family)
Protein:	Chicken (Pheasant Family)
Ice Cream:	Soy (Legume Family)
Vitamin & Mineral Supplement:	IntraMAX®, Russian Formula®
Other:	Cod Liver Oil (Contains FISH)
	Sesame Seeds (Sesame Family)
	Tahini (Sesame Family)
	Quinoa Pilaf & cereal (Goosefoot or Beet Family)

Day 4: Corn & Pork (see note on following page)

Oil:	Sunflower (Composite Family)
Sweetener:	Maple Syrup (Maple Family)
Flours:	Corn (Grain Family)
	Sorghum (Grain Family)
	Flaxseed (Flax Family)
Juice:	Orange (Citrus or Rue Family)
	Lemon (Citrus or Rue Family)
	Strawberry (Berry Family)
	Raspberry (Berry Family)
Milk Substitution:	Sunflower Milk (Composite)
Spices & Flavorings:	Onion & Garlic (Lily Family)
	Lemon & Orange (Citrus or Rue Family)
	Raspberry & Strawberry (Berry Family)
Fruits:	Banana (Banana Family)
	Orange (Citrus or Rue Family)
	Strawberry (Berry Family)
	Raspberry (Berry Family)
Vegetables:	Sweet Potatoes (Morning Glory Family)
	Cauliflower (Mustard Family)
	Broccoli (Mustard Family)
	Cabbage (Mustard Family)
Protein:	Pork (Swine Family)
Ice Cream:	Orange Sorbet; Sunflower Milk Ice Cream
Vitamin & Mineral Supplement:	Isotonix Might-a-Mins®
Other:	Flax Oil
	Sunflower Seeds (Composite Family)
	Ground Sunflower Seed
Butter(Composite Family)	
	Flax Seeds (Flax Family)

Note: Individuals who have problems with corn could substitute other gluten-free flours for corn like buckwheat or teff. Individuals with pork allergies can substitute lamb, or other protein sources. See the food families chart for ideas.

Foods for Our Four Rotation Days

Not every recipe in this cookbook fits neatly into our four rotation diet days. The reason for this is because in the beginning I did not think it was actually necessary to rotate things like sugar, onion, garlic, sweet potatoes, and other foods that we used as spices and flavorings. It was only when it was proven to me otherwise that I finally broke down and began rotating spices, sugars, oils and food items that I had not originally rotated. The following is a list of the foods that you could have on our four rotation diet days with the recipes included in this cookbook.

Potato & Beef Day

Breads

Main Dishes

Any number of cookie, cake & dessert recipes can be made using rice & millet flours.

*Commercially made rice crackers and rice cereals are available for this day.

Chicken & Amaranth Day

Breads

Main Dishes

Other Foods for the Day
        Soy Milk
        Tofu
        Peaches
        Pineapple
        Watermelon
        Spinach
        Beets
        Pumpkin & Squash
        Quinoa Grain

Corn & Pork Day

Breads

How to Figure Out Your Own Rotation Diet

Well, I have 100% compassion for you if you are willing to go the extra mile and do a rotation diet! It seems overwhelming, but it is not as hard as it looks. The first thing you need to decide is how many days you will have in your rotation. If you can have a large variety of foods, go for a longer rotation period than 4 days. If you are very restricted, go for the minimum of 4 days. The second item that you need to consider is what foods you can have and what food families the foods you can have come from. Read through this next section and then you will find charts for you to complete as you move through the process. It may seem confusing at first, but if you fill in the charts provided, it will start to make sense.

To help you along, I have included a food family table. In doing my research for this food family table, it seems as though different families have different common names. I used the most common one found in multiple sources. Write up your list of all the foods that you can have and then look up the food family. You will then sort the foods into groups of foods that come from the same food family. Apples and pears come from the same food family, the Apple or Rose Family, so you would list them together on your list. Amaranth, beets, spinach, beet sugar, quinoa, and chard all come from the Goosefoot or Beet Family so you would list them together on your list of foods assuming you could eat all of those foods.

After you have matched each food with the appropriate food family, and then grouped the foods together by family you will then begin to sort them into four or more food days. For each food day you will want to have a protein source, oil, fruits, vegetables, a milk substitute, flours, spices and a sweetener. The biggest problem that you will have if you are on a gluten-free diet is that many of the gluten-free flours all come from the same food family.

The Grain or Grass Family consists of corn, millet, rice, sorghum and sugarcane/molasses. What that means is that you will need other gluten-free flours like potato, garfava, quinoa, amaranth and tapioca to have enough combinations of flours. What we did in our rotation diet was to take the Grain or Grass Family flours and separate them by one food day. Day 2 of our rotation is the rice and millet flour day. Day 4 is the corn, sorghum and flaxseed/flax meal flour day. Day one is the garfava and tapioca flour day with Day 3 being the amaranth, quinoa and tapioca flour day. So tapioca is used on the first and third day. No other flours are repeated.

It seems more overwhelming than it actually is. Once you list out the foods and start sorting them it gets easier. Safflower and sunflower, two of our oils, come from the same food family, the

Composite Family. So we separated the oils by a day. When your diet is restricted because of food allergies, it is extremely important that you are under the care of a really good physician who can do the proper blood work to look for nutritional deficiencies. I consulted with numerous registered dietitians who were unable to make any positive recommendations due to the restrictions in our food choices. Food is your source of nutrition. Food is your source of life. This is why nutritional supplementation is so vital to individuals suffering from allergies.

Please do not self-medicate. Seek out the proper medical professional to help you with your nutritional needs.

STEP 1:

Fill in the following chart as to the foods that you can eat. List all of the foods that you can have individually. Look up the corresponding food family for each individual food.

Foods That I Can Tolerate	Food Family

STEP 2: Using the first chart that you completed, take any foods that belong to the same food family and mark those foods with a symbol like a star, triangle, square or number (1's, 2's, 3's). For example spinach, beets, amaranth, and quinoa are all from the Goosefoot or Beet Family so these would all go together. You could also use a colored marker on the chart to group foods into the same families. I personally find the colored marker technique to be an easy way to distinguish what foods go together.

STEP 3: The last step is to sort out the foods that you can eat into different days. I have provided the following chart to help you accomplish this task. You should just know up front that you will probably have to do this more than one time, and you may want to do it in pencil. I suggest you make a copy of this chart and not write in your book as this may change for you over time. I have already provided you with a sample of a complete 4 day rotation diet using very limited foods. To complete your own rotation diet, you will take your first chart with the marked foods and put all of the foods that go together on one day. You will have some foods that are not in the same food family as any other. You can save them and use them to fill in as needed.

You will also have several foods from one family. For example, there are many, many grasses or grains in the Grass or Grain Family. You can list them all on one day and then divide them up using them on days 1 and 3 or days 2 and 4. Foods from the same family are best separated by a full day.

	DAY 1	DAY 2	DAY 3	DAY 4
	Rotation Diet Chart *The Super Allergy Girl™ Allergy & Celiac Cookbook*			
Protein				
Oil				
Sweetener				
Flours				
Flours				
Flours				
Fruit				
Fruit				
Fruit				
Vegetable				
Vegetable				
Vegetable				
Vegetable				
Spices				
Spices				
Milk Substitution				
Flavorings				

Foods, Food Families, and Other Food Lists

The following food charts are provided in two ways. The first chart lists foods from all food families alphabetically. The second food chart lists foods alphabetically within their specific food family. This information is a compilation of many different resources. I was amazed at how some listings changed things a bit. I took several reputable lists, made comparisons and summarized them in the following chart. What is interesting to note is how, in my opinion, mass production of foods as we live in society today has reduced the numbers and varieties of foods available. We have seen this in our family through our participation with our local organic farm. We were introduced to foods like blue potatoes and other varieties of foods that you don't find in the grocery store. You can find local organic farmers in your area by looking on the Internet under Community Supported Agriculture (CSA) and through other organizations that are listing and tracking organic farming like Local Harvest (*www.localharvest.org*) or Sustainable Agriculture Research and Education (SARE) which is part of the USDA's Cooperative State Research Education and Extension Service. Look up *www.sare.org* on the Internet. You can find charts like this one on-line through agriculture schools and through the United States Department of Agriculture among other sites.

Because this cookbook may be used as a reference for many people with different needs, including physicians and other medical professionals, I did include tree nuts, plants containing gluten and other allergens that are not otherwise contained in this cookbook. That decision was made to be helpful to the general user and also because while this cookbook contains recipes with no tree nuts, eggs, milk, gluten, etc., some consumers purchasing this cookbook will indeed be able to eat some of those foods and will substitute. Using the following alphabetical chart, you can quickly find a food item and its family. The chart is for rotation diet planning and other measures.

ALPHABETICAL FOOD FAMILIES CHART
The Super Allergy Girl™ Allergy & Celiac Cookbook

FOOD	FAMILY
abalone	Mollusks
acacia (gum)	Legume Family
acorn squash	Gourd Family
agar-agar	Algae Family
agave	Amaryllis Family
albacore	Mackerel Family
alfalfa	Legume Family
algae	Algae Family
allspice	Myrtle Family
almond	Plum Family
aloe vera	Lily Family
American eel	Eel Family
anchovy	Anchovy Family
angelica	Parsley Family
anise	Parsley Family
annatto	Bixa Family
antelope	Pronghorn Family
apple	Apple Family
apple cider	Apple Family
apple mint	Mint Family
apple pectin	Apple Family
apple vinegar	Apple Family
apricot	Plum Family
arrowroot, Brazilian	Spurge Family
arrowroot, *Maranta*	Arrowroot Family
arrowroot, Queensland	Canna Family
artichoke flour	Composite Family
asparagus	Lily Family
aspergillus	Fungi Family
avocado	Laurel Family
bacon	Swine Family (Pork)
baker's yeast	Fungi Family
banana	Banana Family
barley	Grass Family

basil	Mint Family
bass (black)	Sunfish Family
bass (yellow)	Bass Family
bay leaf	Laurel Family
bean	Legume Family
bear	Bear Family
bearberry	Heath Family
beef	Bovine Family
beet	Goosefoot Family
beet sugar	Goosefoot Family
bell pepper	Nightshade Family
bergamot	Mint Family
birds	Birds
black bass	Sunfish Family
blackberry	Berry Family
black-eyed peas	Legume Family
black pepper	Pepper Family
black walnut	Walnut Family
blueberry	Heath Family
bluefish	Bluefish Family
borage	Borage Family
boysenberry	Berry Family
brandy	Grape Family
Brazil nut	Sapucaya Family
breadfruit	Mulberry Family
brewer's yeast	Fungi Family
broccoli	Mustard Family
Brussels sprouts	Mustard Family
buckwheat	Buckwheat Family
bulgur	Grass Family
burdock root	Composite Family
buttercup squash	Gourd Family
butterfish	Harvestfish Family
butternut	Walnut Family
butternut squash	Gourd Family
cabbage	Mustard Family
cacao	Chocolate Family
cane sugar (white sugar)	Grass Family

cantaloupe	Gourd or Melon Family
caper	Capers Family
caraway seed	Parsley Family
cardamom	Ginger Family
cardoon	Composite Family
caribou	Deer Family
carob	Legume Family
carp	Minnow Family
carrageen	Algae Family
carrot	Parsley Family
casaba melon	Gourd or Melon Family
caserta squash	Gourd or Melon Family
cashew	Cashew Family
cassava	Spurge Family
castor bean	Spurge Family
castor oil	Spurge Family
catfish	Catfish (Fish)
catnip	Mint Family
cauliflower	Mustard Family
caviar	Sturgeon Family
cayenne pepper	Nightshade (or Potato) Family
celeriac	Parsley Family
celery	Parsley Family
chamomile	Composite Family
chard	Goosefoot or Beet Family
chayote	Gourd or Melon Family
cherry	Plum Family
chervil	Parsley Family
chestnut	Beech Family
chia seed	Mint Family
chicken	Pheasant Family
chickpea	Legume Family
chicle	Sapodilla Family
chicory	Composite Family
chili pepper	Nightshade or Potato Family
Chinese cabbage	Mustard Family
Chinese gooseberry	Dillenia Family
Chinese potato	Yam Family

Chinese water chestnut	Sedge Family
chinquapin	Beech Family
chives	Lily Family
chocolate	Chocolate Family
cinnamon	Laurel Family
citric acid	Fungus Family
citron	Citrus or Rue Family
citronella	Grass Family
clam	Mollusks (Pelecypod)
clove	Myrtle Family
clover, red	Legume Family
cocoa	Chocolate Family
cocoa butter	Chocolate Family
coconut	Palm Family
cod (scrod)	Codfish Family
coffee	Coffee Family
cola nut	Chocolate Family
collards	Mustard Family
coltsfoot	Composite Family
comfrey	Borage Family
coriander	Parsley or Carrot Family
corn	Grass Family
costmary	Composite Family
cottonseed oil	Macadamia Family
crab	Crustaceans
crabapple	Apple Family (part of the larger *Rosaceae* Family)
cranberry	Heath Family
crappie	Sunfish
crayfish	Crustaceans
cream of tartar	Grape Family
Crenshaw melon	Gourd or Melon Family
croaker	Croaker (Fish) Family
crookneck squash	Gourd or Melon Family
cucumber	Gourd or Melon Family
cumin	Parsley or Carrot Family
currant	Gooseberry Family
cushaw squash	Gourd or Melon Family

dandelion	Composite Family
dasheen	Arum Family
date	Palm Family
date sugar	Palm Family
deer	Deer Family (Mammals)
dewberry	Berry Family (Part of the larger *Rosaceae* Family)
dill	Parsley or Carrot Family
dittany	Mint Family
dolphin	Dolphin Family
dove	Dove Family (Birds)
dried "currant"	Grape Family
drum (saltwater)	Croaker Family (Fish)
drum (freshwater)	Croaker Family (Fish) Freshwater
duck	Duck Family (Birds)
dulse	Algae Family
eggplant	Nightshade or Potato Family
eggs (chicken)	Pheasant Family (Birds)
elderberry	Honeysuckle Family
elk	Deer Family (Mammals)
endive	Composite Family
English walnut	Walnut Family
escarole	Composite Family
eucalyptus	Myrtle Family
fava bean	Legume Family
fennel	Parsley or Carrot Family
fenugreek	Legume Family
fig	Mulberry Family
filbert	Birch Family
finocchio	Parsley or Carrot Family
flaxseed	Flax Family
flounder	Flounder Family (Fish)
French endive	Composite Family
freshwater drum	Croaker Family (Fish)
frog (frogs' legs)	Amphibian (Frog)
fungi	Fungus Family

garbanzo	Legume Family
garden sorrel	Buckwheat Family
garlic	Lily Family
gherkin	Gourd or Melon Family
gin	Conifer Family
ginger	Ginger Family
ginseng	Ginseng Family
globe artichoke	Composite Family
goldenrod	Composite Family
goose	Duck Family (Birds)
gooseberry	Gooseberry Family
gotu kola	Parsley or Carrot Family
granadilla	Passion (Flower) Family
grape	Grape Family
grapefruit	Citrus or Rue Family
grenadine	Pomegranate Family
grits (from corn)	Grass Family
groundnut	Sedge Family
grouper	Sea Bass (Fish)
grouse (ruffed)	Grouse Family (Birds)
guava	Myrtle Family
guinea fowl	Guinea Fowl (Birds)
gum acacia	Legume Family
gum tragacanth	Legume Family
haddock	Codfish Family (Fish)
hake	Codfish Family (Fish)
halibut	Flounder Family (Fish)
ham	Swine Family (Pork/pig)
harvest fish	Harvest Family (Fish)
hazelnut	Birch Family
heartnut	Walnut Family
hibiscus	Mallow Family
hickory nut	Walnut Family
hog	Swine Family (pig/pork)
hominy (grits, from corn)	Grass Family
honey	Not categorized – may contain pollen or spores from a variety of floral plants

honeydew	Gourd or Melon Family
hop	Mulberry Family
horehound	Mint Family
horse	Horse Family (Mammals)
horseradish	Mustard Family
horsetail	Horsetail Family
Hubbard squash	Gourd or Melon Family
huckleberry	Heath Family
hyssop	Mint Family
Jerusalem artichoke	Composite Family
jicama	Legume Family (or Morning Glory Family depending upon who you speak to)
juniper	Pine Family
kale	Mustard Family
kelp	Algae Family
kidney bean	Legume Family
kiwi berry	Dillenia Family
kohlrabi	Mustard Family
kumquat	Citrus or Rue Family
lamb	Bovid or Bovine Family
lamb's quarters	Goosefoot or Beet Family
lavender	Mint Family
lecithin (soy)	Legume Family
leek	Lily Family
lemon	Citrus or Rue Family
lemon balm	Mint Family
lemon grass	Grass Family
lemon verbena	Verbena Family
lentil	Legume Family
lettuce	Composite Family
licorice	Legume Family
lima bean	Legume Family
lime	Citrus or Rue Family
litchi	Soapberry Family
lobster	Crustaceans (Seafood)
loganberry	Berry Family (Part of the larger

loganberry (continued)	*Rosaceae* Family)
lovage	Parsley or Carrot Family
macadamia	Macadamia Family
mace	Nutmeg Family
mackerel	Tuna Family (Fish)
malanga	Arum Family
malt(from barley)	Grass Family
maltose(from barley)	Grass Family
mango	Cashew Family
maple sugar	Maple Family
maple syrup	Maple Family
Maranta starch	Arrowroot Family
marjoram	Mint Family
milk (cow's)	Bovid or Bovine Family
milk, goat	Bovid or Bovine Family
milk, rice	Grass Family
milk, sheep	Bovid or Bovine Family
milk, soy	Grass Family
millet	Grass Family
molasses(cane sugar)	Grass Family
mold	Fungi Family
moose	Deer Family (Mammals)
morel	Fungi Family
mulberry	Mulberry Family
mullet	Mullet Family (Fish)
mung bean	Legume Family
muscadine	Grape Family
mushroom	Fungi Family
muskmelon	Gourd or Melon Family
mussel	Mollusks (Pelecypods)
mustard greens	Mustard Family
mustard seed	Mustard Family
mutton	Bovid or Bovine Family
navy bean	Legume Family
nectarine	Plum Family
New Zealand spinach	Carpetweed Family
northern scup	Porgy Family (Fish)

nutmeg	Nutmeg Family
nutritional yeast	Fungi Family
oat	Grass Family
oatmeal	Grass Family
ocean catfish	Sea Catfish Family (Fish)
ocean perch	Scorpionfish Family (Fish)
octopus	Mollusk
okra	Mallow Family
olive	Olive Family
onion	Lily Family
opossum	Opossum Family (Mammal)
orange	Citrus or Rue Family
oregano	Mint Family
oyster	Mollusk (Pelecypods)
palm cabbage	Palm Family
papaya	Pawpaw Family
paprika	Myrtle Family
paradise nut	Sapucaya Family
parsley	Parsley Family
parsnip	Parsley Family
partridge	Grouse Family (Birds)
passion fruit	Passion Flower Family
pattypan squash	Gourd or Melon Family
pawpaw	Pawpaw Family
pea	Legume Family
peach	Plum Family
peanut	Legume Family
pear	Apple Family (Part of the larger *Rosaceae* Family)
pecan	Walnut Family
pectin (apple)	Apple Family (Part of the larger *Rosaceae* Family)
pennyroyal	Mint Family
pepino (melon pear)	Nightshade or Potato Family
pepper, sweet	Nightshade or Potato Family
peppercorn	Pepper Family
peppermint	Mint Family

perch (ocean)	Scorpionfish Family (Fish) (also called Rosefish)
perch (white)	Bass Family (Fish)
perch (yellow)	Perch Family (Fish)
Persian melon	Gourd or Melon Family
persimmon	Ebony Family
pheasant	Pheasant Family (Bird)
pickerel	Pike Family (Fish)
pigeon (squab)	Dove Family (Bird)
pigweed	Purslane Family
pike	Pike Family (Fish)
pilchard (sardine	Herring (Saltwater) Family (Fish)
pimiento	Nightshade or Potato Family
pineapple	Pineapple Family
pine nut	Conifer Family
pistachio	Cashew Family
plantain	Banana Family
plum	Plum Family
poi	Arum Family
poison ivy	Cashew Family
pomegranate	Pomegranate Family
pompano	Jack Family (Fish)
popcorn	Grass Family
poppy seed	Poppy Family
porgy	Porgy Family (Fish)
pork	Swine Family (Mammals)
potato	Nightshade or Potato Family
prawn	Crustaceans (seafood)
preserving melon	Gourd or Melon Family
prune	Plum Family
puffball	Fungi Family
pummelo	Citrus or Rue Family
pumpkin	Gourd or Mellon Family
pumpkinseed (sunfish)	Sunfish Family (Fish)
quail	Pheasant Family (Birds)
Queensland arrowroot	Canna Family
Queensland nut	Protea Family
Quince	Apple Family (Part of the larger

quince (continued)	*Rosaceae* Family)
quinoa	Goosefoot or Beet Family
rabbit	Hare Family (Mammal)
radish	Mustard Family
raisin	Grape Family
rape	Mustard Family
raspberry	Berry Family (Part of the larger *Rosaceae* Family)
rattlesnake	Snake Family (Reptile)
red clover	Legume Family
reindeer	Deer Family (Mammal)
rhubarb	Buckwheat Family
rice	Grass Family
romaine	Composite Family
rosefish	Scorpionfish Family (Fish)
rosehips	Apple Family (Part of the larger *Rosaceae* Family)
rosemary	Mint Family
ruffed grouse	Grouse Family (Bird)
rutabaga	Mustard Family
rye	Grass Family
safflower oil	Composite Family
saffron	Iris Family
sage	Mint Family
sago starch	Palm Family
sailfish	Marlin Family (Fish)
salmon species	Salmon Family (Fish)
salsify	Composite Family
sarsaparilla	Lily Family
sassafras	Laurel Family
sauger (perch)	Perch Family
savory	Mint Family
scallop	Mollusks (Pelecypods)
sea grape	Buckwheat Family
sea herring	Herring Family, saltwater (Fish)
sea trout	Croaker Family, Saltwater (Fish)
seaweed	Algae Family

senna	Legume Family
sesame	Sesame Family
shad(roe)	Herring Family, freshwater (Fish)
shallot	Lily Family
shave grass	Horsetail Family
sheep	Bovid or Bovine Family
shrimp	Crustacean Family
silver perch	Croaker Family, saltwater (Fish)
sloe	Plum Family (Part of the larger *Rosaceae* Family)
smelt	Smelt Family (Fish)
snail	Mollusks (Gastropods)
soap plant	Lily Family
sole	Flounder Family (Fish)
sorghum	Grass Family
sorrel, garden	Buckwheat Family
soy	Legume Family
soybean	Legume Family
spaghetti squash	Gourd or Melon Family
spearmint	Mint Family
spinach	Goosefoot or Beet Family
spotted sea trout	Croaker Family (also called weakfish), (Fish)
squash	Gourd or Melon Family
squid	Mollusks (Cephalopod)
squirrel	Squirrel Family (Mammal)
strawberry	Berry Family (Part of the larger *Rosaceae* Family)
string bean	Legume Family
sturgeon	Sturgeon Family (Fish)
sucker	Sucker Family (Fish)
sugar beet	Goosefoot or Beet Family
sugar cane	Grass Family
summer savory	Mint Family
sunfish	Sunfish Family (Fish)
sunflower oil & seeds	Composite Family
sweet corn	Grass Family

sweet pepper	Nightshade or Potato Family
sweet potato	Morning Glory Family
swordfish	Swordfish Family (Fish)
tahini	Sesame Family
tamarind	Legume Family
tangelo	Citrus or Rue Family
tangerine	Citrus or Rue Family
tapioca	Spurge Family
taro	Arum Family
tarragon	Composite Family
tea	Tea Family
tequila	Amaryllis Family
thyme	Mint Family
tilefish	Tilefish Family (Fish)
tobacco	Nightshade or Potato Family
tomatillo	Nightshade or Potato Family
tomato	Nightshade or Potato Family
tonka bean	Legume Family
tree tomato	Nightshade or Potato Family
triticale	Grass Family
trout species	Salmon Family
truffle	Fungi Family
tuna	Tuna Family (Fish)
turban squash	Gourd or Melon Family
turkey	Turkey Family (Bird)
turmeric	Ginger Family
turnip	Mustard Family
turtle species	Turtle Family (Reptile)
vanilla	Orchard Family
venison	Deer Family (Mammal)
vinegar(from apples)	Apple Family (Part of the larger *Rosaceae* Family)
walnuts	Walnut Family
watercress	Mustard Family
watermelon	Gourd or Melon Family
weakfish	Croaker Family, saltwater (Fish)
whale	Whale Family (Mammal)

wheat	Grass Family
wheat germ	Grass Family
whitebait	Silverside Family (Fish)
whitefish	Whitefish Family (Fish)
white pepper	Pepper Family
white perch	Bass Family
wild rice	Grass Family
wine berry	Grape Family
wine vinegar	Grape Family
wintergreen	Birch Family
winter savory	Mint Family
yam	Morning Glory Family
yarrow	Composite Family
yellow bass	Bass Family (Fish)
yellow jack	Jack Family (Fish)
yellow perch	Perch Family (Fish)
youngberry	Berry Family (Part of the larger *Rosaceae* Family)
yucca	Lily Family
zucchini	Gourd or Melon Family

FOOD LISTED ALPHABETCIALLY WITHIN THEIR FAMILY
The Super Allergy Girl™ Allergy & Celiac Cookbook

PLANT FAMILY (*Botanical plant family name*)	FOODS IN THE FAMILY
Algae (*Algae*)	agar-agar, carrageen, kelp (kombu), dulse
Amaryllis Family (*Amaryllidaceae*)	agave, mescal, pulque and tequila
Apple Family (*Rosaceae*) This is part of a larger food family that is often broken down into the apple, plum and berry families	apple, apple cider, apple vinegar, apple pectin, crab apple, quince, pear, rosehips*
Arrowroot (*Marantaceae*)	arrowroot (Maranta starch)

Arum Family	dasheen, poi, taro, malanga, yautia
Banana Family *(Musaceae)*	banana, plaintain
Beech *(Fagaceae)*	beechnut and chestnut
Berry *(subfamily of Rosaceae)*	blackberry, boysenberry, dewberry, loganberry, raspberry, black raspberry, red raspberry, purple raspberry, strawberry, wineberry
Birch *(Betulaceae)*	filbert or hazelnut, oil of birch (wintergreen flavor)
Bixa Family *(Bixaceae)*	annatto (natural yellow dye)
Borage *(Boraginaceae)*	(herbs) borage, comfrey* leaf & root
Brazil Nut *(Lecythidaceae)*	Brazil nut
Buckwheat *(Polygonaceae)*	buckwheat, garden sorrel, rhubarb, sea grape
Canna Family *(Cannaceae)*	Queensland arrowroot
Caper *(Capparidaceae)*	caper
Carpetweed Family *(Aizoaceae)*	New Zealand spinach
Cashew *(Anacardiaceae)*	cashew, mango, pistachio, poison ivy, poison oak, poison sumac
Chocolate *(Sterculiaceae)*	chocolate (cacao), cocoa*, cocoa butter, cola nut
Citrus or Rue *(Rutaceae)*	citron, grapefruit, kumquat, lemon, lime, orange, pummelo, tangelo, tangerine
Coffee *(Rubiaceae)*	coffee
Composite *(Compositae)* [These foods are all related to ragweed and may bother people highly allergic to ragweed pollens.]	cardoon, chamomile, chicory*, coltsfoot, costmary, dandelion, endive, escarole, globe artichoke, goldenrod*, Jerusalem artichoke, and artichoke flour, lettuce,

Composite (continued)	pyrethrum, romaine, safflower oil, sunflower seeds, sunflower oil, sunflower meal, tansy (herb), tarragon (herb), witloof chicory (French endive), yarrow*
Conifer *(Coniferae)*	juniper berry (used in Gin) and pine nuts
Custard-Apple *(Annonaceae)*	pawpaw and cherimoys
Dillenia Family *(Dilleniaceae)*	Chinese gooseberry (kiwi berry)
Ebony *(Ebonaceae)*	persimmon
Flax *(Linaceae)*	flaxseed
Fungus *(Fungi)* § See note at the end of this chart	mushrooms, truffle, morel, puffball, Baker's yeast, brewer's yeast or nutritional yeast, citric acid, and molds in certain cheeses
Ginger *(Zingiberaceae)*	cardamom, ginger, turmeric
Ginseng Family *(Araliaceae)*	American ginseng*, Chinese ginseng*
Gooseberry *(Saxifragaceae)*	currant and gooseberry
Goosefoot or Beet *(Chenopodiaceae)*	amaranth, beet, chard, lamb's quarters, spinach, sugar beet, quinoa, tampala
Gourd or Melon Family *(Cucurbitaceae)*	chayote, melon, cucumber, gherkin, cantaloupe, honeydew, Persian melon, Crenshaw, casaba, pumpkin, pumpkin seed, pumpkin meal, acorn squash, buttercup squash, butternut squash, Boston marrow squash, caserta squash, cocozelle squash, crookneck & straight neck squashes, Hubbard squashes, pattypan squash, spaghetti squash, zucchini, watermelon

Grape *(Vitaceae)*	grape, brandy, champagne, cream of tartar, dried "currant" (dried black grapes), raisin, wine, wine vinegar
Grass Family *(Graminaea,* sometimes called the Grain Family) [Several of these flours contain gluten. Please refer to the Flours section to distinguish gluten-free flours.]	bamboo shoots, barley, barley malt, maltose (from Barley), corn, maize (corn), corn meal, corn oil, cornstarch, corn sugar, corn syrup, hominy grits, popcorn, sweet corn, kamut, lemongrass, citronella, millet, oats, oatmeal, rice, rice flour, rye, sorghum grain, sorghum flour, spelt, sugarcane, cane sugar, raw sugar, molasses, teff, triticale, wheat, wheat bran, bulgur, wheat flour, wheat gluten, graham, whole wheat, wheat germ, wild rice
Heath *(Ericaceae)*	blueberry, cranberry, huckleberry, bilberry
Honeysuckle *(Caprifoliaceae)*	elderberry, elderberry flowers
Horsetail Family *(Equisetaceae)*	*shavegrass (horsetail)
Iris *(Iridaceae)*	saffron
Kiwi *(Actinidiaceae)*	kiwiberry, kiwifruit
Laurel *(Lauraceae)*	avocado, bay leaf, cinnamon, sassafras
Legume *(Leguminoseae)*	alfalfa*, alfalfa sprouts, fava beans, lima beans, mung beans, navy beans, string beans, kidney beans, black-eyed peas, carob*, carob syrup, chickpea (garbanzo bean), fenugreek*, gum acacia, gum tragacanth, jicama, kudzu, lentil, licorice*, peas, peanuts, peanut oil, red

Legume (continued)	clover*, senna*, soybeans, soy lecithin, soy grits, soy flour, soy milk, soy oil, tamarind, tonka bean, and all sprouts sprouted from the above listed beans, and all flours made from the above listed beans or plants
Lily *(Liliaceae)*	aloe vera, asparagus, chives, garlic, leek, onion, ramp, sarsaparilla*, shallot, yucca (soap plant)
Macadamia *(Protea)*	macadamia nuts
Mallow *(Malvaceae)*	cottonseed, hibiscus, okra
Maple *(Aceraceae)*	maple syrup, maple sugar
Melon or Gourd *(Cucurbitaceae)*	chayote, melon, cucumber, gherkin, cantaloupe, honeydew, Persian melon, Crenshaw, casaba, pumpkin, pumpkin seed, pumpkin meal, acorn squash, buttercup squash, butternut squash, Boston marrow squash, caserta squash, cocozelle squash, crookneck & straight neck squashes, Hubbard squashes, pattypan squash, spaghetti squash, zucchini, watermelon
Mint *(Labiatae)*	apple mint, basil, bergamot, catnip*, chia seed*, horehound*, dittany*, hyssop*, lavender, lemon balm*, marjoram, oregano, pennyroyal*, peppermint*, rosemary, sage, spearmint*, summer savory, thyme, winter savory
Morning-Glory *(Convolvulaceae)*	jicama and sweet potato

Mulberry *(Moraceae)*	breadfruit, fig, mulberry, hop*
Mustard *(Cruciferae)*	arugula, broccoli, bok choy, Brussels sprouts, cabbage, cardoon, cauliflower, Chinese cabbage, collards, colza shoots, curly cress, daikon, horseradish, kale, kohlrabi, mustard greens, mustard seed, radish, rape, rutabaga, sea collards, turnip, upland cress, watercress
Myrtle *(Myrtaceae)*	allspice *(Pimenta)*, clove, eucalyptus*
Nightshade or Potato *(Solanaceae)*	eggplant, pepino (melon pear), bell peppers, sweet peppers, cayenne peppers, chili peppers, paprika, pimiento, potato (all varieties), tobacco, tomatillo, tomato, tree tomato (This family **DOES NOT** include black or white peppercorns.)
Nutmeg *(Myristicaceae)*	nutmeg and mace
Olive *(Oleaceae)*	olive
Orchid *(Orchidaceae)*	vanilla
Palm *(Palmaceae)*	coconut, coconut milk, coconut oil, coconut meal, dates, date sugar, sago starch, palm cabbage
Papaya *(Caricaceae)*	papaya
Parsley or Carrot Family*(Umbelliferae)*	angelica, anise, caraway, carrot, carrot syrup, celeriac (celery root), celery, celery seed, celery leaf, chervil, coriander, cumin, dill, dill seed, fennel*, gotu kola*, lovage*, parsley*, parsnip, sweet cicely

Passion Flower Family (*Passifloraceae*)	granadilla (passion fruit)
Pepper (*Piperaceae*)	peppercorns, white pepper, black pepper
Pineapple (*Bromeliaceae*)	pineapple
Plum (*Subfamily of Rosaceae*)	almond, apricot, cherry, nectarine, peach, plum, prune, wild cherry, sloe
Pomegranate(*Punicaceae*)	pomegranate, grenadine syrup
Poppy (*Papaveraceae*)	poppy seed
Protea Family (*Proteaceae*)	macadamia, macadamia nut
Purslane (*Portulacaceae*)	purslane
Sapodilla Family (*Sapotaceae*)	chicle (chewing gum)
Sapucaya Family (*Lecythidaceae*)	Brazil nut, sapucaya nut (paradise nut)
Sedge(*Cyperaceae*)	Chinese water chestnuts, chufa (groundnut)
Sesame (*Pedaliaceae*)	sesame seeds, sesame oil, tahini
Soapberry (*Sapindaceae*)	litchi nuts
Spurge (*Euphorbiaceae*)	cassava or yucca (*Manihot*), cassava meal, tapioca (Brazilian arrowroot), castor bean, castor oil
Tea (*Theaceae*)	tea
Verbena (*Verbenaceae*)	lemon verbena*
Walnut (*Juglandaceae*)	black walnut, butternut, English walnut, hickory nut, pecan
Yam (*Dioscoreaceae*)	Chinese potato, yam

MAMMAL FAMILY	MAMMALS
Bear	bear
Beaver	beaver
Bovid (*Bovine*)	beef cattle, beef suet, gelatin, rennin (rennet), sausage casings, veal, buffalo, goat, sheep, lamb, mutton, bison, and all milk products coming from beef, buffalo, goats, sheep, lamb and bison
Camel	camel and llama
Cat	mountain lion
Deer	caribou, deer, venison, elk, moose, reindeer
Hare	hare and rabbit
Hippopotamus	hippopotamus
Horse	horse
Opossum	opossum
Pronghorn	pronghorn (also known as pronghorn antelope)
Squirrel	squirrel
Swine	hog (pork or pig), bacon, ham, lard, pork gelatin, pork sausage, scrapple

BIRD FAMILY	BIRDS
Dove	dove and pigeon (squab)
Duck	duck, goose, and their eggs
Grouse	ruffed grouse (partridge)
Guinea Fowl	guinea fowl
Pheasant	chicken, Cornish hen, pheasant, quail, peacock, and their eggs
Turkey	turkey and their eggs

FISH FAMILY	FISH
Anchovy	anchovy
Anglerfish	monkfish

Bass	white perch and yellow bass
Bluefish	bluefish
Catfish	catfish, minnows, carps
Codfish	cod (scrod), cusk, haddock, hake, pollack, whiting, toadfish, codfish, and allies
Croaker (freshwater)	freshwater drum or croakers
Croaker (saltwater)	croaker, drum, sea trout, silver perch, spot, weakfish (spotted trout)
Eel	American eel
Flounder	dabs, flounder, halibut, plaice, sole, turbot
Harvestfish	butterfish and harvestfish
Herring (freshwater)	shad (roe)
Herring (saltwater)	pilchard (sardine) and sea herring ("anchovies")
Jack	amberjack, pompano, yellow jack (family *Carangidae)*
Mackerel	albacore, bonito, mackerel, skipjack, tuna
Marlin	marlin and sailfish
Minnow	carps, chubs
Ostariophysi	catfish, minnows, carps
Mullet	mullet
Perch	sauger, walleye, yellow perch
Pike	muskellunge, pickerel, pike
Porgy	Northern scup (porgy)
Salmon	all salmon species and all trout species
Scorpionfish	rosefish (ocean perch)
Sea Bass	grouper and sea bass
Sea Catfish	ocean catfish
Shark	shark, skates, rays
Silverside	silverside (whitebait)
Smelt	smelt
Sturgeon	sturgeon (caviar)
Sucker	Buffalo fish and sucker

Sunfish	black bass, crappie, sunfish
Swordfish	swordfish
Tilefish	tilefish
Tuna	mackerel, tuna
Whitefish	whitefish

MOLLUSK FAMILY	MOLLUSK
Gastropods	abalone, snail
Cephalopod	squid
Crustaceans	crab, crayfish, lobster, prawn, shrimp
Pelecypods	clam, cockle, mussel, oyster, scallop

AMPHIBIAN FAMILY	AMPHIBIAN
Frog	frogs and frog legs
Reptiles	reptiles
Snakes	rattlesnake
Turtle Family	terrapin, turtle species

*Plant parts used as a beverage (leaf, root, seed, etc).

§ Items in this food family are technically a division of plants and not a plant family. For use with the rotation diet, physicians consider them to be in one food family.

Important

WARNING for FOOD ALLERGY& CELIAC Consumers

It is extremely important that you read food labels. Food manufacturers have the right to change their food product formulation at any time without notification. A food made gluten-free, egg-free, nut-free or dairy-free today, may not be gluten-free, egg-free, nut-free or dairy-free tomorrow. This warning cannot be emphasized enough. Please read your food labels on an on-going basis to be responsible and avoid serious health problems.

Kids in the Kitchen

Letting your kids in the kitchen can create a big mess! However, if you are willing to allow for some messes, there can be huge benefits from allowing your children to be involved in food preparation. I have encouraged my children to help out in the kitchen since they were toddlers. This is a fantastic chance to spend quality time with your children and help them learn life skills. At age 7, my son Noah, could sauté onions and make hash browns with adult supervision. It encourages creativity, helps to grow self-confidence and there is the opportunity for your children to learn about nutrition. I find it amazing how children are excited to eat what they help to prepare.

With more schools eliminating home economics classes, there are fewer chances for children to learn important life skills such as how to cook. You do need to have some patience as your children learn how to measure, chop, and mix. You do need to be prepared for mistakes and spills; however, this has been a rewarding experience for my family and it could be for yours. Everyone can get involved; my 5 year old daughter, Anne, loves to help add ingredients and stir. My oldest, Luke, can now make rolls and other baked goods from scratch which makes me think that my early investment has a pretty big pay-off!

Meal Ideas

Main Dish Ideas

Main Dish Ideas (continued)

Breakfast Dish Ideas

Lunch Dish Ideas

Snack Ideas

Hunger in the World

One child in the world dies from hunger every five seconds. If you add adults into the statistics, worldwide, approximately 25,000 people die each day from hunger or lack of nutrition and food. According to the United Nations, more than 850 million people around the world do not have enough food to eat right now. That equals one out of every seven people.

The tragedy is that we can do something to interrupt this cycle. Hunger is a problem that is an issue in the U.S. See page 86 for information on helping hungry Americans. I am committed that we raise the consciousness of those who can help to this life and death issue. Internationally, there are many organizations working to end hunger. Two organizations that you may consider are:

The Hunger Project   *www.thp.org*
15 East 26th Street
New York, NY 10010
(212) 251-9100

HEIFER® International   *www.heifer.org*

1 World Avenue
Little Rock, AR 72202
1-800-422-0474

Appetizers and Snacks

Appetizers

Party & Snack Mixes

Granolas

Crispbreads

Appetizers

There are twelve different soup recipes in the Soup Section starting on page 163, all of which make excellent appetizers. In addition to soups, there are many different recipes in this cookbook that would make fine appetizers for a dinner party, buffet, or festive occasion. Here are ideas for 18 different appetizers!

Bread Sticks

Any roll recipe in this cookbook can be used to make bread sticks. Bread sticks are a festive appetizer. You can spice up your roll batter with garlic, onions, rosemary, thyme and other herbs. Or you can make plain bread sticks and serve a nice olive oil for dipping. The easiest way to make bread sticks is if you can invest in a bread stick pan which will save you a great deal of time and energy. If you don't have a bread stick pan, you can use aluminum foil to create a bread stick form. Imagine folding up your aluminum foil into peaks and valleys. The roll batter will then be piped into the valleys of your aluminum foil. You can also just pipe roll batter onto a greased baking sheet and pipe the batter into strips as this will give you a similar effect although both alternatives will give you a flat bottom instead of a round bottom. I did this for a short time to make not only bread sticks, but also to make hot dog rolls. A bread stick pan is a great little invention.

Fresh Vegetables & Dip

The fancy name for fresh vegetables is crudités (pronounced kroo-da-tey), which simply means pieces of raw vegetables served as an hors d'oeuvre usually with a dip. Many restaurants will offer crudités on the menu as an appetizer with a dip. The following six dip recipes are a wonderful match for fresh vegetables. Arrange the fresh vegetables on a platter and you are set to go.

Fresh Fruits and Smashing Fruit Dip
During my Penn State college days, I worked at <u>The Deli</u> in State College, Pennsylvania. One of their appetizers was a fruit platter with a cool fruit dip. While I have no idea of what they put in their fruit dip, the following fruit dip should please almost any guest. Use any fruits that you like, or that are in season.

Garlic Rounds
This appetizer is another idea born from a restaurant. For garlic rounds, simply slice up any rolls that you have made and lightly drizzle with your favorite oil. Then sprinkle lightly with garlic salt and onion salt. Use a dash of paprika and a bit of crushed up parsley to give your garlic rounds that restaurant look. Broil under the broiler until nice and toasty.

Potato Skins
Most of us don't make potato skins at home, however if you are having guests or a party, they make a nice finger food. Potato Skins can be made as half a potato, or one-third or one quarter of a potato. Determine how many actual potato skins you would like per person, and what size. Then bake that number of potatoes. Cut the potatoes into the desired size. Place on a baking sheet and top with non-dairy cheese, bacon bits, or any other toppings that you like. Broil under the broiler until piping hot, or until the non-dairy cheese melts. We serve our potato skins with Tofutti non-dairy sour cream.

Chicken Wings
This cookbook contains three recipes for barbecue sauce that can be used on chicken wings. Cook your chicken wings completely and drain off any excess fat or liquid. Then apply your barbecue sauce and heat until piping hot. Chicken wings are excellent with the Mock Ranch Dip or dressing recipe in this cookbook. This is a wonderful party food or appetizer.

Nachos
Nachos are another food that many people on the gluten-free and dairy-free diet do not think of making at home. Nachos are a

great finger food for festive parties or for pre-dinner munchies. Grease a baking sheet and place corn chips on a single layer making sure that the corn chips overlap each other. Add ground beef, hot peppers, non-dairy cheese, or any other topping that delights you. Now add a second layer of corn chips and repeat with the topping. Add a third layer and then broil until hot and bubbly. Serve with salsa and Tofutti non-dairy sour cream.

Stuffed Celery

Celery can be stuffed with Tofutti's non-dairy cream cheese or ground sunflower seed butter (ground sunflower seeds that look like peanut butter for those of us who have to skip tree nuts and peanuts). You can even add some taco seasoning to the Tofutti non-dairy cream cheese for a special kick. A recipe for taco seasoning is included in this cookbook for those who are allergic to commercially made taco seasoning mixes.

Mini Pizzas

Any of the pizza recipes in this cookbook can be made as mini pizzas, which can be served whole as an appetizer, or can be served as slices for an appetizer. You can also make large pizzas and cut them into slices and serve that as an appetizer. We also occasionally cut rolls in half and use them as a pizza crust base for mini pizzas. If you are using rolls cut in half for mini pizzas, toast the rolls well before applying sauce and toppings.

Onion Rings

My husband came up with this recipe, which is delightful!

    1 cup corn flour or other flour
    ⅓ cup sorghum flour or other flour
    1 teaspoon salt
    1 teaspoon baking powder
    2 teaspoons sugar
    1 tablespoon Ener-G Egg Replacer™
    1 tablespoon sunflower oil or other oil
    ¾ cup pure water
    2 large onions

    high temperature sunflower or other oil for frying

Heat the sunflower oil to about 370°. Use a thermometer and try to get the temperature stabilized. I use a small saucepan on the stove top and have it set at medium heat. There is organic sunflower oil available that is specifically for high heat applications (up to 460°)

Mix dry ingredients and then add 1 tablespoon oil. Add water until the batter is somewhere between creamy and runny. It should drip off a spoon in flat triangular drips. If time allows, refrigerate the batter for an hour or so.

Slice the onions into pieces about ⅜ inches thick and separate into individual rings. If the onion has a "slimy" skin between the rings, remove it. Dip a few rings into the batter so that they are evenly coated and carefully drop into the hot oil. The rings may stay at the bottom at first. I let them cook for about 15 seconds before I nudge them off the bottom, and then let them float. Cook until they just begin to turn brown, somewhere between 1 and 2 minutes. Remove from the oil and drain on a paper towel or wire rack.

Vegetable Tempura

Use the preceding recipe on the previous page, to coat small vegetable pieces instead. We use broccoli and cauliflower, cut carrots (either thin sticks or slices), zucchini slices, asparagus tips, or green beans also work. It is important that the pieces be dry so that the batter will stick and the hot oil won't spatter. Remember, the oil is 370°, so be careful.

Yummy Sticks

This is a great snack item for children or adults. It is fairly easy and straightforward to make. My children named this snack in case you are wondering where the name came from.

> **2 cups gluten-free flour of your choice (sorghum and amaranth work well for this)**
> **2½ teaspoons paprika**
> **1½ teaspoons garlic salt**
> **1½ teaspoons onion salt**
> **1½ teaspoons xanthan gum**
> **1 teaspoon garlic powder**
> **⅓ cup acceptable oil**
> **1½ cups water**

Mix flour and spices. Add oil and water and mix well. Heat oil in a large frying pan until hot. Cut a very, very small diagonal corner off of a ziplock bag and place some of the batter into the ziplock bag. Use the bag to pipe the batter into the hot oil. Fry the batter until very light brown in color. Drain on a paper towel.

A Word about Party and Snack Mixes

If you have never made a party or snack mix, I need to say just a few things here. These are the most flexible and easy to make foods on the planet. They keep for relatively long periods in airtight containers, and they are a ready to go snack food. They are especially nice to take to parties and other gatherings. But be sure to take your own stash of your party mix because people will scarf these mixes right up!

The following party and snack mixes as well as granola recipes will take well to substitutions, so feel free to change them to meet your food needs and allergies.

All Purpose Party Mix

Preheat oven to 250°.

> 7 tablespoons acceptable margarine or oil
> 3 tablespoons GFCF Worcestershire sauce
> ¾ teaspoon onion powder
> ¾ teaspoon garlic salt
> 5 cups Health Valley™ Rice Crunch-Ems cereal or
>   other GFCF cereal
> 3 cups Health Valley™ Corn Crunch-Ems cereal or
>   other GFCF cereal
> 1¾ cups pretzels (1 small bag of Glutano™ or Ener-G™
>   gluten & dairy-free pretzels)
> ½ package (3½ ounces) brown rice snaps - <u>broken into
>   pieces</u> (about 1 cup or so)

Bake for 1 hour, stirring every 15 minutes. This mix can be made to be "stronger" in flavor by increasing the spices and Worcestershire sauce. The fat can also be decreased or increased depending upon dietary needs (our kids need more fat). Also, for a spicy version, you can add chili powder to the mix (starting with about ½ teaspoon and adding more if desired).

Rice Party Mix

This recipe uses all rice based cereal and crackers, so it works for one of our rotation diet days. You can substitute other cereals or crackers as your diet allows.

Preheat oven to 250°.

> ½ cup safflower oil or other acceptable oil
> 3 tablespoons GFCF Worcestershire sauce
> ¾ teaspoon onion powder
> ¾ teaspoon garlic salt
> 8 cups Health Valley™ Rice Crunch-Ems cereal or
>   other GFCF cereal
> 1¾ cups pretzels (1 small bag of Glutano™ or Ener-G™
>   gluten & dairy-free pretzels)
> ½ package (3½ ounces) brown rice snaps - <u>broken into
> pieces</u> (about 1 cup or so)

Bake for 1 hour, stirring every 15 minutes. This mix can be made to be "stronger" in flavor by increasing the spices and Worcestershire sauce. The fat can also be decreased or increased depending upon dietary needs (our kids need more fat). Also, for a spicy version, you can add chili powder to the mix (starting with about ½ teaspoon and adding more if desired).

Corn Party Mix

This recipe uses a mix of cereal and crackers, but you can limit it to one type (e.g. corn) for one of your rotation diet days.

Preheat oven to 250°.

> ⅓ cup corn oil
> 3 tablespoons GFCF Worcestershire sauce
> ¾ teaspoon onion powder
> ¾ teaspoon garlic salt
> 8 cups Health Valley™ Corn Crunch-Ems cereal or
>   other GFCF cereal
> 1 to 2 cups gluten-free pretzels
> 1 cup corn tortilla chips (broken into pieces)

Bake for 1 hour, stirring every 15 minutes. This mix can be made to be "stronger" in flavor by increasing the spices and Worcestershire sauce. The fat can also be decreased or increased depending upon dietary needs (our kids need more fat). Also, for a spicy version, you can add chili powder to the mix (starting with about ½ teaspoon, adding more if desired).

Sweet Treat Snacks

This is a sweet treat that is a snack food. This sweet snack is great for parties, but be sure to make a double batch because it will go fast!

1 cup gluten-free/dairy-free chocolate chips
¼ cup ground sunflower seed butter or other acceptable peanut butter substitute
½ cup sunflower seeds or other crunchy cereal
6 cups Health Valley™ Corn Crunch-Ems or other cereal
1 cup confectioners' sugar

Measure the confectioners' sugar and place in a one-gallon ziplock bag. Set aside. Measure out the cereal and place in a large mixing bowl and set aside. Place the chocolate chips in a glass container and microwave for 45 seconds. Remove and stir the chocolate chips. They may not look like they're melted, but they will be melted. If the chocolate chips are not melted, return to microwave for another 15 to 20 seconds. When melted, add the ground sunflower seed butter and sunflower seeds to the melted chocolate and stir well. Add the melted chocolate mixture to the dry cereal and gently stir to coat the cereal. Then take all of the coated cereal and add it to the ziplock bag containing the powdered sugar. Gently shake the sealed bag until all of the cereal is coated with the powdered sugar.

Honeyed Snack Mix

Preheat oven to 250°.

6 cups acceptable cereal
2 cups gluten-free pretzels
1 cup sunflower seeds OR 1 cup other crunchy cereal
   or seed
⅓ cup oil
⅓ cup honey
1 teaspoon garlic powder
½ teaspoon onion powder
¼ teaspoon dried ginger
2 tablespoons Bragg™ Liquid Aminos (or soy sauce)

Place the oil, honey and all of the spices and Bragg™ Liquid Aminos into a saucepan over medium heat. Grease a 9" x 13" baking pan. Place the cereal, pretzels and sunflower seeds in the baking pan. Bring the honey and oil mixture to a light boil. The mixture will get all light and foamy. Remove from heat and pour over the cereal mixture in the baking pan. Stir well to coat all of the ingredients. Bake for 1 hour and 30 minutes, stirring every 15 minutes. If I was making this for adults only I would kick up the spices a bit by adding more ginger, onion and garlic.

Dijon Style Party Mix

Snack mixes or party mixes are something that you can really have fun with. This uses honey and Dijon mustard for flavoring.

Preheat oven to 250°.

> 3 tablespoons Dijon mustard
> ⅓ cup oil
> 2 tablespoons honey
> 8 cups dry cereal
> 1 cup roasted sunflower seeds or other cereal or seeds
> 1½ cups gluten-free pretzels or other snack (like corn chips broken up)

Place cereal in a greased 9" x 13" baking pan and set aside. In a small pan, cook oil, honey and mustard over medium heat until foamy. Pour over cereal in baking pan and stir well to coat. Bake 1 hour, stirring every 15 minutes. After baking, allow cereal to cool. Then add 1 cup of roasted sunflower seeds or other acceptable seeds or cereal, and 1½ cups pretzels or other snack item like broken up corn chips.

Rice Granola

Preheat oven to 225°.

⅓ cup honey
⅓ cup sunflower or other acceptable oil

Mix the following dry ingredients together in a large mixing bowl:

1 cup Perky's™ Nutty Rice cereal
3 cups Health Valley™ Rice Crunch-Ems cereal or
    other rice cereal substitute
3 cups puffed rice cereal
1 cup sunflower seeds (or other acceptable nuts or
    seeds)
2 cups Barbara's Bakery Rice Puffins® (or 2 cups rice
    cereal)

To be added after baking:

1 cup dried cranberries (or other acceptable dried
    fruit)
1 cup raisins (or other acceptable dried fruit)

Grease a 9" x 13" pan with acceptable oil or fat. Mix the dry cereals and seeds or nuts in a large bowl and set aside. Heat oil and honey in a saucepan until it is nice and foamy. Once it begins to get foamy, cook about 1 more minute and then pour over all of the dried cereals and seeds or nuts. Mix well to coat. Pour into baking pan and bake for 2 hours, stirring well every 30 minutes. Once the cereal mixture is removed from the oven, let it cool completely before adding the 2 cups of dried fruit.

Corn Granola
Preheat oven to 225°.

⅓ cup honey
⅓ cup corn oil

Mix the following dry ingredients together in a large mixing bowl:

1 cup Perky's™ Nutty Flax cereal or other cereal
3 cups corn cereal substitute
3 cups puffed corn cereal
1 cup sunflower seeds (or other acceptable nuts or
seeds)
2 cups acceptable corn flake cereal

To be added after baking:

1 cup dried cranberries (or other acceptable dried
fruit)
1 cup raisins (or other acceptable dried fruit)

Grease a 9" x 13" pan with acceptable oil or fat. Mix the dry cereals and seeds or nuts in a bowl and set aside. Heat oil and honey in a saucepan until it is nice and foamy. Once it begins to get foamy, cook about 1 more minute and then pour over all of the dried cereals and seeds or nuts. Mix well to coat. Pour into baking pan and bake for 2 hours, stirring well every 30 minutes. Once the cereal mixture is removed from the oven, let it cool completely before adding the 2 cups of dried fruit.

Good Morning Granola

I'll be perfectly frank with you, I invented this recipe to use up expired cereal! What started as a lark, turned out very well! The use of sunflower seeds and flax meal add nutrition and fiber. We've used a variety of dried fruits in this granola. This recipe fits with our fourth rotation day completely since we use dried strawberries and raspberries.

Preheat oven to 225°.

> 1 cup sunflower seeds or other seed
> 6 cups Health Valley™ Corn Crunch-Ems cereal or other acceptable dry cereal
> 2 cups Perky's™ Nutty Flax cereal or other acceptable dry cereal
> ½ cup flax meal
> ⅛ teaspoon ground cinnamon
> ½ cup sunflower or other acceptable oil
> ½ cup maple syrup or other liquid sweetener
> 2 cups dried fruit of your choice, bite size pieces

Grease a 9" x 13" baking pan. Measure the sunflower seeds, and cereals into a very large mixing bowl. On top of the dry ingredients place the flax meal. Do not mix. Place oil and maple syrup in a small saucepan and bring to a boil until it is nice and foamy. Boil for 2 minutes and remove from heat. Pour over cereal and flax mixture. Stir well to coat. Add cinnamon to taste. Pour into your greased baking pan and bake for 1½ to 2 hours, stirring every 30 minutes or so. Once the mixture has cooled completely, add 2 cups of dried fruit of your choice. There are now a wide variety of dried fruits commercially available that lend themselves well to dry granola recipes like this one.

Feel Good Granola

Yes, I was using up more expired cereal! I used some different cereals which don't exactly fit with our rotation days. But since my husband and I are the only ones eating the granola, it works.

Preheat oven to 225°.

½ cup sesame seeds
6 cups Health Valley™ Corn Crunch-Ems cereal or
    other acceptable dry cereal
2 cups puffed rice or other acceptable dry cereal
2 cups Nu-World Foods™ Amaranth Cereal Snaps
Dash of ground cloves
½ cup sesame or other acceptable oil
½ cup honey or other liquid sweetener
2 cups dried fruit of your choice, bite size pieces

Grease a 9" x 13" baking pan. Measure the cereals into a very large mixing bowl. On top of the dry ingredients place the sesame seeds. Do not mix. Place oil and honey in a small saucepan and bring to a boil until it is nice and foamy. Boil for 2 minutes and remove from heat. Pour over cereals and sesame seed mixture. Stir well to coat. Add a dash of cloves. Pour into your greased baking pan and bake for 1½ to 2 hours, stirring every 30 minutes or so. Once the mixture has cooled completely, add 2 cups of dried fruit of your choice. There are now a wide variety of dried fruits commercially available that lend themselves well to dry granola recipes like this one.

Dehydrator Crackers or Crispbread

These kinds of crackers or flatbreads are easy to make, but you will have to have specific equipment; namely a temperature controlled dehydrator (that is one where you can set the temperature), plastic dehydrator sheets to line the trays of the dehydrator, a juicer, and a food processor. This type of food falls into the raw foods diet area because the crackers are dried at a temperature lower than an oven can handle. I will give you a basic recipe for the crackers, and then specific ones that we have used and like.

Bear in mind that these crackers are often used with spreads, ground sunflower seed butters, jams and jellies. You can also top them with non-dairy cream cheese, lunch meats, etc. I would recommend that you skip the spices until you have tried these recipes. The spices get stronger when the crackers or crispbreads are done, so go easy on them or they will be too spicy to eat. We had plenty of failures in the beginning as we discovered that you had to have enough root pulp in the recipe to hold the grain together! These are especially good if you are watching your weight, or have trouble with processed foods. Christine Schaefer taught us this delightful new process, and my husband, Randy Garrett, has been the cracker king!

Basic Cracker or Crispbread

> 4 cups root vegetables (e.g. 3 carrots, 2 turnips, 1 beet, 1 radish)
> 1 cup gluten-free grain or seed *soaked in 2 cups of pure water for 24 hours*
> 1 teaspoon salt
> ¼ cup oil

Optional:

> Spices like onion powder, garlic powder, cayenne pepper; use ¼ teaspoon except for cayenne pepper which I would only use ¼ teaspoon or a dash

Prior to starting, soak your 1 cup of gluten-free grain or seeds in water for 24 hours. Peel and cut root vegetables into chunks that will fit into your juicer. Measure about 4 cups of the root vegetables. Juice the root vegetables saving the juice and the pulp. Drain your grain or seeds from the water that they have been soaking in and combine the grain or seeds, vegetable juice, vegetable pulp and oil in a food processor. Blend until smooth. Add spices if you are using them.

Oil the dehydrator sheets and spread the vegetable mixture to about ¼ inch thick. Score mixture into wedges to have better cracker or crispbread shapes. Dehydrate until crisp and dry, which is about 24 hours. Store in an air-tight container.

If you use sweet root vegetables like squash or beets, you will end up with a sweeter cracker or crispbread. Beets add a lot of color!

Root Vegetables: carrots, beets, turnips, parsnips, radish, celery root or celeriac, squash, or pumpkin.

Gluten-Free Grains or Seeds: millet, amaranth, sorghum, rice, sesame seeds, sunflower seeds.

Carrot & Celery Crackers or Crispbread

Here is one of Randy's winning recipes for dehydrated crackers or crispbread.

3 medium carrots
1 stalk celery
⅓ cup millet grain, *soaked in 2 cups water for 24 hours*
¼ teaspoon garlic powder
¼ teaspoon salt
¼ teaspoon dried minced onion
½ teaspoon Worcestershire sauce (if tolerated)
1 teaspoon acceptable oil

Drain the millet grain and set aside. Juice the carrots and celery keeping both the juice and pulp. Combine the juice, pulp, and remaining ingredients in a food processor and purée until a paste is formed. Generously oil the dehydrator sheet and fill with vegetable/grain mixture to ¼ inch thick. Score to make better shaped crackers. Dehydrate until crisp, about 24 hours.

Broccoli Celeriac Crackers or Crispbread

This is another recipe from Randy, my husband. We now have a great use for the organic broccoli stems that our children won't eat!

2 stalks broccoli (minus the florets)
1 large parsnip
½ large celeriac root
1 cup millet grain, *soaked in 2 cups pure water for 24 hours*
⅛ cup acceptable oil
¼ teaspoon salt

Optional:

To taste: black pepper

Drain the grain and set aside. Juice the broccoli, parsnip and celeriac keeping the juice and pulp. Combine the juice, pulp, and remaining ingredients in a food processor and purée until a paste is formed. Generously oil the dehydrator sheet and fill with vegetable/grain mixture to ¼ inch thick. Score to make better shaped crackers. Dehydrate until crisp, about 24 hours.

Roasted Sunflower Seeds

These are easy to make and can be flavored with salt, or you can dress them up with additional spices.

Preheat oven to 350°.

1 tablespoon sunflower oil or other acceptable oil
1 cup organic sunflower seeds

Place the oil and sunflower seeds in a stainless steel or other roasting pan which ideally is about 9" x 13". Salt lightly. You may also lightly sprinkle with onion or garlic salt. Bake for 15 to 20 minutes. Set the timer and check every 5 to 8 minutes because the seeds will turn light brown, and once they do, they are done. They can burn easily, so watch them.

Soups

Soups

Creamy Cauliflower Soup

This soup is excellent and reminds me of the creamy cauliflower soup my mother made for my cousin's bridal shower which was of course, delicious and contained dairy. I do not feel deprived with this creamy soup.

> **6 cups pure drinking water**
> **1 head cauliflower**
> **2 tablespoons oil**
> **1 teaspoon salt (more or less to taste)**
> **To taste: pepper**

Place the water in a medium to large stockpot over medium to high heat. Wash and cut cauliflower florets into medium to small pieces and place in the stockpot. Bring to a boil and reduce to medium heat. Cook for 10 minutes. Check to make sure that the cauliflower is knife tender. Remove from heat. Remove 2 cups of the water from the stockpot and dispose of this excess cooking water. Pour the cauliflower and remaining cooking liquid into a second saucepan or mixing bowl. Then place ½ of the cauliflower and ½ of the cooking liquid in a blender and purée until creamy. Pour this creamy cauliflower back into your original stockpot. Take the remaining cauliflower and cooking liquid and place this in the blender. Add 2 tablespoons of acceptable oil in the blender with 1 teaspoon of salt and a few grinds of pepper. Purée until smooth and pour back into your original stockpot with the existing cauliflower soup. Stir well and taste. This recipe is sensitive to salt since it has very little other flavoring. If you need more salt, and only then, add more to taste. If you are one of the very few Americans who needs to gain weight, you can add more oil to this recipe to add fat and calories. However, we like it with just the minimal amount of oil.

Cream of Broccoli Soup

Use the preceding recipe for Creamy Cauliflower Soup but substitute broccoli. Use one very large bunch of broccoli or 2 frozen bags (10 to 12 oz. Size). Follow the same directions.

Tomato Basil Soup

My sons tasted some tomato basil soup at our local co-op store and begged me to make some. We had no idea what the ingredients were except for tomatoes and basil. We kept adding ingredients until it tasted and looked like the soup that they had tried and loved so much!

One 15 ounce can tomato sauce
One 28 ounce can crushed tomatoes
2 cups Dari-Free™ or other non-dairy milk substitute
1 large onion, finely diced
2 cloves garlic, minced
2½ teaspoons dried basil
1 tablespoon acceptable oil

Sauté chopped onion in oil over medium to medium high heat until soft and cooked through. Add dried basil and minced garlic and stir constantly for 1 to 2 minutes over medium low heat. Add remaining ingredients and cook over medium heat for 30 minutes to 1 hour. Purée soup in a blender and return to the saucepan. My children prefer a creamy consistency. If you like chunks of tomato in the soup then don't purée it. This recipe makes a large quantity good for family gatherings or parties. For a smaller number of guests, this recipe may be cut in half.

Lisa Lundy's Vegetable Soup

1 tablespoon olive oil
1 large onion, chopped
3 cloves garlic, minced
3 carrots, chopped
3 celery stalks, chopped

In a large pot sauté the above vegetables for 10 minutes in the olive oil.

Add the following ingredients to the vegetables:
8 cups water
One 15 ounce can white kidney beans (drained & rinsed well)
One 28 ounce can diced tomatoes (if you want chunks) or tomato sauce
½ cup green beans
½ cup lima beans
⅔ cup frozen corn
To taste: salt and pepper
2 teaspoons oregano
2 teaspoons basil
1 tablespoon parsley
1 teaspoon rosemary
¼ teaspoon cayenne pepper (or more)

Optional:

Tomato paste (to thicken)
2 pinches Wakame (a seaweed found in health food stores)

Simmer all the ingredients for about 1 hour to blend the flavors. You may want to add 1 to 2 cups water as the soup cooks down. We sometimes add tomato paste to make the soup a little thicker. This makes a lot so we freeze some for another day!

Lisa Lundy's 5 Bean Soup

You can use canned or dried beans for this hearty and nutritious soup. The orange zest is what makes the soup so special!

One 19 ounce can red kidney beans
One 15 ounce can white kidney beans
One 15 ounce can black beans
One 14 ounce can pinto beans
One 15 ounce can Navy beans or white northern beans
One 28 ounce can tomato sauce
One 6 ounce can tomato paste
1 tablespoon olive oil
1 medium red pepper, chopped (optional)
1 large onion, chopped
2 medium carrots, chopped
2 cloves garlic, minced
¾ cup white or brown rice
4 cups water (and more later)
1 tablespoon salt
1 teaspoon ground cinnamon
1 teaspoon ground cumin
½ teaspoon cayenne pepper
⅓ cup vinegar
Zest from 1 orange (the peel of 1 orange grated)-this
   will completely change the taste!

Sauté the pepper, onion, and carrots, in the olive oil for about 5 minutes adding the garlic at the end of the cooking so as not to burn it. Meanwhile, drain and rinse all of the canned beans. In a large pot, combine the vegetables and canned beans. Add all of the remaining ingredients. Simmer for 1 hour. As the soup cooks down, you will need to add more water.

Please note, for the proper taste, the grated orange peel (zest from one orange) is a required ingredient! Trust me. After the soup has simmered for about an hour, purée it in a blender. Since there is more soup than will fit in any blender, purée it in "batches". We leave a small amount of the soup not puréed so that it has more texture to it.

This soup will be thick and you will need to thin it to a consistency that suits you. Some people like it thicker than others. Also, it thickens sitting in the refrigerator so you will need to add water prior to reheating.

Makes a large amount, so freeze some! If you would like to use dried beans instead of canned, they work well for this soup and are even more nutritious. When we use dried beans, we use the quick soak method. Rinse your beans and place in a large stock pan filled with pure drinking water. Cover and boil for 10 minutes. Remove from heat and let sit for 1 hour. This process produces about the same result as soaking the beans in water for 24 hours. Drain beans and add to the large pot with the sautéed vegetables. Follow the recipe from there.

Chicken Noodle Soup

8 cups chicken stock (canned or homemade, see below)
1½ cups carrots, chopped
1 cup celery, chopped
2 cups onion, chopped
1 clove garlic, minced
½ cup peas (canned, frozen or fresh)
2 teaspoons salt
¼ teaspoon celery seed (whole)
½ teaspoon seasoning salt (see page 368)
½ teaspoon rosemary
1 teaspoon basil
1 teaspoon oregano
2 teaspoons parsley flakes
2 to 3 cups cooked, gluten-free noodles of your choice
To taste: pepper
2 or more cups cooked chicken, cut into small pieces

Simmer all of the above ingredients in a large pot. As the soup cooks, the liquid will cook down. Add more water as needed. Simmer for 1 hour (or more) to blend the flavors.

Soup Stock

Cook the following ingredients in a large pot filled with at least 10 to 12 cups of water. The vegetables should be cleaned and cut into LARGE chunks – meaning 2 or 3 inch pieces.

1 large chicken breast (with the bone)
1 large onion
2 stalks celery
2 medium carrots
1 teaspoon dried rosemary
½ teaspoon salt

Simmer on medium heat until the chicken is fully cooked. Remove the chicken from the pot, let it cool, and cut it into pieces for the soup. Remove the vegetables from the soup stock and strain the remaining liquid through a cheese cloth or fine linen towel. Straining is important as it will clarify your soup stock and also because it removes fat. You can add water to make 8 cups for the recipe above.

Potato Chowder

The idea for this recipe came from a Potato & Cheese Soup given to me by my mother-in-law, Sally Mathews. Following along the guidelines of the "Galloping Gourmet" when you remove an ingredient from a recipe for fat or in this case allergies, replace the ingredient with another that adds flavor. It ended up being different from the original recipe, but it has a lot of flavor, and none of the allergens that we avoid.

1 onion, chopped
1 clove garlic, minced or crushed
3 to 4 medium potatoes, chopped
2 stalks celery, sliced
1 medium red pepper, seeded, halved and sliced
4 tablespoons acceptable oil
5 cups stock or water
To taste: salt and pepper
2 cups DariFree™ milk substitute or other non-dairy
   milk substitute
One 15 ounce can corn (with juice)
Pinch of dried sage

Place the oil in a large skillet over medium-high heat. Add the onion, celery, red pepper and sauté for 2 to 3 minutes. Add the potatoes, cover the pan and reduce the heat. Because you are cooking potatoes, they will need a lower heat for a longer amount of time. Add the garlic and cook the potatoes and vegetables for approximately 10 minutes on low heat (not your lowest setting, however). Add the stock or water, salt and pepper, and simmer for 15 minutes, stirring occasionally. Add the milk substitute, corn and sage, and cook for 10 more minutes. Different milk substitutes have different flavors. If the milk substitute you are using has a stronger flavor, this will change the flavor of the soup, and you may have to add more spices to compensate, or try adding more onion, garlic and red pepper.

Gourmet Butternut Squash Soup

3½ cups cooked squash, mashed
1 cup DariFree™ or other milk substitute
2 cups water
1 tablespoon oil (optional)
Dash of marjoram
Dash of ground sage
Dash of crushed rosemary
To taste: salt and pepper
2 tablespoons brown sugar

Optional Garnish:

Dash of cayenne pepper and/or
1 teaspoon non-dairy sour cream

Mix squash, milk substitute and water together in a food processor or blender. Place in a saucepan and add spices, salt and pepper and brown sugar. You will be surprised at the great taste of this healthful soup! Makes about 4 servings.

Simple Squash Soup

2 cans or 4 cups cooked, puréed squash
4 cups water
3 tablespoons brown sugar
½ teaspoon ground cinnamon
1 teaspoon salt

Mix well and cook until all ingredients meld together. If desired, you may sprinkle the top of the soup with cayenne pepper as a garnish and to add a bit of zip! Makes about 8-10 servings.

Hot & Sour Soup

This is one of my all time favorites! Many hot & Sour soup recipes call for ingredients that you simply don't have on hand and some that are hard to come by. The ingredients for my version of Hot & Sour Soup are stocked in most standard grocery stores.

2 tablespoons sesame oil (or other acceptable oil)
1 cup julienned cooked pork
One 8 ounce can sliced bamboo shoots
2 cups julienned carrot strips
½ cup sliced mushrooms
1 can water chestnuts, drained
8 cups chicken broth
One 16 ounce package firm tofu, drained and sliced
   into strips
⅓ cup Bragg™ Liquid Aminos
2 tablespoons sugar
¼ cup vinegar
½ cup green onions or leeks sliced thin
3 tablespoons chili and garlic sauce (or any
   combination of garlic and hot sauce)

6 tablespoons corn starch dissolved in
3 cups cold water (or other thickener)

This recipe makes a very large quantity of soup which suits us just fine. If you live alone or are making it for the first time and are not sure how you will like it, feel free to cut the recipe in half. This soup does not freeze well unless you omit the tofu and water chestnuts. Trust me, the tofu and water chestnuts will not be pleasant after freezing! Without them, it survives freezing fairly well. To make the soup, sauté the cooked pork and raw carrots in the oil until hot and sizzling. Then add the chicken broth. Add all remaining ingredients saving cornstarch dissolved in water for last. Add the cornstarch and simmer for 30 minutes. Makes one large stockpot of soup, or approximately 17to 20 cups of soup.

Look for the Chili and Garlic Sauce in the oriental section of the grocery store. If you can't find it, you may substitute hot sauce or chili oil, however my caution here is that you will be missing the garlic flavor. So if you substitute any hot sauce or chili oil, then please be sure to add a good hit of minced garlic or your soup will come up short on flavor.

Red Carrot Soup

This is a simple soup that you can leave plain or add additional ingredients to.

> 2 cups carrots, chopped finely
> 2 red peppers, diced finely
> 1 large onion, diced
> 1 tablespoon acceptable oil
> 4 cups pure drinking water
> 3 tablespoons maple syrup (or sweetener of your
>   choice)
> ½ teaspoon ground ginger
> Dash of cayenne pepper
> Dash of ground cinnamon
> 1 teaspoon salt

Sauté the diced carrots, onions, and red peppers in oil over a medium to high heat. Sauté for 3 to 4 minutes or until soft. Add 4 cups of water, ground ginger, dash of cayenne, dash of ground cinnamon, salt and maple syrup or other sweetener. Simmer for 20 minutes. Place half the stock in a blender and purée. Pour other half into a large bowl. Return puréed stock to pan and place the other half of the soup in the blender and purée. Add to pot. Makes about 4 cups depending upon how long you let it simmer.

Black Bean Soup

This soup has a great flavor and is a food that some young children will eat. At least some of mine did!

> 4 cups chicken or vegetable broth
> 2 cups black beans, cooked or canned (if canned, rinse and drain)
> ½ cup diced celery
> ½ cup diced carrots
> ¾ cup diced onion
> ¼ cup vinegar
> 1 teaspoon orange zest
> ½ teaspoon ground cinnamon
> ½ teaspoon cayenne pepper
> 2 teaspoons minced garlic

Bring ingredients to a boil and then reduce heat to a medium simmer. Simmer for at least one hour. Then purée either all or some of the soup in a blender. My children prefer a smooth and creamy soup so I purée all of the soup. For adults you could purée ½ to ¾ of the soup leaving the balance, giving the soup more texture. This soup can be served with rice for a complete protein. If you like a thinner soup you may add additional broth or pure drinking water. You may garnish the top of the soup with a sprinkle of green onion slices or a dollop of Tofutti non-dairy sour cream.

Rolls, Muffins, Bagels, Pancakes, Waffles & Pizza Crust

Gluten-Free Breads vs. Rolls

I have baked gluten-free breads for many years and this is my outlook: my gluten-free breads were fabulous the day that they were baked, but disappointing on the second day. If the breads were frozen, they just didn't hold together and thaw or defrost in a way that I found acceptable. In other words, the breads after being frozen had to be toasted to be acceptable. I experimented with ascorbic acid and soy lecithin as preservatives, but nothing seemed like the good old gluten days. So I turned to rolls to experiment and see if I could get a better result for day two or for defrosting, and I did. It is for that reason that you will only find one bread recipe in this cookbook. It's an awful lot of work for a baked good that is really only best on the day it is baked. For my money and efforts we are happy with rolls that can be defrosted or microwaved and have the same texture and taste as the day that they were baked.

Hamburger & Hot Dog Rolls

To make these rolls, you can purchase special hamburger and hot dog roll pans. If you are going to be doing much baking, I highly recommend these pans. To make hamburger or hot dog rolls you simply select any of the roll recipes listed in this cookbook and pipe the batter into a greased pan. I recommend that you smooth the tops of the rolls with a spatula or a wet finger to give a more polished look. They will also be easier to slice if smoothed. If you do not have the hamburger or hot dog pans you can still make rolls in this shape. Simply pipe the batter of your choice onto a greased baking sheet and then smooth the top of the roll. Either method will work and produce a beautiful roll, however having the hot dog and hamburger bun pans will save you a lot of time. Most of the roll recipes in this cookbook will make about 8 to 10 hot dog rolls or 6 to 9 hamburger rolls which is completely driven by the size of the roll that you make.

Cloverleaf Specialty Rolls

To make the special cloverleaf rolls simply pipe three balls of batter into a greased regular size muffin cup or tray. The size of the balls should be somewhat uniform and will be about the size of a large marble. When the rolls bake, the three balls of batter will come together and form one nice roll. This is the way to make old-fashioned cloverleaf dinner rolls. Any of the roll recipes in this cookbook will work great for cloverleaf rolls, and they will freeze very well in a tightly sealed ziplock bag or other sealed container. Most of the roll recipes in this cookbook will make approximately 22 to 24 cloverleaf rolls if you use the standard size muffin tin.

Savory Onion & Garlic Rolls
Use any of the roll or bread recipes in this cookbook and add ½ teaspoon onion powder, ½ teaspoon garlic powder, and 1 to 2 tablespoons minced, dried onion to the batter. If you wish you can use fresh garlic put through a garlic press. Other herbs can be added as your tastes dictate. We've used dried rosemary, oregano, basil and thyme.

Anne's Breadstick Mix
Preheat oven to 375°.

  1½ cups tapioca flour (generous, full cups)
  1½ teaspoons xanthan gum
  1 tablespoon baking powder (corn-free if needed)
  ½ teaspoon salt
  3 tablespoons hot water mixed with 1 heaping
    tablespoon Egg Replacer™
  ⅓ cup olive oil (or other acceptable oil)
  ½ cup DariFree™ milk (or other milk substitute)
  ⅓ cup club soda (plus enough to make a creamy batter,
    about a tablespoon)

Mix all dry ingredients in a large bowl. Then add liquid ingredients. Mix well. Batter should be thick and creamy, but also light. If it is not, then add a touch more club soda. Cut a corner off of a ziplock plastic bag (about ½ inch or less of an opening). Place batter into the plastic bag and pipe out onto a breadstick pan (see below). Bake about 11 to 12 minutes, then turn bread sticks over and bake another 4 to 6 minutes. Baking time depends on how thick the breadsticks are. In addition to using this batter to make breadsticks, you can cut a tiny hole out of a ziplock bag and pipe out tiny pretzel sticks. Bake pretzel sticks for only 3 to 5 minutes or so depending upon the thickness of the stick.

When measuring the tapioca flour, tap the bottom of the measuring cup repeatedly as that will help settle the tapioca into the measuring cup to give you a "full cup". Instead of that technique, you may opt to use my "lazy measuring technique" which is to use a heaping cup with the tapioca flour heaped as high as possible on the cup, almost a mini-mountain cup full.

A breadstick pan can be purchased on-line, or from a kitchen specialty store. Xanthan gum is an essential ingredient. Xanthan gum can be purchased on-line (try Bob's Red Mill or Authentic Foods), or at a health food store that carries a good line of gluten-free products. Xanthan gum is the binding ingredient that keeps the breadsticks from crumbling. Xanthan gum is used in most, but not all, gluten-free baked goods to hold them together.

Ener-G Egg Replacer™ is a dry, powder egg substitute that contains no egg components what so ever. It is also typically sold the same places that you find gluten-free baking ingredients like xanthan gum. Olive oil is one of the less "allergenic" oils and I would recommend it unless there are other oils that you are sure are fine for your use. DariFree™ is a dry, non-milk powder that is made from potatoes. See Special Ingredients Section of this book for more information on DariFree™.

For children under two, I recommend that you tear off tiny pieces and hand feed your child - pieces smaller than or about the size of a pea. The breadsticks are only really good on the day that they are made. On day two, when they are "stale", cut the breadstick into slices, and bake them at 350° until lightly toasted. These can then be little crackers for your child, which again can be broken into smaller pieces.

Versatile Roll, Danish, & Pizza Crust Mix (also good for bagels & breadsticks)
Preheat oven to 350°.

- 1 cup garfava flour (or chickpea)
- 1 cup tapioca flour
- 1 cup potato starch (you can substitute other flours for the potato starch)
- 2½ teaspoons xanthan gum
- 3 teaspoons baking powder
- ½ teaspoon salt
- 4 teaspoons dry powdered Egg Replacer™ (OR 2 eggs if you can tolerate eggs)
- ⅔ cup oil
- 1 cup DariFree™ milk or milk substitute of any type
- 1+ cup sparkling water or club soda until the *batter is creamy*

Mix dry ingredients in a bowl. Add liquid ingredients and mix well. Batter will be light and kind of fluffy. If necessary, add more club soda or water.

To make rolls:
Grease muffin tins. This will make about 18 rolls (+/-) depending upon how full you fill the muffin tins. Take the batter you have mixed up and put it into a plastic ziplock bag. Cut off one corner of the bag (about ½" or less of an opening). Pipe the batter into the muffin tins filling about ½ or ⅔ for smaller rolls, and more for larger rolls. Bake about 18 to 24 minutes or until lightly golden but not too brown. The baking time for the rolls depends upon the size of the rolls and the accuracy of your oven temperature. These will freeze well, and are o.k. on day two as well. You can use English muffin rings or hamburger bun pans to make larger rolls. Smooth out the tops of the rolls with either a spatula or wet fingers.

To make pizza crust:
This recipe will make two medium sized pizza crusts or several mini pizza crusts depending upon whether you like thin or thick crust. Place ½ of the batter on a greased cookie sheet or baking sheet. Using either your wet fingers or a greased or wet spatula, spread the batter out to the thickness you desire. You will have to experiment a bit on this the first or second time. Bake the crust for about 10 or more minutes until it starts to look fairly well baked. It will be slightly golden brown in color. Then top with your favorite sauce, and toppings. Return to the oven and bake another 10 minutes more or until done. If you are using the non-dairy "mock cheeses" you can return your pizza to the oven and broil it as that will help the non-dairy cheeses melt better.

To make Danish:
Grease a baking sheet. Place the batter into a ziplock bag with a corner cut off. Pipe the batter into circles on your greased baking sheet; start in the center and wind around the center circle until you have made the desired size circle. This will make about 18 or more medium size Danish. Make a small indentation in the center and fill with about ¼ teaspoon of your favorite jam or jelly. Bake 18 or so minutes until the bottom starts to just turn light

golden color. Let cool, then drizzle with a confectioners' glaze (see page 334). These freeze well and are delicious.

Cloverleaf Rolls:
Grease regular size muffin tins. Place batter in a ziplock bag with a corner cut off on a diagonal. Pipe three balls of batter into each muffin tin so that the balls of batter meet in the center. Smooth off the points or tips of any of the batter. These three balls of batter will then bake together forming a cloverleaf dinner rolls. They are wonderful for dinner parties or for when you want something a little fancy. You can also add rosemary, garlic, onion or other herbs to add more taste and pizzazz.

Amaranth Pizza Crust
Preheat oven to 400°.

1 cup amaranth flour
1 cup quinoa flour
2 cups tapioca flour
1 teaspoon salt
1 tablespoon baking powder
3 teaspoons dry Egg Replacer™ powder
1 teaspoon onion powder
1 teaspoon garlic powder
1½ teaspoons dried oregano
1 teaspoon dried sweet basil
3 teaspoons xanthan gum
1 cup acceptable oil
2 to 2½ cups water(add half, then remaining as needed)

Mix dry ingredients together in a large mixing bowl. Add oil and half of the liquid. Mix and add remaining liquid as needed to make a creamy batter. On a greased baking sheet spoon the batter into pizza shapes. Use either oiled hands or fingertips or an oiled spatula to smooth the batter into the pizza shape and make a rim around the crust. Bake in a 400° oven for 15 to 20 minutes depending upon the thickness of your crust and the size of your pizza and which oven rack you are using. The top of the pizza crust should be lightly browned and baked fairly well through. Top with your favorite toppings and return to the oven. If you are using non-dairy (or dairy) cheeses, broil for 3 to 5 minutes or until the cheese is melted. Otherwise, bake an additional 5 to 8 minutes or until the toppings are hot. Makes 8 to 9 mini-pizzas, 4 to 5 small or 2 larger pizzas.

Donut Store Coffee Rolls

Preheat oven to 350°.

1½ cups garfava flour (or chickpea)
1½ cups tapioca flour
3 teaspoons xanthan gum
3 teaspoons baking powder
½ cup sugar
2 teaspoons ground cinnamon
½ teaspoon salt
4 teaspoons Egg Replacer™ dry powder (OR 2 eggs if you can tolerate eggs)
⅔ cup oil
1 cup DariFree™ milk or milk substitute of any type
1+ cup sparkling water or club soda until the *batter is creamy*

Additional sugar and ground cinnamon as needed for topping and centers

Grease the pan you will be using. If you want large coffee rolls like those sold at the various donut stores, use either a very large muffin tin or what we use is a hamburger roll pan. Mix dry ingredients in a bowl. Add liquid ingredients and mix well. Batter will be light and kind of fluffy. If necessary, add more club soda or water.

Place a quantity of batter into a ziplock plastic bag and cut off one corner on the diagonal (about ½ inch size). Place a small amount of batter in the center of the pan. Then sprinkle the center batter with both the ground cinnamon and sugar. This center mound of batter will constitute the center of the coffee roll. Once you have generously covered the center batter mound, pipe more batter into the pan swirling it around the center mound of batter. Here is where you get the coffee roll shape. If you omit adding ground cinnamon and sugar or some other spice over the mound, the swirl effect will be lost as the batter will blend together.

Top the batter with additional ground cinnamon and sugar. Baking time will be determined by the size of the pan that you use. For standard muffin tin size, bake coffee rolls for about 20 minutes. Bake larger muffin tins or hamburger roll pans for 24 or so minutes, checking for color. These freeze well, and are delightful grilled. You can also drizzle some confectioners' icing or glaze (see page 334) on these to make them extra sweet!

Rice & Millet Rolls, Danish & Waffles
Preheat oven to 350°.

1¼ cups rice flour
1 cup tapioca flour
¾ cup millet flour
3 teaspoons xanthan gum
4 teaspoons baking powder
1 teaspoon salt
4 heaping teaspoons Egg Replacer™ (OR 2 eggs if you
   can tolerate eggs)
⅔ cup oil
1 cup rice milk or other milk substitute of any type
1+ cup sparkling water or club soda until the *batter is*
   creamy

Mix dry ingredients in a bowl. Add liquid ingredients and mix
well. Batter will be light and kind of fluffy. If necessary, add
more club soda or water. You may use other gluten-free flours
than the three listed.

To make rolls:
Grease muffin tins. This will make about 18 rolls (+/-) depending
upon how full you fill the muffin tins. Take the batter you have
mixed up and put it into a plastic ziplock bag. Cut off one corner
of the bag (about ½" or less of an opening). Pipe the batter into
the muffin tins filling about ½ or ⅔ for smaller rolls, and more for
larger rolls. Bake about 18 to 24 minutes or until lightly golden
but not too brown. These will freeze well, and are good on day two
as well. You can use English muffin rings or hamburger bun pans
to make larger rolls. Smooth out the tops of the rolls with either a
spatula or wet fingers.

To make Danish:
Take the batter and place into a ziplock bag with a corner cut off. Pipe the batter onto a greased cookie sheet. Pipe the batter into circles; start in the center and wind around the center circle until you have made the desired size circle. This will make about 18 or more medium size Danish. Make a small indentation in the center and fill with about ¼ teaspoon of your favorite jam or jelly. Bake 18 or so minutes until the bottom starts to just turn light golden color. Let cool, then drizzle with a confectioners' glaze (see page 334). These freeze well and are delicious.

To make waffles:
Use a greased and preheated waffle iron. The waffles will be done when they start to brown just slightly. Do not overcook or the waffles will burn. These waffles freeze well and make a fast breakfast or snack.

Millet Rolls, Danish & Waffles

Preheat oven to 350°.

1½ cups millet flour
1½ cups rice flour
3 teaspoons xanthan gum
1 tablespoon baking powder
½ teaspoon salt
4 teaspoons Egg Replacer™ (OR 2 eggs if you can
 tolerate eggs)
¾ cup oil
1 cup rice milk or other milk substitute of any type
1+ cup sparkling water or club soda until the *batter is
 creamy*

Mix dry ingredients in a bowl. Add liquid ingredients and mix well. Batter will be light and kind of fluffy. If necessary, add more club soda or water. You may use other combinations of gluten-free flours than those listed.

To make rolls:
Grease muffin tins. This will make about 18 rolls (+/-) depending upon how full you fill the muffin tins. Place the batter into a plastic ziplock bag. Cut off one corner of the bag (about ½" or less of an opening). Pipe the batter into the muffin tins filling about ½ or ⅔ for smaller rolls, and more for larger rolls. For a finished look, smooth the top of the rolls with a wet spatula. Bake about 18 to 24 minutes or until lightly golden but not too brown. The baking time is dependent upon the size of the rolls and the accuracy of your oven. These will freeze well, and are good on day two as well. You can use English muffin rings or hamburger bun pans to make larger rolls.

To make Danish:
Place the batter into a ziplock bag with a corner cut off. Pipe the batter onto a greased cookie sheet. Pipe the batter into circles; start in the center and wind around the center circle until you have made the desired size circle. This will make about 18 or more medium size Danish. Make a small indentation in the

center and fill with about ¼ teaspoon of your favorite jam or jelly. Bake 18 or so minutes until the bottom starts to just turn light golden color. Let cool, then drizzle with a confectioners' glaze (see page 334). These freeze well and are delicious.

To make waffles:
Use a greased and preheated waffle iron. The waffles will be done when they start to brown just slightly. Do not overcook or the waffles will burn. These waffles freeze well and make a fast breakfast or snack.

Garfava Roll, Danish, & Pizza Crust Mix (also good for bagels & breadsticks)

Preheat oven to 350°.

1½ cups garfava flour (or chickpea)
1½ cups tapioca flour
3 teaspoons xanthan gum
3 teaspoons baking powder
1 teaspoon salt
4 teaspoons Egg Replacer™ (OR 2 eggs if you can
    tolerate eggs)
⅔ cup oil
1 cup DariFree™ milk or milk substitute of any type
1+ cup sparkling water or club soda until the *batter is creamy*

Mix dry ingredients in a bowl. Add liquid ingredients and mix well. Batter will be light and kind of fluffy. If necessary, add more club soda or water.

To make rolls:
We like to add *dry, minced onion flakes and garlic powder/salt* to our batter for a different taste. You can add any or no herbs to yours. Try a taste test by dividing the batter in half and add herbs, onion flakes, etc. to half the batter and leave half of the batter plain. Grease muffin tins. This will make about 18 rolls (+/-) depending upon how full you fill the muffin tins. Place the batter into a plastic ziplock bag. Cut off one corner of the bag (about ½" or less of an opening). Pipe the batter into the muffin tins filling about ½ or ⅔ for smaller rolls, and more for larger rolls. Bake about 18 to 24 minutes or until lightly golden but not too brown. The baking time depends upon the size of your rolls and the accuracy of your oven. These will freeze well, and are good on day two as well. You can use English muffin rings or hamburger bun pans to make larger rolls. Smooth out the tops of the rolls with either a spatula or wet fingers.

To make pizza crust:
This recipe will make two pizza crusts and the size will depend upon whether you like thin or thick crust. Place ½ of the batter on a greased cookie sheet or baking sheet. Using either your wet fingers or a greased or wet spatula spread the batter out to the thickness you think that you desire. You will have to experiment a bit on this the first or second time. Bake the crust for about 10 or more minutes until it starts to look fairly baked. Then top with your favorite sauce, and toppings. Return to the oven and bake another 10 minutes more or until done.

To make Danish:
Place the batter into a ziplock bag with a corner cut off. Pipe the batter onto a greased cookie sheet. Pipe the batter into circles; start in the center and wind around the center circle until you have made the desired size circle. This will make about 18 or more medium size Danish. Make a small indentation in the center and fill with about ¼ teaspoon of your favorite jam or jelly. Bake 18 or so minutes until the bottom starts to just turn light golden color. Let cool, then drizzle with a confectioners' glaze (see page 334). These freeze well and are delicious.

Delicious Corn Bagels, Waffles or Cornbread

Preheat oven to 350°.

1½ cups corn flour
1½ cups cornstarch
½ cup white sugar
4 teaspoons baking powder
2½ teaspoons xanthan gum
½ teaspoon salt
2 tablespoons Egg Replacer™
One 12 ounce can club soda or sparkling water
¾ cup acceptable oil
¼ cup water, more only if needed

Mix all dry ingredients together. Add liquid (either additional club soda or water) as needed to make a smooth batter. The batter should be smooth and creamy.

To make cornbread:
Grease an 8" x 8" baking pan. Place batter into the baking pan and smooth the top with a wet spatula. Bake for 20 to 25 minutes.

To make bagels:
We use mini-bundt pans to make our bagel shapes with this recipe. You could also use a large donut shaped pan to make bagels with this batter. Bake 18 to 22 minutes or until just starting to show color. Do not overbake.

To make waffles:
Use a greased and preheated waffle iron. The waffles will be done when they start to brown just slightly. Do not overcook or the waffles will burn. These waffles freeze well and make a fast breakfast or snack.

Sorghum Bagels

Preheat oven to 350°.

1½ cups sorghum flour
½ cup flax meal or other GF flour
1 cup corn flour or other GF flour
1 tablespoon baking powder
2½ teaspoons xanthan gum
½ teaspoon salt
3 teaspoons Ener-G Egg Replacer™
½ cup maple syrup
One 12 ounce can club soda or sparkling water
⅔ cup acceptable oil
¼ cup water, more only if needed

Mix all dry ingredients together. Add additional club soda or water as needed to make a smooth batter. Do not add too much water. We use mini-bundt pans to make our bagel shapes with this recipe. You could also use a large donut shaped pan to make bagels with this batter. Place batter into a ziplock bag with the corner cut off on a diagonal and pipe into greased mini-bundt pans or large donut pans. Bake 18 to 22 minutes or until just starting to show color. Do not overbake.

Banana Muffins
Preheat oven to 350°.

1½ cups corn flour or other acceptable flour
1½ cups cornstarch or other acceptable flour
2 teaspoons xanthan gum
¾ cup sugar
1 tablespoon baking powder
¼ teaspoon salt
4 teaspoons dry Egg Replacer™ powder
2 to 2½ cups mashed bananas
¾ cup oil of your choice
1½ teaspoons ground cinnamon
Dash of ground cloves

Additional liquid to make a nice creamy batter: about ⅔ cup of water.

Mix dry ingredients. Add liquid ingredients. Place into either greased muffin tins or muffin tins with baking papers. These muffins are delightful and freeze well. This recipe makes about 24 muffins with sometimes a little batter to spare which we put in an individual loaf pan. If you do not use enough liquid, you will get dense muffins. Too much liquid will not produce the best muffins either. You want a nice creamy batter that is neither too stiff nor too runny. Bake muffins in a 350° oven for 15 to 18 minutes.

Banana Bread

This is a nice treat when you need to use up bananas or when you are looking for a food to serve guests!

Preheat oven to 350°.

2½ cups sorghum flour or other gluten-free flour
½ cup flax meal or other gluten-free flour
2½ teaspoons xanthan gum
1 tablespoon baking powder
1 to 2 teaspoons ground cinnamon
Dash of ground cloves
½ cup maple syrup or other sweetener
6 medium bananas, mashed (equals about 2 cups
    mashed bananas)
½ cup acceptable oil

Place all dry ingredients in a large mixing bowl. Peel and mash bananas and add to the dry ingredients. Add maple syrup or other sweetener to the dry ingredients. If you are using a sweetener other than maple syrup, you may need to add a little water to your batter to compensate for the substitution. Add oil. Mix all the ingredients by hand until the batter is moist. This will be a fairly thick batter. Place in a greased 5" x 9" loaf pan. Bake for 35 to 40 minutes, making sure that the center is done by testing with a cake tester. Larger or smaller loaf pan sizes will decrease or increase your baking times.

Allergy Sourdough Bread

This bread is inherently gluten-free, dairy-free, egg-free, rice-free, soy-free and corn-free. When you remove all of these ingredients, you are left with a very bland, flavorless product, which is why you need something to inject flavor. The sourdough starter provides that flavor. I realize that it will initially seem like a huge problem to make sourdough starter just to be able to make bread, however if you are really allergic to many foods there are not a tremendous amount of options. This recipe is a modified version of one of Bette Hagman's many great recipes!

Preheat oven to 400°.

Sourdough Starter:

> **1 packet dry yeast granules**
> **1 cup potato starch (if you can tolerate rice flour at all, the sourdough starter will be better with ½ cup of potato starch and ½ cup of rice flour in place of the 1 cup potato starch)**
> **½ cup tapioca flour**
> **1½ teaspoons sugar**
> **1 cup hot water (105°F - 115°F)**

Combine the flours, sugar and yeast in a mason jar with a lid, a crock with a lid, or other glass container. It is best to have a clear glass container so that you can see what is happening to the sourdough starter. Choose a container that is at least 1 quart in size, however a 1½ quart container would be better. Add the hot water and stir. Water that is over 115° will kill the yeast. Water that is below 105° will probably not be warm enough to activate or wake up the yeast. Therefore, the temperature of your water is very important. Stir the batter every few hours. If you are using only potato starch and tapioca flour in the starter, the batter will have a huge tendency to separate, and therefore needs more stirring. Use the sourdough starter in the first 3 days of when it is made. See Technical Know-How Section for more information on proofing your yeast.

Dry Ingredients:

2½ cups potato starch
1½ cups tapioca flour
1 tablespoon xanthan gum
1 teaspoon salt
1 teaspoon Egg Replacer™
1 teaspoon unflavored gelatin
6 tablespoons DariFree™ powder (non-milk substitute)
1 to 2 teaspoons ascorbic acid crystals (optional)

Liquid Ingredients:

Entire container of sourdough starter as made above
Generous ⅓ cup oil (any type tolerated)
Generous ⅓ cup honey
¾ cup hot water combined with 4 tablespoons of Egg
**   Replacer™ (mix this very well)**
½ cup warm water combined with 1 packet of dry yeast
**   granules and 1 teaspoon of sugar**
½ cup warm water (more or less)

Grease your baking pan and dust with rice flour. We use this recipe to make one regular sized loaf and one smaller loaf. The size pans we use are: 5"x 9"x 3" loaf pan, and a 4½" x 9" x 2 ½" loaf pan. Instead of making two loaves, you can make one loaf and use the remaining batter for breadsticks or rolls. Mix the dry ingredients together in a large mixing bowl. Mix the liquid ingredients together in a separate bowl. Then add the liquid ingredients into the dry ingredients and mix well. This will be a very, very thick batter. And I mean thick like cookie dough. You will probably think that the dough is too thick and that it will not turn out. Too much liquid in this bread, however, will cause the loaf to fall when it is removed from the oven. Depending upon your measurement of the ingredients however, you may need to add a few extra tablespoons of water.

Allergy Sourdough Bread

Place the batter in the loaf pan(s). If only making one loaf, use the remaining batter to make dinner rolls or breadsticks. The larger loaf pan should only be filled to the ⅔ mark, and no higher. After you have the batter in the pan, smooth out the top and take a very sharp knife and make diagonal cuts deep into the loaf of the bread. This will help reduce the amount of air pockets as the bread rises. If making two loaves, repeat this process with the smaller loaf.

Cover the loaf with a piece of greased waxed paper and place in a nice warm environment for the bread dough to rise. Allow to rise about 30 minutes if you are using fast-acting yeast. Allow to rise 60 minutes if you are using regular yeast. Bake at 400° for 15 minutes and then cover the bread with foil to reduce the browning. Bake for 45 more minutes at 400°. Then use a cake tester to determine if the bread dough is finished as it most likely will not be done. Reduce oven temperature by 75° to 325° and bake for another 10 to 20 minutes until the loaf is done. Using a long metal cake tester is a very reliable method for determining how "gummy" the inside of the bread is during baking. When the cake tester comes out clean, the loaf is done. If your loaf sinks in the middle after it is cooling, that is a sign that you used too much liquid or over-proofed your yeast.

Corn Bagels

Preheat oven to 375°.

    1½ cups corn flour
    1½ cups cornstarch
    2½ teaspoons xanthan gum
    1½ teaspoons unflavored gelatin
    1 teaspoon Egg Replacer™
    ⅓ cup sugar
    ¾ teaspoon salt
    3 tablespoons DariFree™ powder

Liquid ingredients:

    ½ cup warm water with 1 packet yeast and 1 teaspoon
      sugar (water between 105°F to 115°F)
    4 tablespoons corn oil
    ½ cup hot water combined with 3 tablespoons Egg
      Replacer™

    Additional 2 to 4 tablespoons hot water, just enough to
      make a nice batter (batter should be somewhat stiff)

Mix the dry ingredients together. Add the liquid ingredients and mix either by hand or with a mixer until well combined. You should be able to handle the dough with very well greased hands. The dough should *not* be too soft, but a bit on the firm side. If you cannot, then add more flour, 1 tablespoon at a time.

Greasing your hands with oil, form the dough into balls. Poke a hole in the ball to form a bagel and place on a greased baking sheet. This recipe makes about 8 to 9 small to medium sized bagels or 5 to 6 large sized bagels. Cover the bagels with a greased sheet of waxed paper and place in a warm spot to rise for 30 minutes if you are using rapid rise yeast, and 60 minutes for regular yeast. Make sure the bagels are in a warm spot, but not one that is too hot. After the bagels have had time to rise, place them 3 or 4 at a time in a pot of boiling water to which 1 to 2 teaspoons of sugar has been added. Boil for only 1 minute, turning the bagels at 30 seconds. Drain on paper towels. Return to greased baking sheet and bake for 20 minutes or until done.

Half-Grain Bagels

The reason that I have coined the term "half-grain" here is because while both the amaranth and quinoa flours are whole grain, the tapioca flour would not qualify as a whole grain. I have used the tapioca flour to cut the taste of the amaranth and quinoa to make them more appealing for children. ⁔If you use a whole grain flour in place of the tapioca, you will have whole grain bagels.

Preheat oven to 375°.

1 cup amaranth flour
1 cup quinoa flour
1½ cups tapioca flour
½ teaspoon salt
½ cup sugar
3 teaspoons Egg Replacer™ dry powder
1½ teaspoons gelatin
3 teaspoons xanthan gum
⅓ cup oil
¾ cup water, more only if needed

1 package active dry yeast
½ cup warm water
1 teaspoon sugar

Grease a baking sheet. In a mixing bowl, combine flours, salt, sugar, dry powdered Egg Replacer™, gelatin, and xanthan gum. If you are not familiar with proofing yeast, please read about proofing yeast in the Technical Know-How Section as it is important to proof the yeast the correct way. In a separate measuring cup, mix yeast with warm water and 1 teaspoon sugar. When the yeast has been proofed, add the yeast mixture, oil, and some of the water to the flour mixture. Mix well. You may need to add more water, however add it carefully. The dough for the bagels should not be too soft. The dough should be very, very firm and thick. If you add too much water by mistake, simply add more flour. If the dough is too soft, the bagels will fall apart.

Greasing your hands with oil, form the dough into balls. Poke a hole in the ball to form a bagel. Place on a greased baking sheet. This recipe makes about 8 to 9 small to medium sized bagels or 5 to 6 large sized bagels. Cover the bagels with a greased sheet of waxed paper and place in a warm spot to rise for 30 minutes if you are using rapid rise yeast, and 60 minutes for regular yeast. Make sure the bagels are in a warm spot, but not one that is too hot. After the bagels have had time to rise, place them 3 or 4 at a time in a pot of boiling water to which 1 to 2 teaspoons of sugar has been added. Boil for only 1 minute, turning the bagels at 30 seconds. Drain on paper towels. Then bake on a greased baking sheet for 20 minutes or until done.

Blueberry Half-Grain Bagels
Use the recipe above, but delete the ¾ cup of water and add 1 to 2½ cups of blueberries according to taste. Do not add any water until after you add the blueberries. If they are drained well, you can add water, a few tablespoons at a time until the dough is firm and thick. If you use store-bought, frozen blueberries, and they are not drained, you may not need to add any water. The dough for these bagels should not be too soft or moist – it should be very firm and thick. If you add too much water by mistake, simply add more flour. If the dough is too soft, the bagels will fall apart. In addition, you may choose to add another 2 to 4 tablespoons of sugar. These blueberry bagels are simply delightful!

Cinnamon Raisin Half-Grain Bagels
Use the above recipe and add 2 teaspoons of ground cinnamon and ½ to ¾ cup raisins depending upon how much you like raisins. You may add an extra tablespoon or two of sugar if you like.

Everything Half-Grain Bagels
Use the above recipe except cut the sugar to 2 tablespoons. For the coating, use ingredients that you can tolerate. The basic recipes we use is 2 tablespoons of sesame seeds, 3 tablespoons of ground sunflower seeds, 2 tablespoons of dried minced onion, a clove or two of pressed garlic, and 2 tablespoons of poppy seeds. Mix these ingredients and set aside since this is not added to the dough. Once you boil the bagels, use this mixture to coat the outside of the bagel just before baking.

Sesame Amaranth Rolls

My husband, Randy, came up with these rolls for our rotation diet. The kids really enjoy them. They can be made without the sesame if you have a problem with sesame.

Preheat oven to 350°.

> 1 cup amaranth flour
> 1 cup quinoa flour
> 2 cups tapioca flour
> 3 teaspoons xanthan gum
> 1 tablespoon baking powder (corn-free if needed)
> ½ teaspoon salt
> 2 tablespoons Egg Replacer™
>
> ⅔ cup oil (sesame if tolerated)
> One 12 ounce can club soda
> 4 to 6 ounces water (enough to make a creamy batter)
>
> Sesame seeds for topping (if tolerated)

Mix dry ingredients together. Add oil and club soda and mix well until batter is creamy but not runny. Place batter in a piping bag or plastic bag with the corner cut off on a diagonal and pipe into greased baking pan. We use a hamburger bun pan to make rolls for sandwiches. Top the rolls with sesame seeds if tolerated. Bake for 20 minutes or until lightly golden.

Pumpkin Chocolate Chip Muffins

These are a delightful treat for parties! I have taken these muffins to many gatherings and they are devoured by both children and adults. They are sweet enough to be a dessert, but they can also be used for breakfast! It is one way to get pumpkin into your children. Mini-muffin tins work very well for this recipe.

Preheat oven to 350°.

In a large bowl combine:

> ½ cup garfava flour
> 1 cup tapioca flour
> ¾ cup sugar
> 2 teaspoons ground cinnamon
> Dash of ground cloves
> Dash of ground ginger
> ½ teaspoon baking soda
> 1 tablespoon baking powder
> 1½ teaspoons xanthan gum

In a separate bowl, combine:

> 6 tablespoons hot water mixed with
> 4 teaspoons Egg Replacer™ (or 2 eggs)
>
> ¾ cup GFCF mini-chocolate chips
> One 15 ounce can of pumpkin
> 1 stick GFCF margarine (½ cup), melted OR ½ cup oil

Use either greased muffin tins or paper baking cups. Pour liquid ingredients over dry ingredients and mix until just moistened. Fill muffin tins 2/3 full. Bake for 20 to 25 minutes for regular size muffins or 12 to 16 minutes for mini muffins---until puffed and springy to touch in the center. Makes 12 regular or 48 mini muffins. These muffins freeze well.

Half-Grain Blueberry Muffins

The reason that I have coined the term "half-grain" here is because while both the amaranth and quinoa flours are whole grain, the tapioca flour would not qualify as a whole grain. I have used the tapioca flour to cut the taste of the amaranth and quinoa to make them more appealing for children. If you use a whole grain flour in place of the tapioca, you will have whole grain muffins.

Preheat oven to 350°.

> 1 cup sorghum flour
> 1 cup amaranth flour
> 1¼ cups tapioca flour
> 2 tablespoons baking powder
> 2½ teaspoons xanthan gum
> ¼ teaspoon salt
> ½ cup sugar
> ½ cup applesauce or mashed pears
> 1 to 2 cups blueberries
> ½ cup oil
> 1 to 1½ cups water
>
> **Sugar to top muffins**

Mix dry ingredients. Add liquid ingredients. Place batter in either greased muffin tins or tins with baking papers. Top muffins with sugar before baking. Bake 18 to 25 minutes depending upon whether you are making mini-muffins or regular sized muffins. Makes about 40 mini-muffins or 8 to 9 regular sized muffins. In addition to being delicious these muffins freeze well.

Luscious Lemon Poppy Seed Muffins

This recipe was oh, so hard to perfect! I tried converting recipes and no matter what I did, they were just unacceptable to us. After many failed attempts, we were finally successful! This is another recipe that works well if you want to take food to a party that will be popular.

Preheat oven to 350°.

> 1½ cups rice flour
> 1½ cups tapioca flour
> 2 teaspoons xanthan gum
> 1½ cups sugar
> 1½ tablespoons baking powder
> ¼ teaspoon salt
> 1½ tablespoons poppy seeds
> 1 tablespoon lemon peel (optional)
> 1 stick unsalted margarine (or acceptable margarine substitute) room temperature
>
> ½ cup water mixed with
> 4 teaspoons Egg Replacer™ (or 2 eggs if you can use them)
> 1 tablespoon lemon extract
> 1½ to 1¾ cups rice milk (or other acceptable liquid such as water or club soda)

Mix dry ingredients in a large mixing bowl. Cut margarine or margarine substitute into the dry ingredients. Add liquid ingredients and mix well. Bake for 20 to 24 minutes for mini-muffins and about 25 to 30 minutes for regular sized muffins or until done. We have used this primarily for mini-muffins, which I highly recommend. It makes 48 mini-muffins and 2 small mini-loaves. It would make approximately 24 regular sized muffins with some extra batter. The batter should be nice and creamy-not too stiff, and not too runny. The muffins freeze well.

Best Ever Blueberry Muffins

Preheat oven to 350°.

    1¾ cups rice flour (or other gluten-free flour)
    1½ cups tapioca flour (or other gluten-free flour)
    1½ teaspoons xanthan gum
    1 teaspoon salt
    2 tablespoons baking powder
    ½ cup oil
    ½ cup mashed pear or applesauce
    1 to 2 cups blueberries, either fresh or frozen
    1¾ cups water (approximate – batter should be thick)
    ½ cup sugar
    Sugar for topping

Mix dry ingredients well. Add liquid ingredients and place batter into greased mini-muffins tins or regular muffin tins. The batter consistency will be on the thick side. Sprinkle tops with sugar before baking. Bake for 15 to 18 minutes or until done. Makes 18-24 regular sized muffins or about 48 mini-muffins.

Chocolate Chocolate Chip Muffins

These delightful muffins are good enough to serve as dessert! Children and adults just eat them right up.

Preheat oven to 350°.

2 cups gluten-free flour (your choice or use a blend)
2 teaspoons xanthan gum
1½ tablespoons baking powder
½ cup cocoa powder
¼ teaspoon salt
1 cup sugar
¾ cup oil
6 tablespoons hot water mixed with
4 teaspoons Egg Replacer™
1 to 1¼ cups rice milk or other liquid, more only if needed
½ to ⅔ cup GFCF chocolate chips

Mix dry ingredients well. Add liquid ingredients and chocolate chips. Mix well. Spoon batter into greased mini or regular sized muffin tins. Bake at 350° for 15 to 20 minutes or until done for mini-muffins. Bake regular sized muffins for 25-28 minutes or until done. These freeze well.

Sweet Potato Donuts or Muffins

These are good for breakfast or a treat on the run. With sorghum flour and flax meal, you have got some whole grain goodness. Add sweet potatoes and you've got a sweet treat with some nutritional value. We make them in mini-donut pans and mini-muffin pans for that gourmet look.

Preheat oven to 350°.

2 cups sorghum flour
½ cup corn flour
½ cup ground flax meal
1 tablespoon xanthan gum
1 tablespoon Ener-G Egg Replacer™
1 tablespoon baking powder
Dash of ground cloves

¾ cup oil
One 15 ounce can sweet potato purée (or pumpkin or squash)
1 cup maple syrup (or other sweetener)
1 to 3 tablespoons water (only if needed)

½ to ¾ cup gluten-free, dairy-free chocolate chips

Mini muffin baking pans or mini-donut pans are recommended. If you don't have these pans, you can use a regular muffin baking pan. Grease baking pans and set aside. Mix dry ingredients in a large bowl and stir well. Add oil, sweet potato or other purée, and maple syrup. Stir to incorporate well, but do not over mix. Add chocolate chips. Clip corner of a gallon size plastic bag and place ⅓ of the batter in the plastic bag. Using the plastic bag for piping, and fill donut pan or muffin tins ¾ full or more. Bake for 20 to 22 minutes for mini donuts or mini-muffins, and 26 to 30 minutes for regular size muffins. Do not over bake. These freeze well.

Flax Sorghum Sweet Potato Waffles

Preheat waffle iron.

½ cup flax meal
1½ cups sorghum flour
1 cup corn flour or other flour
1 cup maple syrup
1 tablespoon baking powder
3 teaspoons xanthan gum
3 teaspoons Egg Replacer™
Dash of ground cloves
One 15 ounce can sweet potato purée
¾ cup oil
¼ cup water (more if necessary)

Combine dry ingredients. Then add wet ingredients, adding more water only if necessary. These were invented once our rotation diet become more solid and we changed from using cane sugar every day to the four different sweeteners that we now use. This batter will be very thick. If the batter is too runny, the waffles will come apart. If you use a different sweetener, you will need to adjust the liquid (i.e. add more water or reduce the water). Place the batter in a plastic bag with the corner cut on a diagonal. Squeeze the batter onto a greased and pre-heated waffle iron. Cook until lightly browned. Remove gently. Makes about 10 to 12 waffles.

Sorghum Rolls

Preheat oven to 375°.

 2 cups sorghum flour
 1 cup corn flour
 1 tablespoon baking powder
 3 teaspoons xanthan gum
 3 teaspoons Egg Replacer™
 ½ teaspoon garlic salt
 1 teaspoon onion powder
 One 12 ounce can club soda
 ⅔ cup oil
 ¼ +/- cup water

Mix dry ingredients. Add liquid ingredients and mix well. Grease muffin tins. This will make about 18 rolls (+/-) depending upon how full you fill the muffin tins. Take the batter you have mixed up and put it into a plastic ziplock bag. Cut off one corner of the bag (about ½" or less of an opening). Pipe the batter into the muffin tins filling about ½ or ⅔ for smaller rolls, and more for larger rolls. Smooth out the tops of the rolls with either a spatula or wet fingers. Bake about 18 to 24 minutes or until lightly golden but not too brown. The baking time for the rolls depends upon the size of the rolls and the accuracy of your oven temperature. You can use English muffin rings or hamburger bun pans to make larger rolls. These will freeze well.

Sweet Potato Chocolate Chip Muffins or Waffles

Preheat oven to 350°.

> 1 cup millet or rice flour or other gluten-free flour
> 1½ cups tapioca flour or other gluten-free flour
> 1 cup white sugar
> 1 tablespoon baking powder
> 1¼ teaspoons xanthan gum
> 4 teaspoons Egg Replacer™
> One 15 ounce can sweet potato purée
> ¾ cup safflower oil (or other acceptable oil)
> 1 teaspoon ground cinnamon
> Dash of ground cloves
> 1 to 1¼ cups water (enough to make a smooth batter)
> ½ to ¾ cup GFCF chocolate chips

Mix all dry ingredients in a large bowl and set aside. Mash the canned sweet potatoes well with a fork in a large bowl. Add oil and water and combine. Add liquid ingredients to the dry ingredients and mix to incorporate, but do not over mix. (If you can have eggs, then use 2 large eggs in place of ⅔ cups warm water and the Egg Replacer™.)

To make muffins:
Spoon the muffin batter into greased muffin tins. Mini muffin tins work very well with this recipe. Bake at 350° for 16 to 20 minutes for mini-muffins and 25 to 30 minutes for regular sized muffins. These freeze well.

To make waffles:
Place the batter in a ziplock bag with the corner cut off on a diagonal. Squeeze the batter onto a greased and pre-heated waffle iron. Cook until lightly browned. Remove gently. Makes about 10 waffles.

French Toast

My children love French toast! This recipe can be broiled or pan fried and is excellent with maple syrup or just some powdered sugar.

¼ cup DariFree™ milk substitute (or other acceptable liquid)
¼ teaspoon ground cinnamon
2 teaspoons Egg Replacer™

Bread or rolls
Oil
Additional ground cinnamon

Mix the Egg Replacer™ with one half of the DariFree™ milk until smooth and creamy. Then add the remaining DariFree™ milk and ground cinnamon. You can use sliced bread, or use rolls that you slice into pieces. We use hot dog rolls sliced into small round slices which the kids love, and have a nice gourmet look to the end result. Either pan fry the French toast on the top of the stove, or broil them under the broiler. In either case, dip the slices of bread into the liquid mixture and coat well. If pan frying, place a small amount of acceptable oil in your frying pan and heat on medium heat. Fry until just slightly golden on both sides. If using the broiler, place slices of French toast on a well greased baking sheet and top with a dash of ground cinnamon. Broil one side for 3 to 4 minutes, turn and top other side with cinnamon. Broil for another 3 to 4 minutes. The French toast usually does not brown that much under the broiler which is why we use a dash of ground cinnamon when we make them under the broiler.

Rice & Millet Pancakes

1½ cups rice flour
½ cup millet flour
1 teaspoon salt
1 ½ teaspoons xanthan gum
2 tablespoons Egg Replacer™

2 cups water
¼ cup safflower oil or other acceptable oil
¼ cup rice syrup or honey

2 teaspoons baking powder

Combine all dry ingredients together *except* baking powder. Add liquid ingredients and mix well. Add the baking powder and stir. Drop batter into a large, oiled skillet and cook on medium to medium-high heat until lightly brown. Turn pancakes over and brown on the other side.

Chocolate Chip Pancakes
Use the above pancake recipe and add either chocolate chips or carob chips to the batter.

Blueberry Pancakes
Use the above pancake recipe and add blueberries to the batter. Dry blueberries off before adding them to the batter or the water will make the batter too runny. If that happens, just add a bit more flour to thicken it up.

Garfava & Tapioca Pancakes

1 cup garfava flour
1 cup tapioca flour
1 teaspoon salt
1 ½ teaspoons xanthan gum
2 tablespoons Egg Replacer™

2 cups water
¼ cup olive oil or other acceptable oil
¼ cup cane sugar syrup or honey

2 teaspoons baking powder

Combine all dry ingredients together *except* baking powder. Add liquid ingredients and mix well. Add the baking powder and stir. Drop batter into a large, oiled skillet and cook on medium to medium-high heat until lightly brown. Turn pancakes over and brown on the other side. This batter yields "puffy" pancakes, so spread the batter out thinly to ensure that they cook all the way through by the time they are browned.

Chocolate Chip Pancakes
Use the above pancake recipe and add either chocolate chips or carob chips to the batter.

Blueberry Pancakes
Use the above pancake recipe and add blueberries to the batter. Dry blueberries off before adding them to the batter or the water will make the batter too runny. If that happens, just add a bit more flour to thicken it up.

Corn & Sorghum Pancakes

1½ cups corn flour or other acceptable flour
½ cup sorghum flour
1 teaspoon salt
1½ teaspoons xanthan gum
2 tablespoons Egg Replacer™

2 cups water
¼ cup sunflower oil or other acceptable oil
¼ cup honey or maple syrup

2 teaspoons baking powder

Combine all dry ingredients together *except* baking powder. Add liquid ingredients and mix well. Add the baking powder and stir. Drop batter into a large, oiled skillet and cook on medium to medium-high heat.

Chocolate Chip Pancakes
Use the above pancake recipe and add either chocolate chips or carob chips to the batter.

Blueberry Pancakes
Use the above pancake recipe and add blueberries to the batter. Dry blueberries off before adding them to the batter or the water will make the batter too runny. If that happens, just add a bit more flour to thicken it up.

Cornmeal Griddle Cakes

½ cup cornmeal
½ cup cornstarch (heaping)
2½ teaspoons baking powder
¾ teaspoon xanthan gum
3 tablespoons sugar

8 tablespoons hot water with
2 tablespoons Egg Replacer™

2 tablespoons corn oil
1 cup club soda

Mix dry ingredients. Add liquid ingredients and mix well. Cook on a hot griddle oiled with corn oil or other acceptable oil. Makes about 16 small to medium size pancakes (child size). This recipe can be doubled, cooked and then the pancakes frozen for later use. Double all ingredients except for the Egg Replacer™ and accompanying water.

Chocolate Chip Pancakes
Use the above pancake recipe and add either chocolate chips or carob chips to the batter.

Blueberry Pancakes
Use the above pancake recipe and add blueberries to the batter. Dry blueberries off before adding them to the batter or the water will make the batter too runny. If that happens, just add a bit more flour to thicken it up.

Half Grain Chocolate Chip Waffles

The reason that I have coined the term "half-grain" here is because while both the amaranth and quinoa flours are whole grain, the tapioca flour would not qualify as a whole grain. I have used the tapioca flour to cut the taste of the amaranth and quinoa to make them more appealing for children. If you use a whole grain flour in place of the tapioca, you will have whole grain waffles.
Preheat waffle iron.

    1½ cups quinoa flour
    1 cup amaranth flour
    ½ cup tapioca flour
    1 cup sugar or other sweetener*
    1 tablespoon baking powder
    3 teaspoons xanthan gum
    3 teaspoons Egg Replacer™
    3 teaspoons ground cinnamon
    Dash of ground clove

    One 15 ounce can pumpkin or squash purée (OR 2 cups
       fresh squash or pumpkin, that has been baked)

    ¾ cup oil
    1 to 1¼ cups water
    ½ to ¾ cup acceptable chocolate chips

Mix dry ingredients together. Add oil and some of the water and the squash or pumpkin. You do not want this batter to be too runny. In other words, the batter should not run or drip off of your mixing spoon. Put batter into a ziplock bag with the corner cut diagonally and pipe onto a greased and hot waffle iron. Follow waffle iron instructions. Remove carefully as these waffles are slightly more delicate. It is most important not to add too much liquid to the batter. The water added to this recipe will also vary by how much water content is in your pumpkin or squash purée as some cooked pumpkin/squash has more water content than others. Makes 10 to 12 waffles depending on the waffle iron and batter

* Note: We use beet sugar. If using a liquid sweetener, reduce the amount of water.

Half-Grain Chocolate Chip Muffins
Preheat oven to 350°.

Use the Half-Grain Chocolate Chip Waffle recipe except you will use less water for the muffins. Use ¾ cup to 1 cup water for muffins. Place muffins in a greased or paper lined muffin tin and bake at 350° for 20 or so minutes for mini-muffins or 25 to 30 minutes for regular sized muffins.

Half-Grain Carob Waffles
Use the Half-Grain Chocolate Chip Waffle recipe above except delete the chocolate chips from the recipe. Add ⅓ cup carob powder and ⅓ cup sugar to the recipe. All other ingredients and instructions remain the same.

Restaurant Style Croutons

It's easy to make gluten-free, dairy-free, allergen-free croutons and they are such a nice addition to salads and some soups. These croutons can be made for any rotation day. Just use the bread or rolls from a given day. For example to have croutons for Day 1, use the rolls made with garfava and tapioca flours. To have croutons for Day 2, use rolls made from rice and millet flours.

Preheat oven to 425°.

4 cups bread cubes
¼ teaspoon onion powder
¼ teaspoon garlic powder
¼ teaspoon paprika
½ teaspoon sweet basil
½ teaspoon salt
To taste: black pepper (go easy on this)
1 tablespoon acceptable oil

You can use any bread for this. If you are using up dried or stale bread, you will need to alter the baking time as this recipe is for freshly made bread or rolls cut into cubes. Place bread cubes in a 9" x 13" baking pan and sprinkle dry spices over the bread cubes. Drizzle 1 tablespoon of oil over bread cubes and bake in a 425° oven for 10 minutes. Remove from oven and stir. Return to oven and bake until completely toasted which will be about 20 minutes or so for fresh bread cubes. If you are watching your weight you can omit the oil. If your spices do not adhere to the bread without oil, you can lightly spray the bread cubes with a spritz of water which will help the spices adhere to the bread cubes. This may lengthen the baking time just a bit. If you have a love of other spices, you can use whatever you like. This is a general crouton recipe that we love.

Fast and Easy Stuffing

We created this recipe to use up some gluten-free, dairy-free cereal that we had which had expired. The kids loved it. And it freezes well.

    6 cups bread crumbs or crushed cereal
    2 tablespoons acceptable oil
    1 medium onion, diced
    1 clove garlic
    1 teaspoon sage (or to taste)
    1½ teaspoons thyme (or to taste)
    1 teaspoon salt
    5 to 6 cups broth of choice (or more)

Place bread crumbs or crushed cereal in a large mixing bowl and set aside. Sauté onion in the oil of your choice. When onion is very soft and cooked through, add 1 clove garlic minced or put through a garlic press. Sauté 1 minute longer, then remove from heat. Add sautéed onion and garlic to bread crumbs or crushed cereal and mix well. Add sage, thyme, and salt and mix well. Then add 5 cups of the broth of your choice. Some people like their stuffing dry, and some people like their stuffing moist. If you have both types in your household, then divide the stuffing in half and add more broth to one bowl to get it to the right consistency for those members. If you like very moist stuffing, you will continue to add either broth or water to reach the texture/consistency that you prefer. This is now ready to serve as a tasty side dish.

Old Fashioned Stuffing

We call this old fashioned stuffing because we make it just like my Mom used to make. You will either need bread or rolls to cut into pieces and toast or you will need acceptable commercial bread cubes. This recipe makes enough to feed a crowd. If you are having a small gathering, this will freeze well. We make this size batch of stuffing and then freeze it in meal size portions. My children love this! We will use the roll recipes in this cookbook and make a double batch of rolls for this stuffing recipe.

16 cups toasted or dried bread cubes
3 tablespoons acceptable oil
3 large stalks celery, minced
1 medium to large onion, diced
1 clove garlic, minced
2 teaspoons salt (or to taste)
  Pepper to taste
4 to 6 teaspoons thyme
4 to 6 teaspoons ground sage
Up to 8 cups turkey broth (or other broth of your
  choice)

Place bread cubes in either a large mixing bowl or the bottom of a very tall roasting pan and set aside. Sauté onion and celery in oil. When the onion and celery are soft, add minced garlic and sauté one more minute. Add onion mixture to bread cubes. Sprinkle salt, sage, thyme over bread cubes and mix well. Pepper to taste. Add 4 cups of the broth of your choice and mix well. Place bread cubes in a large greased baking pan or two smaller baking dishes and bake in a 375° for 30 minutes. Remove from oven and check moistness. Add additional broth to reach your desired level of moistness. We like very moist stuffing since we typically don't use gravy, so we will use all 8 cups of broth. This freezes well.

Simpler Stuffing

Once we got our rotation diet down solidly, we didn't want to be using onion and garlic as often as before, so I began modifying recipes to remove the garlic and onion and still have the foods be tasty. To make the Simpler Stuffing you will use the Old Fashioned Stuffing Recipe and omit the onion, garlic, celery and oil. To replace the flavor that you have removed, add turkey lard to the turkey broth to add lots of deep, rich flavor. Also increase the sage and thyme to compensate, and a little extra salt. I managed to change from our Old Fashioned Stuffing recipe to this Simpler Stuffing recipe and my children didn't know the difference. And they usually don't miss a trick.

Wild Rice Stuffing

This is a fast way to make stuffing compared to the traditional recipes that I use. This makes about 4 cups of stuffing.

4 cups wild rice, cooked
2 tablespoons acceptable oil
1 large onion, finely chopped
3 stalks celery, finely chopped
½ teaspoon sage
½ teaspoon thyme
1 teaspoon salt
1½ cups broth

Sauté the onions and celery in the oil until soft. Add the rice, broth, and herbs and mix gently. This can be used to stuff a bird or as a side dish. If you like heavily flavored foods, you can increase the sage and thyme to your tastes.

Main Dish Meals

Chicken (continued)

Pasta

Vegetarian

Pizza

Jo Holcombe's Barbecue

This was my grandmother's recipe for barbecue or "sloppy joes" as we called it. My mother made it often when we were growing up and it was a family favorite. My aunt Irene Tubach, my mom's sister, made it when we went to Lake Mokoma for our annual trip, and it was the first time our gluten-free son had ever had it. He was about 14 months old at the time and he loved it! He still likes it! While this recipe will be either a hit or a miss with children, adults usually love it.

> 3 pounds ground beef
> 3 pints chili sauce
> 1 to 2 small onions, finely chopped (depending on your preference)
> ¼ teaspoon ground cloves
> ½ teaspoon ground cinnamon
> 1 tablespoon vinegar
> 1 tablespoon dry mustard powder
> 1 teaspoon sugar
> To taste: salt and pepper
> 8 ounces of water

Fry the meat and onions in some type of fat or oil. Drain off excess fat after the meat and onions are cooked. Add the chili sauce and spices. Add 8 ounces of water to one of the empty chili sauce bottles, cap and shake well. Then pour this mixture into the second empty chili sauce bottle and shake well. Repeat this with the third empty chili sauce bottle and then add the liquid to the barbecue. Simmer slowly for 1 hour. This is a large amount of barbecue, however it freezes very well. Make it and freeze what you don't eat for another meal or two.

Randy's Turkey Meatloaf

Preheat oven to 350°.

2 pounds ground turkey
3 strips turkey bacon (uncooked)
1 medium onion finely chopped (~ 1 cup after being
    chopped)
2 stalks celery, finely chopped (~ ¾ cup after being
    chopped)
4 teaspoons Ener-G Egg Replacer™
6 tablespoons hot water
¼ cup sunflower oil
1 cup cooked rice
1 cup crushed Health Valley™ Rice Crunch-Ems
    (measured before crushing)
1 teaspoon salt
½ teaspoon pepper
1 tablespoon Worcestershire sauce
1 teaspoon dried parsley flakes

In a large bowl, mix hot water and Egg Replacer™ to a frothy
consistency, then add oil. Add all other ingredients except ground
turkey and turkey bacon. Stir to mix. Add ground turkey to the
mix and squish through fingers to mix thoroughly. Put mixture in
a greased loaf pan, smooth and top with turkey bacon slices. Bake
for about 1½ hours (use a meat thermometer to check for
doneness, to about 170°).

Pigs in a Blanket

Remember the days of unrolling a package of refrigerator rolls and placing mini-hot dogs in the center for a fun and tasty treat? This is a recipe to rival the good old days. We use hot dogs that are nitrate, nitrite, BHA, BHT and preservative-free. These can be made in either a mini, appetizer size or a larger, meal size. My children love both. The yield for the recipe varies because you can use a smaller amount of dough or a more generous amount of batter for the blanket part. These are the perfect party treat when made in the mini or appetizer size! This is also a fun food for children to help prepare.
Preheat oven to 350°.

5 to 7 hot dogs
1 batch of roll dough, prepared

Boil the hot dogs in a saucepan of water until done, typically 5 to 8 minutes. While the hot dogs are cooking, prepare one batch of roll batter or dough. We use the garfava roll mix recipe in this cookbook because it contains the flours and ingredients that we use on our beef day. Once the roll batter is prepared set it aside. Remove the cooked hot dogs from the boiling water and drain. Place your dough batter into a plastic bag with a diagonal corner sliced off that is less than ½ inch. The process to actually form the pigs in a blanket is the same if you are making mini ones or larger ones, the only difference being the size of the hot dog and the amount of the baking time.

Mini Pigs in a Blanket

To make the mini pigs in a blanket, slice your hot dog in half crosswise leaving you with 2 round hot dog halves. Then take each round half and cut them in half length-wise, and then again in half length-wise. Following this process will leave you with 8 hot dog pieces that resemble strips. On a greased baking sheet, pipe out a 2 inch strip of batter OR less. This strip of batter will be wider than the strip of hot dog. Place a strip of hot dog in the center of the batter and pipe more batter on top of the hot dog. You can use more or less batter in the forming of the pigs in a blanket. Repeat this process until all of the batter is used.

Once you have made all of the pigs in a blanket, you will need to mend the seams of the top and bottom of the batter. To do this lightly wet your fingers and run them along the side of the pigs in a blanket to meld or mend the seam. You may need to add a bit more batter to some if the seams are not easily meeting. If you do not do this part, and your seams are not meeting, the hot dogs will pop out of the blanket during the baking process.

Large Pigs in a Blanket
Large pigs in a blanket are simply whole hot dogs encased in roll dough. Pipe out the roll batter onto a greased baking sheet. To make the large pigs in a blanket, you will pipe out a strip of batter that is about twice as long. Follow the same process as for the mini pigs in a blanket making sure to mend the seams or the hot dog will pop out. Baking time will be slightly longer. Bake until roll dough is baked through (about 25 minutes).

Yields: 35 to 40 Mini Pigs in a Blanket
8 or more Large Pigs in a Blanket

Slow Cooker Meatballs

2 pounds ground beef, turkey, chicken or pork
To taste: salt and pepper
Two 26 ounce jars of sauce or homemade sauce

Place the ground meat in a mixing bowl and add salt and pepper. Form meatballs and brown in a frying pan until lightly brown on all sides. This helps to hold the meatballs together and to keep the juices in the meatball during cooking. Place browned meatballs in a slow cooker with the sauce of your choice and place on high until it is bubbly. Then turn heat to low and simmer for 3 hours. If you don't have a slow cooker, you can place the meatballs and sauce in a baking dish and bake in the oven at 375° about 1 hour or until the meatballs are done. This recipe does not add any filler. You may add acceptable bread crumbs, crushed cereal or cooked or dried rice as filler. This makes approximately 45 walnut sized meatballs.

Green Bean Hamburgers

This is a great way to add nutrition to your burgers. My husband invented this recipe, and our children love them!
Preheat oven to 375°.

2 tablespoons oil
1 cup green beans, chopped
2 to 2½ pounds ground beef
To taste: salt and pepper

Chop green beans in food processor or by hand into very small pieces. Mix well with beef and shape into patties. Brown on both sides in oil. Place in a baking dish and bake in a 375° oven for 45 to 60 minutes, until done. The baking time depends on the size and thickness of the patties. Two pounds of ground beef will yield 8 four-ounce hamburgers. Larger patties or using more beef will impact your yield.

Lentil Burgers

Becky Flahart, one of my best friends, has had this recipe for a few years now as one of my "early" cookbook testers and she swears by this recipe for her family.

    1¼ cups dry lentils (about ½ pound)
    3 cups pure water
    1 large onion, chopped finely (about 1 cup)
    3 cups fresh gluten-free bread crumbs (about 6 slices)
    1 tablespoon water mixed with 3 teaspoons of Ener-G
        Egg Replacer™ (or 1 egg)
    1 teaspoon garlic salt
    ½ teaspoon oregano
    ½ teaspoon salt
    ½ cup carrots, chopped finely
    3 tablespoons acceptable oil or fat

Cook the lentils in the 3 cups of water for 15 minutes. Add carrots and onions to the lentils and cook 15 more minutes or until tender. Remove from heat and allow to cool slightly. Stir in bread crumbs, Egg Replacer™, garlic salt, and oregano. Form into patties and fry in oil or fat until lightly browned.

Hidden Burgers

This is a fun recipe that was the brainstorm of my son, Luke. The idea for the Hidden Burgers came one day when we were making Pigs in a Blanket. You can use any roll dough for this recipe. The yield for the recipe will depend upon the size of the hamburgers that you make. Larger hamburgers require more roll batter.

Preheat oven to 375°.

1 recipe of roll dough (We use the Garfava Roll recipe on page 190)
6 to 8 cooked beef, turkey, chicken or pork patties

Grease a baking sheet and set aside. Mix up one batch of roll batter of your choice according to its recipe. Drain cooked hamburgers of any excess fat or oil. Place the roll batter in a plastic bag with one corner cut on a diagonal, less than one inch across. Pipe the batter in a round circle about the size of your hamburgers. This circle of batter will become the bottom of the hidden hamburger. If your hamburgers are on the large size, pipe out round circles for just 3 or 4 hamburgers to start with. Place your hamburger in the center of the circle. Now, pipe batter on top of the hamburger being generous so that some of the sides are covered.

With a wet finger or spatula, mend or meld the tops and bottoms of the roll batter together so that the hamburger actually becomes hidden. If you do not mend the seams of the roll batter, the hamburger will "pop" out or become visible during the baking process. Repeat the process until you run out of roll batter or hamburgers.

Bake for 25 minutes in the oven. These will look like large rolls on the outside when they are done because the hamburgers are hidden on the inside. You can make very small hamburgers for a nice party food or hors d'oeuvre. You can also place a slice of non-dairy cheese on the hamburger before you encase it in roll batter if you like.

Black Bean Lasagna

Preheat oven to 350°.

One 10 ounce package of gluten-free lasagna noodles
Two 15 ounce cans black beans (drain & rinse)
Nonstick cooking spray
½ cup chopped onion (1 medium onion)
½ cup chopped red pepper (½ of a pepper)
2 cloves garlic, minced
Two 15 ounce cans of tomato sauce
Two 16 ounce packages firm tofu, drained well and
  puréed with 8 tablespoons of water)
¼ cup non-dairy sour cream topping

Cook lasagna noodles. Mash 1 can of beans. Coat a large skillet with cooking spray. Add onion, pepper and garlic. Cook over medium heat. Add mashed and unmashed beans & tomato sauce. Heat through.

Purée the drained tofu, and if using, the non-dairy cream cheese and then set aside. Spray a 9" x 13" baking dish. Arrange 3 noodles on the bottom and top with ⅓ of the bean mixture, then ⅓ of the Tofu mixture. Repeat next 2 layers ending with the bean mixture. Cover and bake for 1 hour or until done. It should be hot and bubbly the whole way through. Top with a dollop of non-dairy sour cream. Let stand 10 minutes before serving.

Pasta with Broccoli and Bacon

My husband invented this recipe to create a dinner meal that fit with our rotation diet. Our children love this dish!

> 1½ cups broccoli florets, cooked
> 4 slices bacon, cooked
> 1 medium onion, diced
> 8 ounces pasta, uncooked (we like corn tagatelli noodles)

Optional:

> 1½ tablespoons sunflower oil

Cook the broccoli in 4 cups of boiling water until tender, about 6 minutes. I like to cut the florets into small pieces, less than 1 inch. Scoop out the broccoli with a slotted spoon and set aside. Cook the pasta in the "broccoli water", adding more water if necessary.

While the pasta is boiling, cook the bacon in a large skillet until crisp. Remove the bacon and set it aside to cool. In the bacon grease, cook the onions until tender and starting to brown.

When the pasta is done, drain it and add it to the large skillet, along with the broccoli. Crumble the bacon and sprinkle it in over the pasta. Stir the mixture and if desired, drizzle on a bit of sunflower oil.

Turkey Pasta Toss

This is a very popular recipe at our house - my three young children can eat the whole batch! It is also very flexible – you can add other vegetables or tomato sauce for additional variations.

    1 medium onion, chopped (¾ to 1 cup)
    1 pound ground turkey
    3 stalks celery, thinly sliced at an angle
    3 medium carrots, thinly sliced
    1 large clove garlic, minced
    2 tablespoons safflower oil

    12 ounces gluten-free pasta (we like rice penne noodles or spirals)

Optional:

    2 tablespoons safflower oil, additional
    To taste: salt and pepper

Cook the pasta in boiling water. While the pasta is boiling, cook the onions in 1 to 2 tablespoons of oil in a large skillet. Add the ground turkey and sauté into small pieces until well cooked. Add the celery and carrot slices and cook on low heat until desired softness. We sometimes leave the vegetables a little crunchy.

When the pasta is done, drain and add it to the skillet. If desired, add 1 to 2 more tablespoons of oil and salt and pepper to taste. Stir and heat the mixture through.

This makes approximately four, 2-cup servings.   For added variety, you can add or use other vegetables, or add tomato or cream sauce.

Lemon Chicken

Preheat oven to 350°.

¼ cup safflower or other oil
½ teaspoon garlic powder
¼ teaspoon lemon pepper
1 teaspoon parsley flakes
½ teaspoon paprika
1 teaspoon lemon juice
4 boneless chicken breasts

Mix all ingredients together except for chicken to make lemon marinade sauce and set aside. Pound chicken breasts to about ½ inch thick. Sear both sides in a frying pan in safflower or other oil. Spoon ⅓ of marinade onto top of the chicken breast and cover for 10 minutes heating on medium low. Turn chicken over and spoon on remaining sauce. Cover and cook second side for 10 more minutes or until done. Note, if you do not pound your chicken breasts, then you will have a much longer cooking time. It is the thin fillets that cook so quickly. This is one of Randy's original recipes!

Chicken with Peach Salsa

This is an easy way to change up your chicken breasts.

Preheat oven to 350°.

4 boneless chicken breasts
1 cup peach or pineapple salsa (see page 305)

Bake the chicken breasts in the oven for about 45 minutes or until the juice runs clear. Or use a meat thermometer which should read about 190°F. Drizzle about ¼ cup of salsa on each chicken breast and serve.

Chicken Divan

This is a recipe that can be made with uncooked chicken or leftover, cooked chicken.

Preheat oven to 350°.

> **2 pounds chicken breasts and/or thighs**
> **3 large broccoli stalks with florets (or 16 ounces frozen)**
> **¾ cup dry soup base (see recipe on page 371), constituted with**
> **3 cups water**

Constitute the soup base by mixing with water. Cut up the broccoli into large pieces (using as much of the stalks as you like) and lay them into a large baking pan (at least 9" x 13"). Lay the chicken pieces on top of the broccoli and pour the constituted soup base mix on top of the chicken. Bake for 1 to 1½ hours until done. The time will vary depending on the thickness of the chicken. Always check for doneness of poultry by insuring that the juices running out are clear. Better yet, use a meat thermometer which should read about 190°F.

This recipe can be made with leftover chicken, either in large pieces or cut up. If the chicken is already cooked, you can cook the broccoli in a saucepan and just assemble the broccoli, chicken and soup base mix in a baking dish. Bake for 10 to 15 minutes at 350° to warm through.

Spinach Lasagna

I invented this recipe before I had children when I was doing my best to avoid dairy. It was easy to convert it to be gluten free. This is a great dish for dinner parties or special functions.

Preheat oven to 375°.

2 boxes gluten-free lasagna noodles
4 cups (32 ounces) spaghetti sauce
4 to 6 cups fresh spinach, washed & chopped (or 1 to 2
   packages of frozen spinach drained)
Two 16 ounce packages tofu, drained
2 tablespoons oil
1 to 2 cloves garlic, minced
1 large onion, chopped
1 red pepper, diced
2 cups carrots, chopped
2 cups celery, chopped

If using frozen spinach, thaw and drain and set aside. Cook lasagna noodles and drain. Lay out noodles on waxed paper with waxed paper between layers. Grease a 9" x 13" baking pan. Drain tofu. Purée tofu in a food processor with enough water to make a mixture the consistency of ricotta cheese, and set aside. Sauté the onions and red pepper in oil. Add carrots and celery and sauté until soft. Add the spinach. If using fresh spinach, cook just enough to wilt the spinach. If using frozen spinach, sauté to remove any water that did not drain off. Frozen spinach typically holds a lot of water and it will take 2-3 minutes to cook off the excess water. Add garlic and cook for only 1 to 2 minutes being careful not to scorch or burn the garlic.

Place a small amount of spaghetti sauce in the bottom of the greased pan and spread around. Place a layer of noodles on the bottom of the pan. Place a layer of the onion, pepper, carrots and celery mix over the noodles. Add a layer of spinach followed by a generous helping of spaghetti sauce. Finally, add a layer of tofu. Next add another layer of lasagna noodles and repeat the steps until you are at the top of the pan or out of ingredients.

Bake at 375° until hot and bubbly. You can make this in two 8 x 8 pans and freeze one or both if a smaller amount works for your family. I like to make this in two 8" x 8" pans and one we eat that day and one I freeze for another day. You can freeze the lasagna before or after baking it. To use frozen lasagna, simply thaw and heat until hot and bubbly.

This is a recipe you can get creative with. You can use other vegetables. You can add other spices. Have fun with it!

Easy Lasagna Casserole

This has the ingredients of lasagna and tastes just like it, but it's a lot faster and easier to make. As presented here, this is a vegetarian dish; however you can easily add your choice of meat. Additionally, this is a great dish for hiding vegetables.
Preheat oven to 375°.

> **4 to 6 cups acceptable cooked pasta (12 ounce dry package, cooked and drained)**
> **4 cups (32 ounces) spaghetti sauce**
> **Two 16 ounce packages tofu, drained**
> **To taste: salt and pepper**

Cook pasta and drain. Drain the tofu and purée in a food processor with about ¼ cup of water, per package, until the consistency is like that of ricotta cheese, adding more water if necessary. The amount of water varies depending upon the brand and firmness of the tofu that you purchased. In a large bowl, combine cooked pasta, with the tofu, salt and pepper and mix well. Add the spaghetti sauce and stir well. Place the lasagna mixture in a 9"x 13" or other large greased casserole dish and bake for about 45 minutes or until it is hot and steaming. You may add meat and/or vegetables to this fast and easy casserole dish.

Vegetarian Pizza

It often seems if you can't eat cheese, why bother with making a pizza. We think in a narrow box called pepperoni and cheese. This vegetarian pizza has no cheese although you could use the Tofutti Rice non-dairy cheese or another cheese substitute. The recipe is designed to be without cheese or a cheese substitute.

Preheat oven to 400°.

> 1 pizza crust of your choice (see note about this below and page 175)
> 8 ounces spaghetti sauce or other red sauce (this can be omitted if tomatoes are a problem)
> 1 red pepper, sliced very thin in strips
> ½ cup carrot shavings
> 1 clove garlic, minced
> 1 stalk celery, sliced very thinly on an angle
> ½ cup crushed pineapple

Note: Any dough recipe in the cookbook could actually be used as a pizza crust. We frequently use the Garfava Roll dough for our pizza crust unless we are on our Amaranth food day. For dough instructions, see pizza crust recipes.

Pizza crust should be baked and then topped with red sauce. Then layer vegetables on it as thickly as you would like. If you place vegetables on the top too thickly, you will get a heavy and soggy pizza, so a moderate layer is best. The crushed pineapple is an idea from my sister, Sharleen, and the sweetness of the pineapple is a great compliment to the vegetables. You may use any other vegetables for a topping. This is just one combination to give you a starting point. Once your pizza is topped, place it in a 400° oven for 8 to 10 minutes or until you deem it is ready. Leaving it in too long will scorch or burn the vegetable tips.

White Pizza

I was doubtful myself before I made my first white pizza with NO dairy! I used the Tofutti Brand non-dairy rice cheese slices which contain absolutely no dairy at the time of this printing. When baked in the oven, the cheese melted and it looked good enough to serve in a restaurant!

Preheat oven to 400°.

> **Pizza crust of your liking (see page 175)**
> **Acceptable oil**
> **Tofutti Brand Rice Cheese slices**
> **1 clove garlic, minced in a garlic press**

Lightly oil the pizza crust of your choice which has already been baked. Smooth the minced garlic over the top of the pizza crust, spreading as evenly as possible. Tear the Toffuti Brand rice cheese slices into pieces that overlap and cover the top of the pizza. Bake for 8 to 10 minutes until the cheese is melted. You can put other toppings with this white pizza if you desire (meat, other vegetables, etc).

Shepherd's Pie

We make this recipe in a large, deep casserole dish or in individual servings using small (7 ounce) glass baking dishes or small pie plates (4 ½" to 5"in diameter). This will make 10 to14 mini-Shepherd's Pies depending upon which size dish you use. If you make the mini-Shepherd's pie, it will require more mashed potatoes due to the increase in surface area, so we usually make a double-batch.

Preheat oven to 375°.

> 3 pounds ground beef
> 1 onion, finely diced
> 2 tablespoons oil
> 1 cup carrot, shredded or finely diced
> 1 cup celery, diced
> 1 cup frozen peas
> 5 tablespoons Worcestershire sauce*
> Two 15 ounce cans of tomato sauce
> 3 tablespoons sugar
> To taste: salt and pepper

* Contains fish and soy – omit if necessary

Mashed Potato Topping:

> 5 cups water
> 2 teaspoons salt
> 3 tablespoons oil
> 3 cups instant potato flakes (about 8 to 10 ounces)
> OR
> Homemade mashed potatoes

Please note if you reduce the amount of ground beef that this recipe calls for, please reduce the tomato sauce accordingly or it will be too "soupy". Brown the onions in the 2 tablespoons of oil. Then add the ground beef and brown. Drain the fat and any liquid from the beef. Add tomato sauce, sugar, Worcestershire sauce, carrots, celery and peas and cook over medium-low heat until the carrots and celery are soft. If you are in a rush, you can microwave or cook the carrots and celery separately. However, if you have finely chopped the carrots and celery, it will not take long to cook them. While the beef mixture simmers, mix up the mashed potato topping. The topping should be creamy, that is not too stiff and not too runny.

Place the beef, tomato & vegetable mixture in a deep casserole dish or pan and top with the mashed potatoes. We use a casserole dish that is about 4½" deep by 9" in diameter. We make our individual Shepherd's pies in small white Pyrex oven crocks and in small metal pie pans (about 4" diameter). Containers of this size will hold about ⅔ cup of the meat mixture. Then top with a layer of mashed potato topping. If you like a lot of mashed potatoes, then you will want to double the mashed potatoes called for in this recipe. Bake for about 45 to 60 minutes or until the Shepherd's pie is bubbling and hot. If you are making individual Shepherd's pie containers, you will also want to increase the mashed potatoes because it will take more mashed potatoes to cover all the mini pies. You may make this recipe without the vegetables if necessary; it just won't be as flavorful.

Vegetarian Shepherd's Pie

You can use just about any vegetables that you like for your Shepherd's pie! Here is just one way to make it with vegetables. I made this for a dinner guest who just loved it, as did my husband and son.

For the beef, substitute the following or your choice of other vegetables:

1 large or 2 medium zucchini sliced in half-moon pieces
2 red peppers, diced
4 stalks celery, diced
3 large carrots, chopped or diced

Reduce tomato sauce to one can, and add 2 tablespoons of tomato paste to the one can of tomato sauce. The reason for doing this is that the vegetables add a good deal of liquid when they cook. If you use the preceding Shepherd's pie recipe without making any modifications, the result will be a soupy Shepherd's Pie. Follow the preceding recipe directions.

Lisa's Mexican Pie

Preheat oven to 375°.

Sauté in a frying pan:

   1 large onion, finely chopped
   2 cloves garlic, mashed or minced
   1 red pepper, chopped
   2 zucchini, sliced thinly

Sauté the above ingredients until they are soft. The remaining ingredients are:

   3 gluten-free tortillas
   1 cup refried beans
   1 to 1½ cups salsa
   ½ cup non-dairy sour cream

In a 9" pie plate, place one soft tortilla. Cover with ¾ cup refried beans spreading to cover evenly. Cover with ½ of the sautéed vegetables and ½ of the salsa. Place a second tortilla over the mixture and repeat the layers of refried beans and veggies. Use the third tortilla to cover the pie. As much as possible, press the top tortilla to meet the second layer. Place 2 to 3 tablespoons of salsa on top of the pie. Cover with either parchment paper or foil and bake for about 30 minutes or until hot and bubbly. Top with non-dairy sour cream.

Hearty Pot Pies

This is a great recipe for children! The two great things about this recipe are that you can use up what you have on hand and that they freeze well. By deleting the meat and substituting more vegetables of your choice, this dish easily becomes a vegetarian meal. If you don't have individual pot pie containers I would recommend that you invest in them. You can find individual glass containers at your local discount store made by manufacturers like Pyrex and Corning, which are ideal for individual pot pies. While it may seem like it is more work to make individual pot pies, there is less waste. You may also find individual metal pie plates (4 ½" to 5" in diameter) that work well, however they cannot be reheated in microwave ovens. One large, deep casserole dish also works very well with this recipe.
Preheat oven to 375°.

Ingredients (with liberal substitutions allowed):

    1½ cups carrots, diced or chopped
    1½ cups celery, diced or chopped
    1 large onion very finely chopped (about 1 cup)
    1 large potato chopped into small pieces
    2 pounds turkey, beef, chicken or pork(cut up into small pieces or ground)

Additional vegetables as you choose:

    ½ to ¾ cup frozen peas OR
    ½ to ¾ cup broccoli

Broth:

    32 ounces broth of your choice

Thickening agent:

2 tablespoons cornstarch, tapioca or potato starch mixed with
½ cup water
To taste: salt and pepper
1 to 2 cloves garlic, mashed (or through a garlic press)
2½ tablespoons acceptable oil

Topping:

1 batch pie crust (see pages 342 or 343)

Sauté or brown meat and onion in oil until the meat is fully cooked. Sauté carrots and celery over medium heat until soft. In a separate saucepan, boil potatoes until done. Mix ½ cup broth with 2 tablespoons cornstarch or other thickening agent. Add to meat and onion mixture and cook over medium-low heat until thick. Add potatoes and vegetables to meat and gravy mixture and then spoon into the individual pot pie containers or into a deep casserole dish. The size casserole dish we use is 4½" deep by 9" in diameter. Top with a pie crust topping. Make sure to cut steam vents in the pot pie tops before baking in a 375° oven. Bake until the crust is very lightly browned, about 40 to 45 minutes for the individual pot pies and slightly longer for a large casserole dish. This makes more than a family of five can eat at one sitting, which is why we frequently make individual pot pies and freeze the extras.

Chicken Fillets

This is one of my husband's original recipes, and we all love it.

Preheat oven to 350°.

> ¼ **cup corn flour or other gluten-free flour**
> ½ **teaspoon onion salt**
> ½ **teaspoon garlic salt**
> ½ **teaspoon paprika**
> 1 **teaspoon dried parsley flakes (crush in your hand to powder-like consistency)**
> 1 **pound boneless chicken breast or chicken cut off the bone, cut into fillet pieces**

Mix the dry ingredients together and set aside. Cut your chicken into fillet pieces. Fillet pieces can be very small or large depending upon your preference. Dip chicken fillets in water, or milk substitute or other acceptable liquid, and then coat with fillet coating mix. Your chicken fillets can then either be pan fried on top of the stove, or baked in the oven.

Stove top method: fry until brown and then reduce the heat, cooking until done (25 to 40 minutes depending on the size of the pieces). Smaller fillet pieces will cook very quickly (15 to 20 minutes) in oil on the stove top.

Oven method: bake at 350° for 30 to 40 minutes or until done.

We make very small fillets for our children and larger ones if we are having adult guests. This can be made in a larger quantity and stored for future use; however it is very quick to mix up.

Barbecued Chicken

Barbecued chicken is a family favorite. You can cook chicken in a variety of ways. The instructions in this recipe are for broiling your chicken. I've included 3 different barbecue sauce recipes in the Dressings, Dips and Sauces Section of this cookbook.

Preheat oven to Broiling

> **1 broiler chicken (typically 2 ½ pounds or less), cut in half and cleaned**
> **2 tablespoons acceptable oil**
> **1 cup or more of barbecue sauce (see page 302)**

The chicken should be about 5 to 6 inches from the broiling element. Lightly rub oil on both sides of your chicken. Broil them in a baking pan for 15 to 20 minutes per side. The broiling times provided are for a "broiler" chicken which means a chicken that is smaller than 3 pounds. If you use a larger chicken, you will need to increase your roasting times per side. Brush or coat with barbecue sauce and broil each side for an additional 3 to 5 minutes. Makes two or three servings.

Chicken Lasagna

This was a hit with all three of my children surprisingly! It is yet another way to get nutritious greens into your children.

Preheat oven to 350°.

> **24 ounces (1½ pounds) of ground chicken**
> **One 10 ounce package of frozen spinach, chopped well**
> **One 25 ounce jar of spaghetti sauce**
> **One 1 pound package of tofu**
> **To taste: salt and pepper**
> **1 to 2 tablespoons of acceptable oil**

Optional:

> **1 diced onion**
> **Other vegetables**

Fry the ground chicken in the oil until well cooked. While the ground chicken is cooking, purée the tofu in a food processor or blender until smooth and creamy. Chop the spinach into very fine pieces if you are serving this dish to children either by hand or in the food processor. Combine the puréed tofu, spaghetti sauce, spinach and cooked chicken in a very large mixing bowl. Add salt and pepper to taste. Mix well. Place the mixture in a 8" x 12" glass baking dish or other similar sized baking pan. Bake in a 350° oven for 40 minutes or until hot and bubbly. Because the chicken is pre-cooked, you can just heat through until hot.

Vegetarian Tamale Pie

Preheat oven to 400°.

4 cups water
1½ cups yellow cornmeal
¼ teaspoon salt

1 cup cheese substitute, grated (optional)

Cooking spray
1 cup onion, chopped
2 teaspoons dried oregano
1½ teaspoons chili powder
15 ounce can black beans (rinsed & drained)
16 ounce can pinto beans (rinsed & drained)
One 14¾ ounce can no-salt-added cream-style corn
6 tablespoons non-dairy sour cream

Combine 4 cups water, cornmeal, & salt in a large saucepan and bring to a boil. Cook cornmeal mixture over medium heat for 5 minutes or until thick, stirring constantly with a whisk. Stir in cheese substitute if using. Pour half of mixture into a 9"x13" baking pan or dish that has been <u>coated</u> with cooking spray.

Sauté onion until soft. Add spices, beans and corn. Cook for 1 minute. Spoon bean mixture evenly over the cornmeal crust. Drop remaining cornmeal mixture on top. Bake in a 400° oven for 30 minutes or until set. Top with sour cream.

Randy's Terrific Turkey Burgers

Your family will love these tasty turkey burgers which can be made ahead and frozen.

> 2 pounds ground turkey
> 1 cup crushed gluten-free cereal
> ½ teaspoon onion powder
> ¼ teaspoon celery seed
> 1 teaspoon salt
> ¼ teaspoon ground pepper
> 1 tablespoon Worcestershire sauce (contains fish & soy, so omit if allergic)

Mix all ingredients together and form burgers. This will make about 8 four-ounce burger. Fry in oil or bake in the oven until completely cooked.

Ham or Pork in Raisin Sauce

> ½ cup brown sugar, packed
> 2 tablespoons cornstarch
> 1 teaspoon dry mustard
> 1½ cups water
> ¼ teaspoon grated lemon peel (fresh is best, but dried lemon peel works also)
> 2 tablespoons lemon juice
> 2 tablespoons vinegar
> ½ cup raisins

Mix brown sugar, cornstarch, and mustard in 1½ quart saucepan. In a small bowl, mix water, lemon peel, lemon juice and vinegar; gradually stir into sugar mixture. Cook over low heat, stirring constantly, until mixture thickens. Stir in raisins. Makes about 2 cups sauce. Serve with ham or pork. We love it and it keeps well in refrigerator so it can be made ahead of time and heated up. Pour over ham or pork just before serving.

Pork Chops in Raisin Orange Sauce

This is a family recipe that I modified to be gluten free.   My grandmother, Jo Holcombe gave it to my mom, Jean Gottas.

> 4 pork chops
> 3 tablespoons gluten-free flour for coating
> 1 tablespoon fat of any type
> To taste: salt
> 1 or 2 oranges
> 4 tablespoons sugar
> 1 tablespoon cornstarch
> ⅛ teaspoon ground cinnamon
> Dash of ground cloves
> 1¼ cups hot water
> 1½ cups orange juice
> ¼ cup raisins

Roll pork chops in flour and brown in the fat on both sides in a large skillet. Sprinkle with salt. Set aside. Peel and section the oranges and put several sections on each chop. In a saucepan, mix the sugar, cornstarch, and spices. Add water and lemon juice and simmer until thick. Add the raisins and then pour over chops. Cover and simmer 1 hour. Serves 4. This is an excellent recipe and worth the effort.

Barbecued Spareribs

I consider spareribs an adult dish although some children will eat them. While you can cook your ribs on a grill, I've provided instructions for oven cooking in this recipe. Three barbecue sauce recipes are included in the Dressings, Dips and Sauces Section of this cookbook.

Preheat oven to 450°.

4 pounds of spareribs
1 cup or more of barbecue sauce (see 302)

Place spareribs in a baking pan in the oven for 15 minutes. Reduce heat to 350° and baste with barbecue sauce. Continue cooking for 1 hour or until the meat is done, basting with more barbecue sauce two or three times. Makes 4 servings.

Marinated Pork Chops

Preheat oven to 325°.

¼ cup lemon juice
2 tablespoons dried minced onion
1 teaspoon salt
2 teaspoons paprika
1½ to 2 pounds pork chops, 1 inch thick

1 cup water (this is used later in the recipe)

In a small bowl, mix the lemon juice, dried onion, salt and paprika together. Marinate the pork chops in the marinade for 2 to 3 or more hours in the refrigerator. Scrape the marinade off of the pork chops and save this for later. Brown both sides of the pork chops in a skillet with a little bit of oil.

Take the saved marinade and add 1 cup of water. Place browned pork chops in a baking dish and cover with the marinade mixture. Cover the baking dish and bake in a 325° oven for about 1 hour or until completely cooked through.

Beef Stroganoff

This recipe is from my mother, Jean Gottas, who is an excellent cook, baker, home economist, mother and grandmother! Thanks Mom!

1 tablespoon gluten-free flour
½ teaspoon salt
1 pound beef sirloin or other tender cut (cut in ¼ inch strips)
2 tablespoons oil
½ cup chopped onion
1 clove garlic, minced (this is optional)
1 cup thinly sliced mushrooms (this is optional)
2 tablespoons GFCF margarine or fat
3 tablespoons gluten-free flour
1 tablespoon tomato paste or ketchup
One 15 ounce can gluten-free beef broth
2 tablespoons cooking sherry (or red or white cooking wine)
1 cup non-dairy sour cream

Dredge the meat in 1 tablespoon flour and salt. In a skillet, quickly brown the beef on all sides in the oil. Add mushroom if using, onion and garlic. Cook for 3 to 4 minutes or until onion is barely tender. Remove mixture from skillet. Add 2 tablespoons margarine or oil to pan drippings. Blend in the 3 tablespoons flour, add tomato paste or ketchup. Slowly pour in the beef broth stirring until mixture thickens. Return meat mixture to skillet and heat. Just before serving, stir in non-dairy sour cream and sherry. Serve over rice or gluten-free noodles. Makes 4 to 5 servings.

Stuffed Cabbage Rolls

This is a flexible recipe because if you are vegetarian, you can eliminate the meat in this recipe and substitute your favorite mix of vegetables or a pilaf.

Preheat oven to 350°.

> **1 cup chopped onion**
> **1 to 1½ pounds pork sausage or ground beef**
> **1 tablespoon acceptable oil**
> **1 head cabbage**
> **1 teaspoon salt**
> **To taste: pepper**
> **One 26 ounce jar tomato sauce or your favorite sauce topping**

To make this recipe you will need to remove the outer first layer of cabbage leaves. To remove the cabbage leaves from the head, place the head of cabbage in a large stockpot of boiling water for 2 to 3 minutes or until the first layer of leaves are loosened. Remove the cabbage from the boiling water and with a knife, gently remove the outer layer of leaves. Immediately place those leaves back into the boiling water and blanche them for 2 to 3 minutes. Remove the cabbage leaves from the boiling water and immerse them in a bowl of cold water to stop the cooking process.

Place the cabbage head back in the boiling water to loosen the next layer of leaves. Repeat the process until you have more than 12 or 15 large cabbage leaves. How much filling your cabbage rolls will hold depends in part on how large the head of cabbage is. To prepare the filling, salt and pepper the meat and brown the onion and meat in the oil over medium high heat until the meat is fully cooked.

Place 1 to 2 tablespoons of meat filling in the center of each cabbage roll and fold in all of the sides to make a neat package. Place the cabbage roll with the folded side down in a greased baking dish. Repeat the process until all of the filling is used up. If you run out of cabbage leaves and have extra filling, you can use the leftover filling in the sauce that you will place over the cabbage rolls or you can go back and add additional filling to some of your cabbage rolls.

Cover the top of the cabbage rolls with either tomato sauce or your favorite other sauce recipe. Tomato sauce works well with stuffed cabbage rolls; however it is not the only option. Place the baking dish in a 350° oven and bake for 30 to 40 minutes or until sauce is bubbly. Rice is frequently used in stuffed cabbage rolls. We didn't use rice in this recipe because of our rotation diet days. You could easily add rice or another grain to the above recipe. Makes 12 or more cabbage rolls.

Chicken Spinach Burgers

One innovative way to get greens into your children! My children actually like these burgers! I made them as a complete fluke one day, and then the kids requested them again! Now, they are a regular feature for dinner.

> ¼ cup sesame seeds or gluten-free bread crumbs
> 12 ounces of ground chicken
> 1 cup chopped fresh spinach
> 2 tablespoons acceptable oil
> To taste: salt and pepper

Wash the spinach well, and drain. Pat or air-dry the spinach. Chop finely by hand or in a food processor so that the spinach is in tiny pieces. Mix the spinach, ground chicken, sesame seeds (or bread crumbs), salt and pepper. Fry in oil over medium heat for 15 to 20 minutes, reduce heat and continue cooking until cooked through. Makes three, 4-ounce burgers.

General Tso's Chicken

This is a recipe that we love. But if you get General Tso's Chicken from your local Chinese restaurant it isn't going to be organic, and it will most likely contain monosodium glutamate (MSG).

Sauce for Chicken:
> ¼ **cup cornstarch (or other gluten-free flour)**
> 2 **tablespoons pure water**
> ½ **teaspoon dry ground ginger**
> 1 **clove garlic, minced**
> ⅓ **cup sugar**
> ¼ **cup Bragg™ Liquid Aminos (or soy sauce)**
> 1 **cup chicken broth**
> 2 **tablespoons vinegar**
> 2 **tablespoons sherry or cooking wine**
> ¼ **teaspoon cayenne pepper**

Poultry:
> 1½ **pounds boneless chicken, cut into cubes or pieces**
> ½ **cup cornstarch (or other gluten-free flour)**
> **Oil for frying**

Additional Ingredients:
> 2 **cups broccoli**
> 1 **cup green onions OR ½ cup diced onion**
> 4 **small dried hot peppers OR**
> 2 **tablespoons dried hot pepper flakes**
> 3 **cups cooked rice,** *if serving over rice*

Note: cornstarch is intentionally listed twice in the ingredients section as it is used in two places. To make the sauce for this recipe, place all of the sauce ingredients into a container or jar with a lid and shake well to dissolve the cornstarch. Set this aside until later. Place the chicken in water to moisten so that the cornstarch will adhere to it. Using a ziplock bag to coat the chicken works well. Fry the chicken in oil at 350° until crispy. Drain. To finish the sauce, heat 1 tablespoon of oil in a skillet and fry the onions, peppers and broccoli for about 3 minutes. Add sauce mixture. Cook until thick stirring frequently. Add chicken and cook just long enough to heat through. This dish is typically served over rice.

Vegetable Lo Mein

There are many, many recipes and ways to make Vegetable Lo Mein. Besides the ingredients listed below, there are many other vegetables that you could use in place of what is listed or in addition to what is listed. Ideas of additional vegetables to include: celery, snow peas, mushrooms, and zucchini to name just a few. Use your favorite vegetables and have fun.

> 1 tablespoon acceptable oil
> ½ to ¾ cup chopped onion OR 1 cup sliced green onion
> ½ teaspoon ground ginger
> 2 medium carrots, julienned
> ½ sweet red pepper, sliced thin into strips
> 3 cloves garlic, minced
> 1 cup chicken or other broth (divided into two ½ cup servings)
> 1½ cups broccoli florets
> 1 tablespoon cornstarch
> 2 tablespoons Bragg™ Liquid Aminos (or soy sauce)
> 1 tablespoon ground sunflower seed butter
> 1 teaspoon acceptable oil
> ½ teaspoon sugar

Optional:

> ¼ teaspoon cayenne pepper or ¼ teaspoon crushed hot red pepper
> 10 to 12 ounces dry gluten-free spaghetti noodles, <u>cooked</u>

In a heavy skillet, heat 1 tablespoon of oil over moderately high heat and add onions, garlic and ginger. Garlic scorches easily, so be attentive and stir well. Add carrots, sweet red pepper, and stir 2 to 3 minutes longer. Add ½ cup of the chicken broth and cover. Allow to simmer for 3 minutes. Add broccoli and simmer two more minutes.

To make the sauce, in a medium bowl combine the remaining ½ cup broth with the cornstarch, hot pepper, Bragg™ Liquid Aminos, ground sunflower seed butter, oil and sugar. Add this mixture to the skillet and heat, stirring constantly over medium heat until it is thick. This should not take more than 3 to 4 minutes. Turn off heat. Cook pasta and drain. Add drained pasta to sauce in skillet and serve immediately. As the main meal, this will make about 4 servings.

Jambalaya

This is a recipe that is easy to make and good for potluck dinner parties or when you want something different to do with beef.

    2 tablespoons oil
    ½ cup diced onion
    ¼ cup diced green pepper
    1 pound ground beef
    One 28 ounce can crushed or chopped tomatoes
    1 teaspoon salt
    ½ teaspoon sugar
    ¼ teaspoon thyme
    1 small bay leaf
    1⅓ cups rice, cooked

In a large skillet heat oil and then sauté onion, green pepper, and ground beef. Cook, stirring often until meat is browned. Spoon off excess fat. Drain tomatoes; measuring juice, add water to juice to make 1½ cups. Add liquid, tomatoes, salt, sugar, thyme, and bay leaf to the skillet mixture. Cover and simmer for 5 minutes. Stir in rice and simmer for 5 more minutes. Discard bay leaf before serving.

Pork Patties and Meatballs

This is another invention of my husband.   Our children are delighted by this dish!

    1 to 1½ pounds ground pork
    1 clove garlic, minced or finely chopped
    1 teaspoon onion powder
    ⅓ cup Health Valley™ Corn Crunch-Ems cereal or
        other acceptable cereal, crushed
    2 tablespoons sunflower or other acceptable oil

Sauté minced garlic in oil. In a large bowl, mix sautéed garlic, onion powder and crushed cereal with the ground pork. Form into patties or meatballs and brown in a frying pan until done.

Stuffed Peppers

I think we tend to think of stuffed peppers as a more adult dish. My children however loved the idea of stuffed peppers and ate all the filling. Stuffed peppers are great because you can alter the filling to meet your dietary needs and rotation food days. The recipe here is for the more common stuffed peppers. Vegetarians can easily convert this dish to meet their needs by substituting vegetables, a grain or a pilaf for the meat or poultry.

Preheat oven to 350°.

> **4 to 6 red or green peppers**
> **1 pound ground beef, chicken, pork, or turkey (or grain pilaf or vegetables)**
> **1 diced onion**
> **1 tablespoon oil**
> **3 tablespoons Worcestershire sauce (*contains fish & soy, use only if tolerated)**
> **2 cups cooked rice**
> **To taste: salt and pepper**

When making stuffed peppers, I like to make the filling first. For the stuffing for this recipe, brown the beef and onion in the oil until thoroughly cooked. Add the Worcestershire sauce, cooked rice and salt and pepper. Keep on a low heat while you prepare the peppers.

Remove the top of the pepper and gut the inside. Do this carefully to preserve the shape of the pepper. I cut a circle around the stem of the pepper as small as possible, remove the top and using a knife, remove the seeds and guts. The next step is to parboil the peppers. Fill a large stockpot with pure drinking water and bring to a boil. Drop the peppers in the boiling water one at a time and boil for 2 minutes (**See note below about parboiling times). Remove from the boiling water and plunge into cool water to preserve the shape and stop the cooking process. Then turn pepper upside down and drain on a cooling rack. Do this with each of the peppers.

Once your peppers are drained, place them cut side up in a greased baking casserole dish and stuff them with the filling. If you have any extra filling, place it around the peppers in the baking dish. Bake in a 350° oven for 15 to 20 minutes until heated through. This recipe filled 2 large and 2 medium peppers with enough leftover to fill one small to medium sized pepper. How many peppers you fill will depend not only on the size of the pepper but also how stuffed you make them.

**Because you will be baking them in the oven for 15 minutes after they are stuffed, I don't like to overdo the parboiling and have mushy peppers. You will get a feel for this after you make them the first time. Maybe you only want your peppers parboiled for 1½ minutes. Or maybe you would like yours parboiled for 3 minutes.

Smothered Peppers

Smothered peppers are stuffed peppers which you cover with tomato sauce and bake. The reason it is good to use tomato sauce is because both peppers and tomatoes are in the same nightshade family, so it works for rotational purposes to keep the foods in the same family on the same rotation day. If you are not rotating foods, feel free to use any sauce that you love. Follow all other directions.

Honey Mustard Chicken

You can use this recipe for chicken breasts, legs, or a whole chicken cut up. We purchase whole organic chickens and cut them up for this recipe because it represents a huge financial saving. We found this dish to be popular with some children and most adults.

Preheat oven to 350°.

½ cup Dijon mustard
½ cup honey
1 tablespoon dried dill
2 teaspoons fresh orange zest
1 to 2 pounds chicken breasts or legs and thighs

Mix mustard, honey, dill and orange zest well in a small mixing bowl. Reserve ⅓ cup of the honey mustard sauce and set aside. You will use that for serving. Place chicken in a greased baking dish and coat with a thick layer of the honey mustard sauce. Bake chicken until done. Chicken fillets or chicken breasts will take much less time than chicken on the bone. Turn chicken in 20 minutes and coat the second side. Just before serving, add one last coat of honey mustard sauce. Serve with a tablespoon of honey mustard sauce as garnish and dipping sauce.

Spicy Chicken Fingers

My children love this coating mix for chicken fingers! These chicken fingers can be either baked, fried, or grilled depending upon your preference for cooking. The level of spices in this recipe will work for many children. If you love spicy food, you may increase the spices in this recipe.

> 1 to 2 pounds   chicken breasts, sliced into chicken finger size pieces
> 1 cup water
> 2 tablespoons amaranth flour (or other gluten-free flour)
> 4 tablespoons tapioca flour (or other gluten-free flour)
> 2 tablespoons quinoa flour (or other gluten-free flour)
> 1 teaspoon dried parsley flakes
> 1 teaspoon paprika
> 1 teaspoon onion powder
> 1 teaspoon garlic powder
> ½ teaspoon lemon peel
> 1 teaspoon salt
> To taste: black pepper

Optional:

> To taste: cayenne pepper (up to ¼ teaspoon)

Mix the flours and spices together in a small mixing bowl and set aside. Cut chicken breast into chicken finger size pieces. The larger the pieces, the longer the cooking time will be. We have small children, and we typically cut our chicken breast into pieces the size of your thumb or pinky. Dip the chicken pieces into water or other liquid and then coat with the spicy flour mixture. If you are frying the chicken fingers, they are then ready for frying. If however, you are baking or grilling the chicken fingers, you will need to dip them again in water or liquid or spritz with water or oil to moisten the spicy coating mix. Bake, grill or fry until completely cooked. These freeze well.

Spinach Quiche

I first experimented with tofu to replace ricotta cheese in lasagna over 10 years ago before I had my children when I was exploring natural foods. With that success under my belt, I thought that tofu might make a good substitute for the eggs and cheeses in a quiche. I have made this quiche many times and it is a good party food for adults, although my daughter loves it at age five. If you are in a hurry, or don't have a gluten-free pie crust, you can make this dish without the crust as we have done many times!

Preheat oven to 350°.

> 1 pie crust recipe, prepared
> 1 large onion, chopped
> 2 tablespoons acceptable oil
> 3 tablespoons Bragg™ Liquid Aminos or soy sauce
> 1 large clove garlic, minced or pressed
> 2 tablespoons vinegar
> ½ teaspoon salt
> To taste: pepper
> One 16 ounce package firm tofu
> 10 ounces frozen spinach, thawed and very well drained (*OR* 8 very large handfuls of fresh spinach, with the stems removed)

Optional:

> **Oregano, basil, or other spices**

Bake pie crust for 15 to 20 minutes in a 350° oven until just lightly browned. Do not over bake the crust. Open tofu package and drain excess water. In a food processor, purée the tofu with the 2 tablespoons of vinegar and set aside. In a large skillet sauté the onions in the oil until soft and well cooked. Add the Bragg™ Liquid Aminos or soy sauce and then the fresh or frozen spinach. Cook until the excess moisture is evaporated if using frozen spinach, or until the spinach is well wilted if you are using fresh spinach. Add the garlic and tofu mixture and allow to cook down for just about 2 or so minutes. Add the salt and pepper.

Years ago when I made this I used additional herbs like oregano and sweet basil which I've had to omit because of my daughter's food allergies. If you would like to add additional herbs, you can do this now. Pour tofu and spinach mixture into the pie crust and bake in a 350° oven for 1 hour or until the quiche seems firm. If you use frozen spinach and don't cook the excess liquid out of the spinach, this will add a great deal of liquid to the tofu mixture and increase your baking time substantially. Cover the crust of the pie if the edges get too brown with either aluminum foil, or a pie crust cover (a metal rim designed just to cover the edges of a pie crust during baking). Check for doneness using a clean metal knife. When the quiche is done, the knife will come out pretty clean. Allow the quiche to cool for 15 minutes before cutting and serving.

If you are making the quiche without the crust, simply place the spinach mixture into a greased pie plate without a crust! And bake as above.

Vegetable Bean Chili

This is a great vegetarian dish and good for people watching their calories and fat intake.

2 cups dried kidney beans, picked over and rinsed OR
Two 15 ounce cans kidney beans, rinsed & drained
2 tablespoons olive oil
2 red peppers, coarsely chopped
1 medium onion, coarsely chopped
2 medium carrots, chopped
2 stalks celery with leaves, chopped
2 cloves garlic, minced
28 ounce can tomato sauce
6 ounce can tomato paste (add a second can for thicker chili)
2 tablespoons chili powder
2 teaspoons ground cumin
2 teaspoons dried oregano
2 bay leaves
1 teaspoon salt
1½ teaspoons sugar
2 tablespoons water (if desired)
Dash of cayenne pepper (to taste)

Optional:

Frozen, fresh or canned corn or other vegetables

If using dried beans, quick soak by bringing them to a boil in a large pot of water. Boil for 5 minutes. Then cover the pot and let them sit in the pot for 1 hour. Then drain and rinse the beans. Add fresh water and cook for 1 hour to 1 hour and 15 minutes (or until done). Beans should be nice and soft, not crunchy or mealy. Drain cooked beans.

Sauté carrots, celery and onions in olive oil until soft. At the tail end of the sautéing process, add the garlic so as not to burn it. In a large pot, combine the cooked carrots, celery, onions and garlic with the corn, tomato sauce, beans and all the spices. Simmer 1 hour to blend flavors.

Note: This makes a fairly large quantity. We freeze some and eat chili for 2 or 3 days. This is great served over rice or just in a bowl alone! Cornbread or cornbread muffins are also nice with this chili. You can alter the consistency of this chili by adding more tomato paste if you like it thicker or water if you like a more "soupy" chili.

Sunflower Pasta
If you are not familiar with ground sunflower seed butter, then allow me to introduce you to it. This is a product that is peanut-free and tree nut-free that is a replacement for peanut or other nut butters. Ground sunflower seed butter is made from ground sunflower seeds, and our family has found it to be a superb replacement for peanut butter and nut butters. Here is a quick and easy dish that will please many a child and adults as well.

1 cup cooked gluten-free pasta of your choice
2 tablespoons ground sunflower seed butter
1 tablespoon acceptable oil

Mix the ground sunflower seed butter and oil together until you have a creamy sauce. Place warm pasta in the sauce and mix until the pasta is covered with sauce. You can't get any easier than this! This makes one serving. You can double or triple your recipe to make more servings or make a larger serving.

Vegetable Stir Fry

Vegetable stir-fries are easy and fast to make and are versatile because you can use the vegetables that are either in season or that you have on hand. With this stir-fry recipe you can eat it plain, with a tablespoon or two of Bragg™ Liquid Aminos or soy sauce, any commercially made sauces on the market, or the General Tso's sauce recipe included in this section with the General Tso's Chicken recipe.

    2 tablespoons acceptable oil
    1 large onion, sliced into wedge-shaped slices
    1 large red pepper, cut into strips and then cut in half
    5 cups fresh or frozen vegetables

Here is one mix that we often use:

    2 cups carrots
    1 cup celery
    1 cup broccoli
    1 cup cauliflower
    1 clove garlic, minced

Wash and prepare the vegetables. If using broccoli and cauliflower, cut into bite sized pieces. Cut remaining vegetables on a diagonal for a more appealing dish. Put the oil in a large skillet and heat over medium high heat. Add onions and fry for about 2 to 3 minutes. Add all remaining vegetables except the garlic and sauté until crisp-tender. If your vegetables still retain some of their crispness, you are retaining more of the vegetable enzymes, which are good for you. This can be served as a side dish, or over rice or any other cooked grain as a main dish.

Lisa Lundy's TV Chili

This is TV chili because it is a great food to serve while watching TV. It's also great for parties although if you are having a big crowd, you may want to double the recipe.

1 large onion, diced
2 tablespoons oil
2 pounds ground beef
1 tablespoon paprika
2 tablespoons chili powder
3 cloves garlic, grated or pressed
One 8 ounce can tomato sauce
1 teaspoon salt
To taste: ground pepper
1 pint chili sauce (bottled or see the recipe on page 303)
1 tablespoon chili pepper flakes
1 cup water
Two 15 ounce cans red kidney beans, drained and rinsed (or dried beans that have been cooked and rinsed)

In a very large frying pan sauté onion in oil and add ground beef. Fry ground beef and onion over medium high heat until the beef is brown. Add paprika, chili powder, and garlic. Sauté for 2 minutes. Then add tomato sauce, chili sauce, salt, pepper, chili pepper flakes, and water. Simmer for 40 minutes over low to medium low heat. Drain red kidney beans and rinse well with pure drinking water. Add to chili and simmer on low for another 20 to 30 minutes.

This is a family size recipe. If you plan on freezing part of this recipe, do not add kidney beans to the portion to be frozen. The beans do not hold up well to the freeze/defrost cycle. Freeze the chili without beans and add them later when you re-heat the frozen chili.

Beef Paprikash

*This is a fast and easy skillet dinner to make, and one that our children like. Paprikash (**paprikás** in Hungarian) is a traditional Hungarian stew made with either chicken or beef where paprika is the primary seasoning. It is usually served over egg noodles.*

1 tablespoon acceptable oil
2 cups chopped bell peppers (this is about 2 medium peppers)
1 large onion, chopped
1 pound ground beef
3 tablespoons paprika
½ teaspoon thyme
1 teaspoon marjoram (ground)
1 teaspoon salt
To taste: ground pepper
1 clove garlic, minced
2 tablespoons cornstarch, flour, or other thickening agent
3 cups beef broth or other broth
One 10 ounce package of gluten-free pasta, uncooked

Optional:

3 tablespoons non-dairy cream cheese

Brown the ground beef in the oil over medium high heat. Once the meat is brown, add the onion and green pepper, paprika, marjoram, thyme and garlic. Cook for 5 to 10 minutes, stirring frequently to prevent the garlic from scorching. While you are cooking the beef, in a separate pot, boil the gluten-free pasta and then drain when cooked. In a small bowl, mix your thickening agent (cornstarch or other gluten-free flour) to the beef broth and add to beef mixture. Stir well. Add the salt and pepper and then the cooked pasta. Allow the beef and pasta to simmer together on low to medium heat for about 5 minutes. Remove from heat and add the non-dairy cream cheese if you are using it. Makes 6 servings.

Marinated Flank Steak

This delicious recipe comes from an AOΠ Alum by the name of Lois Klotz whom I adore for so many reasons and in so many ways. Lois is a spectacular woman and this recipe is reflective of that.

24 hours in advance:

> 1 cup acceptable oil
> ½ cup vinegar
> 1 teaspoon salt
> ¼ teaspoon pepper
> 2 teaspoons dry mustard
> 2 teaspoons Worcestershire sauce (contains fish & soy)
> Dash of red pepper
> Dash of Tabasco™ sauce
> ¼ cup Bragg™ Liquid Aminos or soy sauce
> 2 to 3 pounds flank steak

Mix the ingredients together and use to marinate the flank steak for 24 hours covered in the refrigerator. Then about 2 to 4 hours prior to cooking, bring out to room temperature and allow the meat to continue to marinate.

Cooking instructions for a flank steak: Preheat the broiler. Place the steak on a greased broiler rack and place under the broiler making sure that it is within 2 to 3 inches of the heating element. This is important. Broil for 5 minutes and then turn steak over and broil for 4 minutes on the other side. This will produce a rare meat because if you cook a flank steak to medium or well done, it will become extremely tough and difficult to eat. Carve in ¼ inch slices cut diagonally across the grain.

Veal Shanks Italian Style

This is a recipe that my mom passed down to me.

2 tablespoons oil
4 shank crosscuts veal (2 to 2¼ pounds)
1 medium onion, chopped
1 medium carrot, chopped
1 medium celery stalk, chopped
3 cloves garlic, minced
1 cup dry white wine
1 medium ripe tomato, peeled, cored and chopped
1 bay leaf, crumbled
½ teaspoon dried basil
½ teaspoon thyme
¼ teaspoon black pepper
1½ teaspoons grated lemon rind
1 teaspoon dried parsley

In a 2" deep skillet or 4 quart Dutch oven, brown the veal over high heat for about 2 minutes on each side. Transfer to a platter. Reduce the heat to moderate and add oil, onion, carrot, celery, and ½ of the garlic to the skillet. Cook, uncovered, for 5 minutes or until the onion is soft. Add the wine and boil, uncovered. Keep stirring to loosen any browned bits from the bottom of the pan (from searing the veal). Stir and boil for 5 minutes or until the liquid has reduced by half.

Return the veal and its juices to the skillet. Add the tomato, bay leaf, basil, thyme and pepper. Cover and simmer over moderately low heat for 2 hours or until the meat is tender but not falling off the bones. Add the parsley, lemon rind and remaining garlic to the skillet just before serving. Makes 4 servings.

Roasting Meats

For beginners, cooking meats can be a daunting challenge! One tool that will give you confidence and help keep you and your family safe is a good quality meat thermometer. Use the meat thermometer to gauge the internal temperature of the meats that you are cooking. A roast can look juicy and nicely browned on the outside, but can be very undercooked on the inside. Meat thermometers are sold in most kitchen stores, large retail stores and even in many grocery stores.

Undercooked meats can easily make you sick, so the following chart gives you some guidelines for cooking your meats. In roasting meats, the idea is to start roasting at a very high temperature so that you sear in the juices of the meats. You roast at 450° for 15 minutes before you turn the temperature down and continue roasting until it is cooked through. A larger, thicker roast will take longer than a thin cut of meat.

Prior to roasting your meat, you can season it with a variety of spices depending upon what you like. You can season your meat with simple salt and pepper, fresh garlic, rosemary, chives, or other herbs. Simply rub the selected spices or herbs around the outside of your meat cut before roasting.

(See chart on the next page)

Meat Roasting Times

	Pork	Beef	Lamb
Roast for 15 minutes at:	450°	450°	450°
Reduce heat to:	350°	350°	350°
Continue cooking for:	18 to 20 minutes per pound	Rib Roasts & Sirloin Top Round: 20 to 25 min/lb Tenderloin Roast: 8 to 11 min/lb	Boneless: 19 min/lb Semi-boneless: 21 min/lb
Internal temperature when meat is done:	150° to 155°	Rare: 125° Medium: 130° Well Done: 145°	Rare: 125° Medium: 130° Well Done: 145°
Resting time before carving:	15 minutes		

Poultry Roasting Times

Weight	Roasting Time	Oven
Under 8 pounds	Less than 2½ hours	325°
8 to 12 pounds	2½. to 3 hours	325°
12 to 14 pounds	2¾ to 4 hours	325°
14 to 18 pounds	3½ to 5 hours	325°
18 to 20 pounds	4 to 5 hours	325°
20 to 24 pounds	4 to 5½ hours	325°
Over 24 pounds	5 to 7 hours	325°

Cooking a Turkey or a Chicken

I include how to cook a turkey in this cookbook because many people simply don't know how to cook one and would not know where to look for instructions. This is the most cost effective way for individuals who want to get hormone-free, antibiotic-free, free-range food. Buying the whole bird and cooking it yourself saves money and time. We typically get a larger turkey so that we have turkey in the freezer to last for 2 to 3 months.

To prepare for cooking a turkey or chicken, make sure that any equipment that you use is clean. Wash your hands very well in hot soapy water before and after handling raw turkey. Remove the giblets and neck from inside the bird and rinse the outside and inside of the turkey or chicken with pure drinking water.

Preheat your oven to 325°. You may choose to rub the outside of your turkey or chicken with oil. Lightly salt and pepper the outside of the bird. Place the bird, breast side up, in a shallow roasting pan. To keep your bird moist, cover the roasting pan. To brown the turkey or chicken, remove the roasting lid (or foil) the last hour of cooking. Use a meat thermometer to check the temperature of the turkey or chicken even if the turkey comes with a pop-up thermometer. Your meat thermometer should read 175° or greater when the turkey or chicken is done cooking. The juices should be clear NOT pink. Allow to sit for 15 minutes before carving.

Roasting times are based on the weight of the turkey or chicken. These figures are given as estimates only and you should check your bird for doneness. The roasting times are provided for a bird that contains NO stuffing. The roasting times also assume that the bird is fresh and not frozen. **(See chart on the previous page)**

Storing turkey or chicken leftovers

All meat should be cut from the bird within 2 hours of cooking, and the sooner the better. Chicken or turkey, stuffing, and gravy should be refrigerated in separate containers. Use leftover turkey and stuffing within 3 to 4 days, and gravy within 1 to 2 days. For longer storage, freeze foods and use within 3 months.

Vegetables & Side Dishes

Hash Brown Potatoes

Hash brown potatoes can be either potatoes cut in cubes or potatoes grated into pieces with a grater or food processor. We make both kinds at our home.

4 large organic potatoes, washed and peeled
½ cup olive oil or acceptable oil for frying
To taste: onion salt
To taste: garlic powder or 1 clove garlic pressed or smashed
To taste: salt

Either cut the potatoes into bite size (½ inch) cubes or grate with food processing blade or hand grater. Fry the potatoes in oil until browned. We use a lot of oil because we are trying to add essential fatty acids to our children's diets, as well as needed calories. If you are trying to reduce your weight, you can use less oil.

Homemade Mashed Potatoes

I have discovered in my travels that the younger generation, who have been raised on instant mashed potatoes, doesn't know how to make mashed potatoes from scratch. So, here is a basic recipe sans the butter and milk, of course.

7 large organic potatoes, washed well and cut into 4 to 5 pieces each
2½ tablespoons acceptable oil
¼ cup liquid (water or broth)

Fill a large stock pot with water and place the potatoes into the pot. Bring to a boil and cook for 15 to 20 minutes until just **knife tender**. Do not overcook potatoes or they will get gummy. The cooking time will vary depending on how fast your stove element heats up (gas or electric) and the size of potato slices you cut. Cool slightly and peel or leave the skins on for more nutrition as some gourmet restaurants do. Mash with a potato masher. Add acceptable oil. Start mixing with either a stand mixer or a hand held mixer. To the potatoes you will need to add just a little bit of liquid to make them creamy. You can add water, or broth, about ¼ to ⅓ cup, more or less depending upon how thick or thin you like your mashed potatoes.

Summer Squash Medley

This delicious dish is listed under vegetables; however it can easily be served as a main dish. To serve it as a main dish, you can put the vegetables over rice or over a cooked grain.

2 medium zucchini (4 cups), cut in half lengthwise and then cut into slices
1 medium red pepper, sliced into strips and cut into 2 inch pieces (1 to 1½ cups)
1 medium onion, cut in half and then cut into wedge slices (1 cup)
1½ tablespoons acceptable oil
To taste: salt and pepper
¼ cup pure water

In a very large skillet, sauté the onion and red pepper in the oil. Sauté until the onion is fairly soft and beginning to caramelize. Add the sliced zucchini or summer squash and continue cooking until the zucchini is soft but not mushy and overcooked. Add salt and pepper to taste. We love this dish made just this way. If you use fresh vegetables and don't overcook them, it will have a delicious taste with just a bit of salt and pepper. As a side dish, this will make 6-8 servings. As a main dish, this will make 2 generous servings, but you will need to add some grain, rice, or bread to make it a complete meal. Have other fresh vegetables on hand? You can combine additional vegetables as you have them!

Restaurant Style Broiled Home Fries

If you can eat potatoes, this is one way to dress up a bland food. I got the idea from a restaurant as the name implies.

5 washed potatoes, (peel if desired), sliced thinly
1½ tablespoons acceptable oil (you can use more if desired)

Select one of the following spices:

Lisa's Special Seasoning Salt (see page 368)

Rosemary, basil and parsley
Paprika, cayenne pepper, garlic and onion salt
Or use acceptable commercial seasoning mixes as you tolerate them

Do you want spicy home fries? Or perhaps home fries with just a hint of flavor? Choose one of the seasoning options and sprinkle over the potatoes. Broil until done, approximately 30 minutes depending on how you slice your potatoes stirring occasionally.

Sweet Potato French Fries

I included this recipe because many consumers don't think of buying sweet potatoes much less make them into French fries. While you can deep fry any food like this, this recipe gives you the instructions to broil them with a minor amount of fat. This recipe makes a small batch.

1 very large sweet potato, washed and peeled
1 tablespoon of acceptable oil

Slice the sweet potato into French fry sized pieces and place them in a 9"x 13" or similar sized baking dish. Drizzle the oil over the sweet potatoes and place under the broiler. Broil for 20 to 25 minutes or until desired doneness, turning the French fries once during the broiling time. My children will eat sweet potato French fries plain with just a bit of salt.

Scalloped Potatoes

What? Scalloped potatoes without dairy and gluten? Yes! You can have delicious scalloped potatoes without the dairy and gluten!

Preheat oven to 375°.

> **6 to 7 large potatoes, washed well**
> **2 tablespoons oil**
> **2½ tablespoons acceptable flour (rice, or tapioca)* (see note below about flour choice)**
> **2 cups DariFree™ or other milk substitute ** (see note below)**
> **To taste: salt and pepper**
> **1½ tablespoons minced, dried onion**

Wash and peel the potatoes, and soak in pure water while you proceed. If you have never made scalloped potatoes, the basic recipe is to layer peeled and thinly sliced potatoes with slabs of fat and to sprinkle flour, salt and pepper to each layer. In this gluten-free and dairy-free version of scalloped potatoes we are using liquid oil (since the slabs of fat melt anyway) and gluten-free flour. It *does matter* which gluten-free flour you use and *it does matter which liquid* you will use because certain gluten-free flours and dairy-free beverages will alter the taste of the scalloped potatoes.

In a large greased casserole or glass baking dish place a single layer of peeled and sliced potatoes on the bottom of the dish. Lightly sprinkle this layer of potatoes with salt and pepper, a pinch of the dried onion flakes and the gluten-free flour you have selected. Then place a second layer of peeled and sliced potatoes on top of the first layer. Repeat the sprinkling of salt, pepper, minced onion and flour. Continue this layering process until all potatoes are used up. Pour oil over the potatoes and then fill the casserole dish with your non-dairy milk substitute. Add enough milk substitute to come up to the top of the potatoes.

Bake the potatoes in a 375° oven for 60 minutes stirring occasionally. Your potatoes will be done when a knife goes through them easily. The reason that I recommend thinly sliced potatoes is because they will bake more quickly. If you have used thicker slices, you will need to bake your scalloped potatoes longer.

Notes:

*I have recommended rice or tapioca flours for this recipe because they are about as tasteless as you can get. It doesn't mean that these are the only two flours that you can use. I have made this recipe with garfava flour and it tasted great! The only negative about this recipe using garfava flour was that the potatoes turned out a little browner in color because garfava flour is darker in color. So my recommendation for the rice or tapioca flours is not just for taste but also for the sake of appearance.

**Many of the non-dairy beverages will add sweetness or other flavors to foods. So, you may have to compensate if you use a sweetened or stronger flavored beverage. We use DariFree™ non-dairy potato milk for our scalloped potatoes which works well. It adds some flavor, but that flavor is offset by the onions.

No Potatoes Mashed Potatoes a.k.a. Mock Mashed Potatoes

This is a favorite dieter's delight recipe especially formulated for those adults watching their waistlines! Be that as it may, it is one of the best ways to get children to eat their cauliflower! This will freeze, however you will have to drain some of the water off when defrosting.

    1 head cooked cauliflower
    2 tablespoons of acceptable oil
    To taste: salt and pepper

In a food processor or blender purée the cauliflower with a little oil. Add salt and pepper to taste.

German Potato Salad

8 to 10 large potatoes boiled in skins and peeled while
  hot
12 strips bacon fried crisp
2 medium onions
2 teaspoons salt
4 tablespoons sugar
½ cup diced celery
⅔ cup cider vinegar or white vinegar
4 tablespoons potato starch or other thickening agent
  or flour, dissolved in ⅓ cup water
2 cups water

While the potatoes are boiling and the bacon is frying, dice the
onion and celery. Sauté the onion and celery in the bacon fat
when the bacon is done. When the onions and celery are cooked,
remove from the pan and make the sauce for the potato salad in
the remaining bacon fat. Combine the vinegar, water, sugar, and
salt and cook over a low heat. In a small bowl, combine the potato
starch (or substitute thickener) with the water to dissolve. Add to
the sauce mixture and cook, stirring while it thickens. Peel and
cut the potatoes into slices. Add the sauce mixture, crushed or
crumbled bacon, sautéed onion and celery to the potatoes. This is
delicious hot or cold. This is a party or family size recipe. If you
are cooking just for one or two I would cut this recipe in half.

Vegetable Fried Rice

This recipe is for basic fried rice, which our family loves. You can vary this recipe by adding meat, chicken or additional vegetables.

> 3 cups cooked rice
> 5 tablespoons Bragg™ Liquid Aminos (or soy sauce if you can tolerate)
> ⅓ cup onion , finely chopped
> ½ cup carrots, diced
> ¼ cup peas
> 2 cloves garlic, minced
> 2 tablespoons of acceptable oil

Sauté the carrots and onions in the oil until soft. Remove pan from heat and add peas, minced garlic, Bragg™ Liquid Aminos (or soy sauce), and rice. Over medium heat, stir fry the rice mixture until heated through.

Pork Fried Rice

> 3 slices bacon or cooked pork cubes
> 3 cups rice, cooked and cooled
> ½ cup peas, fresh or frozen
> ½ cup canned miniature corn on the cob ears (or just plain corn)
> To taste: salt and pepper

In a large frying pan, fry bacon until fully cooked. Remove and drain bacon. Crumble bacon and set aside. In the frying pan containing the bacon drippings add the rice, vegetables and bacon and fry over medium high heat until heated through. Salt and pepper to taste. You may add soy sauce or Bragg™ Liquid Aminos but they are optional because the bacon and bacon drippings add a lot of flavor to this fried rice. You can substitute pork cubes in place of the bacon. If you are substituting cooked pork, you will need to add a little oil to this recipe.

Eggless Scrambled Eggs

It is amazing how much this dish looks like scrambled eggs. The most important aspect of making this dish is not to add too much turmeric (an uncommon spice that is yellow). Turmeric gives the tofu the color of scrambled eggs, but don't be heavy handed because it does add flavor. This dish is just great with the optional ingredients of vegetables, and the non-dairy cheeses available these days.

1 pound firm tofu
1 tablespoon of acceptable oil
To taste: salt and pepper
Dash of turmeric

Optional:

Sautéed vegetables (onions, peppers, broccoli, cauliflower)
Non-dairy vegetarian cheeses, shredded

Open package of tofu and drain excess water leaving the block of tofu. In a large skillet or frying pan, add oil and bring to a medium heat. Add tofu to frying pan by crumbling into chunks with your hands. Add salt and pepper to taste and just a dash of turmeric. Stir fry until the tofu is heated all the way through and the coloring of the turmeric is blended throughout. If necessary, you can add more turmeric, but only if the "eggless" scrambled eggs need more coloring. If you use the non-dairy vegetarian cheeses, you may want to place the grated or mashed cheeses over the tofu and place under the broiler as this frequently produces the best "melting" of the non-dairy cheeses.

Beets

Yes, I had to include a recipe for beets because most people don't know how to cook beets or what to do with them. It's all a learning process and I didn't know how to cook beets years ago either! My friend, Becky Flahart, got us eating beets, and helped us get into this wonderful food packed with nutrition.

How to get your kids to eat beets? Try the Mock Ranch Dip featured in this cookbook on page 305! All three of my children will eat beets with a little of the Mock Ranch Dip we make. The cooked beets will keep in your fridge for about 3 days. The uncooked (raw) beets however will keep in your fridge for weeks and weeks. So, just cook what you will eat.

Cut off the tops of your raw beets and place in a large pan of water. Bring to a boil and cook until a sharp knife can be inserted easily. Large to medium sized beets will probably need to be boiled for about 1 hour. Watch the pan and add water as needed. Cool beets slightly and then peel outer skin.

Special Green Beans

> 1 medium onion, diced
> 1 clove garlic, minced
> 1½ tablespoons acceptable oil
> 1 pinch crushed rosemary
> Green beans (fresh or frozen)

Heat the onion, garlic and rosemary in the oil over medium heat until very lightly browned and the onions are soft. Add French cut green beans and cook through. This adds a lot of extra taste and not too many calories.

Vegetable Spaghetti a.k.a. Lo-Carb Pasta

If you have never had spaghetti squash this is truly a delight of a vegetable! When cooked, this squash will come out of the skin looking just like spaghetti noodles obviously without the starch. You can then top it with your favorite sauce, a little sprinkle of oil, or whatever you can tolerate. This is a must-serve dish for individuals and families looking to go healthy!

Preheat oven to 350°.

1 spaghetti squash, cut in half lengthwise

Cut your spaghetti squash in half and remove the seeds. Place open side down in a baking dish with 1 to 2 tablespoons of pure drinking water. Bake for 30 minutes or until it is very soft. The baking time will be driven by the size of your squash. When it is very soft it is done. Then simply scrape the spaghetti squash out of its shell and into your serving dishes. Top with your choice of sauce or other dressings.

Cole Slaw

1 head cabbage, grated or shredded(or 1½ bags of
   shredded cabbage)
1 medium onion, chopped
1 red pepper, chopped
1 yellow pepper, chopped
1 orange pepper, chopped
1 cup shredded carrot
½ cup sugar
½ cup white vinegar
¼ cup of acceptable oil
½ teaspoon celery seed
¼ teaspoon dried mustard

In a saucepan, combine sugar, vinegar, oil, celery seed and dry mustard and bring to a boil. Boil for 2 minutes until sugar is dissolved and remove from heat. Let cool. Process cabbage into bite-sized pieces by using a hand grater or a food processor to shred or grate. Place cabbage, chopped peppers and the shredded carrot in a large bowl. Pour the sugar and vinegar mixture over the cabbage mixture and allow to marinate in the refrigerator overnight. Mix well before serving.

Baked Butternut Squash

My good friend, Becky Flahart, taught me about the beauty of butternut squash years ago when my oldest son was a baby. This is an easy food to prepare and it is an excellent side dish for dinners as well as a great baby food. If you make this for your infant or toddler, you can then freeze the baked butternut squash in ice cube trays or other small portions and take out just the right amount when it is feeding time. Butternut squash has a slightly sweet taste, and you may find it palatable scooped right out of the shell.

Preheat oven to 375°.

1 butternut squash

Optional:

You may oil the outside of the squash (we don't do this, however some people do)

If you want to, you can add sugar, brown sugar or any sweetener that suits you

Wash and dry the squash and cut in half lengthwise. Remove the seeds and place open side down in a baking dish. Place in a 375° oven and bake for 1 to 1½ hours depending upon the size. When it is completely soft and tender it is done. Scoop out the insides discarding the shell.

One great way to use squash is for muffin and waffle recipes, which I have included in this book (see pages 203, 209 and 211). Squash adds nutrition, great taste, and is a welcome addition.

Quinoa Grain Possibilities

If you like the quinoa grains, then the possibilities are unlimited. Cooked properly, you can use the quinoa grain like rice and make quinoa pilafs, and quinoa side dishes substituting it for rice. My family is not particularly fond of the quinoa grain taste. But for those with limited food choices, this is a grain worth looking into for its potential. My daughter will eat the following recipe as is with a huge smile.

⅔ cup dry quinoa, rinsed well in pure water
2 cups chicken or other acceptable broth (water could be used)
¼ teaspoon salt

It is important to rinse the quinoa grains well because it helps to remove a possible bitter taste. Rinse the quinoa well and place in a saucepan with either broth or water. Broth adds a great deal of flavor if you can tolerate some broth. Bring to a boil and boil for 2 to 3 minutes. Reduce heat to low and simmer until the grains have "popped" and are nice and soft (about 20 to 25 minutes depending on your heat level). Suggestions for serving: add chopped onion, minced garlic and your favorite vegetables for a nice pilaf.

Cauliflower and Greens Stir Fry

I made this with kale on a whim, trying to increase the number of greens and vegetables that my children would eat. Nothing could have surprised me more than when two of my three children cleaned their bowls and actually asked for seconds! This dish can easily be made as a vegetarian dish by omitting the bacon and using another acceptable oil in place of the bacon fat. You can also add additional vegetables for grown ups!

4 to 6 slices of bacon (free of nitrates, nitrites, and preservatives)
1 small onion, finely diced
½ head cauliflower or more
8 to 10 very large leaves fresh kale, spinach or greens of your choice
To taste: salt and pepper
½ cup water (omit if using frozen spinach or greens)

Prepare cauliflower and greens by washing. Chop or rip greens and cauliflower into very small pieces, removing any coarse or thick stems, and set aside. Fry the bacon in a large skillet. Remove the bacon when fully cooked and set aside. Keep most of the bacon fat in the skillet, only removing 1 or so tablespoons, if the bacon has rendered too much fat. Fry the onion and cauliflower in the bacon fat until soft. Add the small pieces of greens and sauté. Sauté the greens until they are wilted and very soft. Once the vegetables are done, crumble the cooked bacon over the vegetables and serve.

Dressings, Dips & Sauces

Sassy Salad Dressing

This salad dressing is definitely not for everyone. But if you like a sweet and sour type dressing, then this one may just hit the spot. You can alter the tartness or sweetness by changing the vinegar to sugar ratio.

⅔ cup sugar, or other sweetener
1 cup vinegar
½ teaspoon white pepper
1 tablespoon chives
1 teaspoon salt
2 tablespoons Worcestershire sauce
½ cup olive oil (or other acceptable oil)
1 small onion, finely chopped
½ teaspoon paprika
2 teaspoons prepared mustard

Place all ingredients into a blender and mix well. This recipe keeps well in the refrigerator for about 1 week. It is excellent on raw spinach and lettuce greens. Makes about 1½ cups.

French Dressing

This is a recipe that I have had since I started collecting recipes as a child.

½ cup acceptable oil
¼ cup vinegar
1 teaspoon sugar
½ teaspoon salt
½ teaspoon dry mustard
½ teaspoon paprika

Place all ingredients in a glass jar with a lid or any other closed container that you can shake. Shake well before serving. Makes about ¾ cup.

Eggless Mayonnaise

With the new foods commercially available now, you can purchase non-dairy mayonnaise made without eggs. This recipe is offered to the few who cannot tolerate soy, canola, or the other ingredients in the commercially available eggless mayonnaise. This recipe is nothing like mayonnaise made with eggs and dairy ingredients, but it is an acceptable substitute.

1 teaspoon salt
½ teaspoon paprika
¼ teaspoon dry mustard
Dash of cayenne pepper
1 teaspoon plain gelatin
½ cup cold non-dairy milk substitute
½ cup hot non-dairy milk substitute
4 tablespoons lemon juice

Combine gelatin and ½ cup cold milk and dry spices. Mix well. Add ½ cup hot non-dairy milk substitute and lemon juice and refrigerate until well chilled, 2 to 4 hours. Remove from the refrigerator and beat until fluffy in an electric mixer or with a rotary whisk. Chill again for 2 to 4 hours and then remove and beat one more time. Refrigerate until needed. You will need to stir this very well before using, and you may need to thin it a little bit with some lemon juice or water if the consistency is too thick for you. Makes about 1 cup.

Celery Seed Dressing

½ cup sugar or other sweetener
1 teaspoon dry mustard
1 teaspoon salt
1 tablespoon grated onion
⅓ cup vinegar
¾ cup acceptable oil
1 tablespoon celery seed

Combine sugar or other sweetener, mustard, salt, onion, and vinegar in a blender and mix well. Add oil and blend again. Add the celery seed and pulse just to mix well. Makes about 1 cup.

Non-Dairy Ranch Dressing

I invented this for salads so we could have a soy-free dressing that the kids would enjoy. The thickening agent in this dressing is xanthan gum. You will need a blender to make this recipe as it thickens with the whirling motion of the blender. Don't be alarmed if you mix it up and it seems too watery. You can add more xanthan gum, but I would not add more until you have blended it in the blender.

½ cup pure drinking water
⅓ cup acceptable oil
¼ cup milk substitute (see note)
1 tablespoon sugar or other sweetener (see note)
1 tablespoon brown rice syrup (see note)
1 teaspoon apple cider vinegar
1 teaspoon white or red wine vinegar
1¼ teaspoons garlic powder
1¼ teaspoons onion powder
½ teaspoon Dijon mustard
1 teaspoon lemon juice
1 teaspoon dried parsley flakes
Dash of ground black pepper
¼ teaspoon xanthan gum, blend and use ¼ teaspoon more, only if necessary to thicken

Note: You can substitute other natural sweeteners, if needed, as long as you understand that they will alter the taste. Therefore, if you are using other sweeteners (like honey), you may need to adjust your spices. We used DariFree™ as our milk substitute which is already on the sweet side, so you may need to adjust your sweetener if you use another milk substitute.

Combine all ingredients in a blender and blend for 1 to 2 minutes. Add more xanthan gum, only if necessary to thicken to your desired consistency. Store in an airtight container in the refrigerator. Makes about 1 cup.

Poppy Seed Dressing

This is one of my favorite dressings. You can substitute another sweetener for the honey if you need to.

¼ cup apple cider vinegar
¼ cup honey or other sweetener
1 teaspoon dry mustard
1 teaspoon salt
½ medium onion, chopped
¾ to 1 cup oil
1 tablespoon poppy seeds

Place all ingredients in the blender except the poppy seeds. Blend until smooth. Add the poppy seeds and gently blend for a few seconds. Makes about 1½ cups.

Strawberry Vinaigrette

This recipe was Noah's idea and he was there to taste test the first go at it. This is nice for fresh spinach, salads, or as a dipping sauce for fresh veggies.

½ cup acceptable oil
2 tablespoons red wine vinegar
2 tablespoons sugar
5 large fresh strawberries
Dash of salt
To taste: ground pepper

Combine all ingredients in the blender and purée until smooth. Refrigerate until well chilled. If you are using smaller strawberries, use more than five.

Raspberry Vinaigrette

You can use fresh or frozen raspberries for this salad dressing.

½ cup acceptable oil
½ cup raspberries (fresh or frozen)
2 tablespoons sugar or other sweetener
2 tablespoons red wine vinegar
Dash of salt
To taste: pepper

Mix all ingredients in a blender and purée until smooth. Refrigerate until well chilled. We usually use frozen raspberries that we allow to thaw first. We use a combination of raspberries and juice for this recipe.

Hot Fudge Sauce

6 tablespoons cocoa powder
3 tablespoons oil
⅓ cup boiling water
1 cup sugar

Mix cocoa powder and oil in a double boiler. Add ⅓ cup boiling water. Mix well and then add sugar. Bring to a boil. Allow to boil for 3 minutes. Cool just slightly before serving. This sauce will have to be warmed up prior to serving, as it is very thick when cold.

Raspberry Sauce

2 cups raspberries (fresh or frozen, thawed)
1 tablespoon lemon juice
½ cup sugar or other sweetener
⅓ cup water

In a small saucepan combine the sugar and water and bring to a boil over medium high heat. This is the process of making a simple syrup which is sugar and water. Stir constantly until the sugar is completely dissolved which may take 5 minutes. Add the raspberries and cook for 2 more minutes, stirring constantly.

Remove from heat and run through either a blender or a food processor to purée. Then pour the raspberry mixture through a fine wire mesh strainer over a medium bowl to remove the solids and seeds. Press the raspberry mixture through the mesh strainer with the back of a spoon to extract all of the liquid. You can save the raspberry "pulp" from the strainer for raspberry ice cream if you don't mind the seeds.

Add the lemon juice to the raspberry liquid that you collected from the straining process and allow to cool completely before serving. This makes approximately 2 cups. If you are not going to use the sauce in the next three days, freeze it for longer storage.

Cranberry Sauce

> 1 cup sugar
> 1 cup water
> 1 package fresh whole cranberries

Mix the sugar and water in a medium saucepan. Bring to a boil and stir until the sugar is dissolved. Add the cranberries; return to a boil. Reduce heat and boil gently for 10 minutes, stirring occasionally. Remove from heat and cool completely. Refrigerate. Makes about 2 ¼ cups.

Honeyed Cranberry Sauce

> 2 cups cranberries
> ½ cup water
> ½ cup honey

Place all ingredients in a saucepan over medium heat and boil for 5 minutes. Then reduce heat and simmer for a total of 15 minutes. Cool completely and refrigerate. Makes about 2 cups.

Lemon Marinade and Basting Sauce

¼ cup safflower or other oil
½ teaspoon garlic powder
¼ teaspoon lemon pepper
1 teaspoon parsley flakes
½ teaspoon paprika
1 teaspoon lemon juice

Mix well and refrigerate. Use within a week. This recipe is used in the Lemon Chicken recipe in this cookbook.

Homemade BBQ Sauce

¾ cup ketchup
2 tablespoons oil
1 tablespoon vinegar
2 tablespoons honey
2 teaspoons water
1 large clove garlic
¼ teaspoon xanthan gum

Mix all ingredients together. If you can tolerate a lot of garlic or are a garlic lover, you can add more than one clove. If you cannot tolerate commercial ketchup or afford the more expensive organic ketchups, you can use a mix of tomato paste and water in place of the ketchup, but you will need to add more sweetener to compensate. This makes about ¾ cup of sauce. We usually double or triple the recipe.

Fast and Easy Barbecue Sauce

1 cup ketchup
1 tablespoon honey
2 tablespoons barbecue marinade (that you can
   tolerate)

Mix all ingredients together and use to marinate poultry or meats.
Makes one cup. Double recipe if you are cooking for a crowd or
people with big appetites.

Fresh Barbecue Sauce

*There are lots of commercially made barbecue sauces around these
days. If you are looking for something a little bit fresher than
bottled sauce, here is one more recipe for you.*

2 tablespoons oil
½ cup onion, chopped
3 tablespoons Worcestershire Sauce
1 clove garlic, minced
2 full bottles chili sauce (or a double batch of Chili
   Sauce recipe*)
¼ cup apple cider vinegar
¼ cup sugar or other sweetener
¼ cup water
To taste: ground pepper
½ teaspoon paprika
¼ teaspoon chili powder

Sauté the onion in a large frying pan in the oil until it is very soft.
Reduce heat to low and add minced garlic, chili powder, paprika,
and fresh ground pepper. Sauté quickly and constantly as garlic
is easy to scorch. Sauté for 2 minutes. Remove from heat and add
the remaining ingredients. Return to heat and simmer over low to
medium low heat for one hour. Makes about 3½ cups.

*If you do not tolerate commercial chili sauce, you can use a
double batch of the Chili Sauce recipe on page 303 of this
cookbook.

Chili Sauce

I invented this recipe when my daughter required foods that were organic and free of preservatives. It is so much more economical to make some of these foods from scratch!

6 ounces organic tomato paste
1 cup pure drinking water
¼ cup sugar or other acceptable sweetener
2 tablespoons vinegar
1 teaspoon salt
1 tablespoon dried onion flakes
1 teaspoon garlic powder
½ teaspoon onion salt

Dissolve the tomato paste in the water and then add remaining ingredients. Cook slowly for 15 to 20 minutes. Makes 1½ cups. Double if using for barbecue.

Mom's Spaghetti Sauce

2 cups carrots, coarsely chopped
1 cup celery, coarsely chopped
2 cups onion, coarsely chopped
2 tablespoons olive or other acceptable oil
4 cloves garlic, minced (large cloves)
2 tablespoons dried basil
2 tablespoons dried parsley
2 tablespoons dried oregano
12 ounces tomato paste
13 cups tomato sauce
1 cup packed brown sugar

This recipe makes about 15 cups depending upon how long you simmer down the sauce. Sauté onion, carrots, celery in oil in a large stockpot over medium high heat until soft. Add garlic and stir for 1 minute. Add dried spices and sauté 1 more minute. Add tomato paste, tomato sauce and brown sugar. Simmer over low to medium heat for 1 + hour.

Mama Mia Spaghetti Sauce

1¾ cups finely chopped onion
½ cup diced carrots
1 red pepper, diced
2 cloves garlic, minced
¾ cup finely chopped celery
2 tablespoons olive or other oil
1½ tablespoons oregano
1 tablespoon basil
1 tablespoon parsley
4 tablespoons brown sugar
4 cups pure drinking water
24 ounces tomato paste
56 ounces canned tomatoes
1 to 2 teaspoons salt

This recipe makes about 7½ cups or more of spaghetti sauce depending upon how long you simmer it. Sauté onion, carrots, and celery in oil in a large stock pot. Sauté until soft, then add garlic and stir for 2 minutes. Add dried spices and sauté one more minute. Add remaining ingredients and simmer for 1 to 2 hours.

Cowboys Dip

12 ounces non-dairy sour cream
2 tablespoons dried parsley flakes
¼ teaspoon onion salt
¼ teaspoon garlic salt
¼ teaspoon Special Seasoning Salt (recipe on page 368 of this cookbook)
Dash of paprika

Add all ingredients to the non-dairy sour cream and mix well. This dip is great with chips and fresh vegetables.

Mock Ranch Dip

My son, Luke, was the inspiration for this dip mix. We think it is absolutely delightful!

> 12 ounces non-dairy sour cream
> 2 teaspoons sugar
> ½ teaspoon salt
> To taste: fresh ground pepper (e.g. 8 grinds of a small pepper mill)
> 1 to 2 teaspoons vinegar
> ½ teaspoon garlic powder
> ½ teaspoon onion powder
> Dash of xanthan gum
> 1 tablespoon minced dried onion flakes
> 1 tablespoon dried parsley (further crushed in your hands)
> 1 large garlic clove (either smashed or put through a garlic press)
> 2 tablespoons water (add this last, and only to desired consistency)

In a small mixing bowl, combine all ingredients. Stir well. Refrigerate for 2-3 hours before serving to meld the flavors. This dip is great for chips, fresh vegetables, meats and crackers. Makes 1½ cups.

Peach Salsa

This fruit salsa goes well with chicken or fish. It is easy to make and is one way to add some variety to chicken.

> 3 medium peaches, chopped
> 2 green onions, sliced thinly
> 2 teaspoons sugar or sweetener
> 1 teaspoon fresh ginger or 1 to 2 teaspoons chopped ginger from a jar
> 1 tablespoon lime juice

Mix all ingredients together and refrigerate until well chilled. Makes about 1 cup.

Noah's Mock Cheese Sauce or Nacho Dip

When my son, Noah was six years old he invented this recipe. It really is quite good! If you cannot have the real thing this is a great substitute.

This recipe is for an individual serving.

> **2 slices Tofutti Brand™ non-dairy "cheese"**
> **Dash of salt and pepper**

Optional:

> **Dash of cayenne pepper**
> **Dash of garlic or onion powder**

Tear cheese slices into pieces and place in a microwavable bowl. Add salt and pepper and any of the optional spices. Cover bowl with waxed paper and microwave for 10 seconds. If not melted, microwave for 10 seconds more. Microwaves vary greatly in power and your time will be determined by your microwave power. Stir in spices. Use as a chip dip or for crackers. This can also be poured over tortilla chips for nachos.

Pineapple Salsa

We whipped up this recipe one night when we were having chicken and fresh pineapple at the same time. It was popular with both the children and adults.

> **1½ cups fresh pineapple, diced**
> **2 green onions, sliced thinly**
> **1 tablespoon lime juice**
> **1 teaspoon ginger (fresh grated, or from the jar)**
> **1 teaspoon sugar or other sweetener**

Mix all ingredients together and refrigerate until well chilled. This salsa is great with chicken. Makes 1½ cups.

French Onion Dip Mix

This recipe was inspired by my desire to have an onion dip like the one we used to have in the "good old days". This dip's flavors meld overnight, so it will have a stronger flavor the second day, so make sure you make it one day before you need it for optimal taste!

12 ounces non-dairy sour cream
4 tablespoons dried onion flakes or bits
1 teaspoon onion powder
1 teaspoon onion salt
1 tablespoon sugar
1 large clove of garlic, minced

Mix all ingredients together. For the "mock sour cream" for this dip, we use Tofutti Brand soy based non-dairy sour cream. If you can tolerate soy, it is an excellent alternative to dairy sour cream. Instead of the non-dairy sour cream, you could substitute pureed chickpeas.

Spinach Dip

This tastes just like the spinach dip that I used to make for parties. It is excellent with fresh vegetables or crackers.

1½ teaspoons onion powder
1 teaspoon sugar
1 teaspoon salt
3 tablespoons dried onion flakes
1 can diced water chestnuts (if you can tolerate)
12 ounces non-diary sour cream
10 ounces frozen spinach, defrosted and drained well
1 clove of garlic, minced through a garlic press
3 to 5 stalks of green onions, sliced

Place spinach in a colander or mesh drainer and press well to remove additional liquid. Place all ingredients in a mixing bowl and mix well. This looks and tastes just like the real thing, so feel free to take it to parties!

Smashing Fruit Dip

This is a surprisingly simple dip that tastes excellent with fruit!

12 ounces non-dairy sour cream
3¾ tablespoons packed brown sugar

Mix well and refrigerate. The flavors will meld overnight or in a period of several hours, so the taste improves with some time. If you are using a sour cream brand that comes in an 8 ounce size, you will use 2½ tablespoons of packed brown sugar to the 8 ounces of sour cream. You can make individual serving portions if needed, and here are the proportions for an individual serving:

2 tablespoons non-dairy sour cream
1 teaspoon packed brown sugar

The ratio of non-dairy sour cream to sugar is 6 to 1. You can increase the sugar ratio if your sweet tooth isn't satisfied by the 6 to 1 ratio. This is fantastic with fresh strawberries, cantaloupe, grapes, etc.

South of the Border Baked Fiesta Dip

This was a favorite recipe of mine from my old dairy days. The original recipe was filled with dairy and baked in a hollowed out loaf of bread. We like this dip warm with fresh vegetables, on top of a baked potato, or with some crisp crackers.

Preheat oven to 350°.

12 ounces non-dairy sour cream
8 ounces non-dairy cream cheese
6 ounces acceptable salsa

Place all ingredients in a glass baking casserole dish and mix ingredients together until creamy. This will seem too runny and you will think that you have made a mistake. Place the casserole dish in the oven uncovered and bake for 1 to 1½ hours, stirring every 20 minutes or so. The dip will thicken up and have a delightful southwestern taste!

Desserts, Cakes, Cookies and Sweet Treats

Sweet Treats (continued)

Chocolate Brownies

Preheat oven to 350°.

2 sticks margarine
4 ounces GFCF unsweetened baking chocolate
2 cups sugar

4 teaspoons Egg Replacer™ powder mixed with
½ cup water

2 teaspoons pure vanilla extract
1½ cups GF flour mix (use ¾ cup each of two different
     flours)
1 teaspoon baking powder
1 teaspoon salt
1 teaspoon xanthan gum

In a medium saucepan, combine the margarine and baking chocolate and heat on LOW until melted. Stir in the sugar and mix well. Let pan cool slightly, about 5 to 10 minutes while you grease and flour a 9" x 13" baking pan. Mix the water and Egg Replacer™ and mix very well to remove all lumps. Strain the Egg Replacer™ mixture through a wire mesh strainer to remove any remaining lumps. After the saucepan has cooled a little, add the strained Egg Replacer™ (or 2-3 eggs if you can tolerate them omitting the water and Egg Replacer™ mixture). Stir in the pure vanilla extract. Mix the dry ingredients in a separate bowl, and stir well. Then add to the saucepan mixture, stirring only as much as needed to combine. Do not over mix. Pour into the prepared baking pan and bake for 25 to 30 minutes (or more) until a cake tester comes out clean, and the top springs back slightly when touched.

Allergy-Free Chocolate Brownies
Preheat oven to 350°.

> 4 ounces GFCF unsweetened baking chocolate
> (OR ¾ cup cocoa powder and ¼ cup oil if you can't
> find an acceptable baking chocolate)
> ¾ cup olive oil
> 2 cups sugar
> ⅔ cup warm water combined with
> 5 tablespoons Egg Replacer™
> 2 teaspoons pure vanilla extract
> 2 cups GF flour (bland flours work best)
> 2 to 3 teaspoons baking powder
> 1 teaspoon salt
> 1½ teaspoons xanthan gum
> ¼ to ⅓ cup more water or other liquid (as needed)

In a medium saucepan, combine the olive oil and chocolate and heat on LOW until melted. Stir in the sugar and mix well. Let pan cool slightly, about 5 to 10 minutes while you grease and flour a 9" x 13" baking pan. After the saucepan has cooled a little, mix the warm water with the Egg Replacer™ until thick and creamy in a separate bowl. Pour this Egg Replacer™ mixture through a strainer into the chocolate mixture. If you don't strain it, you will most certainly get white lumps in your brownies. Mix well. Stir in the pure vanilla extract. Mix the dry ingredients in a separate bowl, and stir well. Then add to the saucepan mixture, stirring only as much as needed to combine. Mixture will be very thick. Spread into the prepared pan. Bake for 25 to 30 minutes or until a cake tester comes out clean and the top springs back slightly when touched.

Fast and Easy Granola Bars

10 oz bag GFCF marshmallows
   (such as Jet-Puffed™ or other acceptable product)
¾ stick GFCF margarine (Fleischmann's™ unsalted
   margarine)
3 cups puffed corn cereal
4 cups Gorilla Munch™ (or other favorite cereal)
1 cup crushed GFCF cereal – flake type cereal like
   Amazon Flakes™, or sweetened rice flakes
¼ teaspoon ground cinnamon
¾ cup GFCF chocolate chips

Grease a 9" x 13" baking pan. Combine the marshmallows and margarine in a large stock pot and place over a very low heat. Mix all other remaining dry ingredients in a large mixing bowl. Stir the margarine/marshmallow mixture until melted and creamy. Add dry ingredients to the marshmallow mixture. Remove from heat and mix well. Pour into greased baking pan and pat into the pan. We add a few extra chocolate chips to the top of the pan as we pat the mixture to provide some additional texture to the granola bars. Cut into rectangles (split the pan either in half or in thirds length wise) and then cut into acceptable size granola bars. Then individually wrap the granola bars in plastic wrap. These travel well and are a great snack or treat.

These can be made in a more healthful way if you can eat nuts, seeds, and other dried fruits, all of which we have to avoid.

Sugar Cookie Cut-Outs

These can be used on any rotation day depending upon what flour you use. The type of flour used will dramatically alter the taste. In this recipe I have listed rice or millet in combination with tapioca for a very bland flour mix.
Preheat oven to 350°.

1 cup white sugar
2 tablespoons oil
4 tablespoons warm water mixed with
4 teaspoons Egg Replacer™
1½ teaspoons pure vanilla extract
¾ cup rice or millet flour (or any other acceptable flour)
1 cup tapioca flour
1 teaspoon xanthan gum
1 teaspoon baking soda
2 teaspoons baking powder (or cream of tartar)
2 tablespoons water

Mix sugar and oil. In a separate bowl, mix the warm water with the dry Egg Replacer™ powder and stir until it is very thick and creamy. Add the Egg Replacer™ to the sugar/oil mixture and mix well. Add the pure vanilla extract and stir well. Then add all of the dry ingredients and mix well. Add the water last and only if needed. Divide the dough in fourths and refrigerate wrapped in waxed paper or plastic for 1 to 2 hours.

Remove 1 section of dough from refrigerator and roll the dough out between 2 sheets of waxed paper dusted with tapioca flour. Cut out with cookie cutters and place on an Ungreased baking sheet. Sprinkle with acceptable baking colored sugars or white sugar. Bake very tiny cookies for 6 to 7 minutes and larger cookies for 9 to 12 minutes. These will not turn brown or golden but will remain pretty "white" in color. If you over bake these, they will be very crisp and hard. Properly baked, they will have a soft texture, but will not fall apart. These travel well and freeze well. You can also use a confectioners' frosting if you want a more festive cookie.

Moran Spice Cake

This is a family recipe that originates in the depression era when milk and eggs were often in short supply. I converted it to be gluten-free. Other shortening can be used as allergies permit.

Preheat oven to 350°.

1 cup lard (or other acceptable shortening)
2 cups water
1 to 2 cups raisins
1 teaspoon ground cinnamon
½ teaspoon ground cloves
2 cups white sugar
3 cups gluten-free flours (use a mix of flours)
1 tablespoon baking powder
1 teaspoon baking soda
2½ teaspoons xanthan gum

Combine shortening or lard, water, raisins, all spices, and sugar in a saucepan. Simmer for 10 minutes but do not boil or you'll end up with a candy base! Remove from heat and let stand until cool.

Grease one 9" x 13" baking pan. Combine the flour, baking soda, baking powder, and xanthan gum in a small bowl. When the saucepan mixture is cool, add the flour mixture to the liquid and stir until combined well. Pour the batter into your greased baking pan and bake for 45 minutes or until the center is done.

Delicious Chocolate Cake

This makes one great chocolate cake, and it is easy to mix up. This recipe does not work well with some flours like amaranth, sorghum and quinoa. For this recipe I would suggest the rice, tapioca, or potato flours and maybe even the garfava flour.

Preheat oven to 350°.

> 3 cups gluten-free flours (for example 1½ cups rice flour and 1½ cups tapioca flour)
> 2 cups white sugar
> 1 teaspoon salt
> 2 teaspoons baking soda
> ½ cup unsweetened cocoa powder
> 2½ teaspoons xanthan gum
> ¾ cup vegetable oil
> 2 tablespoons distilled white vinegar
> 2 teaspoons pure vanilla extract
> 1¾ cups cold water

Combine all the dry ingredients in a large mixing bowl. Add liquid ingredients and mix well. Pour into a 9" x 13" ungreased baking pan. Bake for 30 to 40 minutes or until cake tests done with a toothpick or cake tester or if top bounces back if touched lightly with your finger. This cake freezes well. Promptly freeze any leftovers.

Chocolate Cupcakes

Use the above recipe for the Delicious Chocolate Cake. Instead of using a cake pan, use muffin tins greased or lined with baking papers. Bake for 22 to 25 minutes. Makes 24 cupcakes. These cupcakes freeze well.

Carrot Cake

Preheat oven to 350°.

1 cup lard (or other acceptable shortening)
2 cups water
2 cups grated carrots
1 teaspoon ground cinnamon
½ teaspoon ground cloves
2 cups white sugar
3 cups GF flour mix (use a mix of whichever flours
    you can tolerate)
1 tablespoon baking powder
1 teaspoon baking soda
2½ teaspoons xanthan gum

Optional:

½ to 1 cup raisins

Combine shortening or lard, water, carrots, all spices, raisins (if using) and sugar in a saucepan. Simmer for 10 minutes but do not boil or you'll end up with a candy base! Remove from heat and let stand until cool. Grease one 9" x 13" baking pan. Combine the flour, baking soda, baking powder, and xanthan gum in a small bowl. When the saucepan mixture is cool, add the flour mixture to the liquid and combine well. Pour the batter into your baking pan and bake for 45 minutes or until the center is done. Cool cake completely and then frost with the Non-Dairy Cream Cheese Frosting recipe on page 318.

.

Non-Dairy Cream Cheese Frosting

This is the perfect addition to the Carrot Cake recipe on page 317. We love this frosting!

> 16 ounces powdered or confectioners' sugar (10X), sifted
> One 8 ounce container of Tofutti Brand ™ non-dairy cream cheese
> 1 teaspoon of pure vanilla extract

Place powdered sugar in a mixing bowl. Place the Tofutti non-dairy cream cheese in chunks on top of the powdered sugar. Add the pure vanilla. Very slowly mix in the lowest speed of your electric mixer until the cream cheese blends with the powdered sugar. Gradually increase the speed of your mixer and blend frosting until it is creamy. I recommend sifting to reduce the lumps in your frosting. Otherwise, you'll need to mix the frosting longer to remove any lumps in the sugar. Refrigerate frosting until ready to use, and refrigerate any cake that you use this frosting on as you would with a regular cream cheese frosting.

Marshmallow Treats

> ¾ stick margarine or margarine substitute
> One 10.5 ounce bag gluten-free/milk-free marshmallows (like Jet-Puffed™)
> 8½ cups gluten-free cereal (one 13 ounce box)

Grease a 9" x 13" baking pan and metal spatula and set aside. In a stockpot, melt margarine or other fat then add the marshmallows. Stir until the marshmallows are melted and the mixture is nice and creamy. Add cereal and quickly mix well. Pour into greased baking pan and press with a greased metal spatula to fill pan evenly.

Microwave directions:
Microwave the margarine in a microwavable bowl for 45 seconds or until melted. Add marshmallows and toss to coat. Return for 45 seconds. Remove from microwave and stir well. Repeat until marshmallows are completely melted. Finish as directed above.

Sun Blossom Cookies

This is a simply delightful cookie that we converted to be allergy friendly. It uses ground sunflower seed butter, which is a peanut-free, tree-nut-free substitute for peanut butter. The original recipe, which was from my Aunt Irene Tubach, called for gluten, dairy, eggs and a Hershey Kiss™ in the center.

Preheat oven to 375°.

Sift together:

> 1¾ cups gluten-free flours
> 1½ teaspoons baking soda
> ½ teaspoon salt
> 1½ teaspoons xanthan gum
> 1 tablespoon Egg Replacer™

Cream together:

> ½ cup Fleischmann's™ unsalted margarine (or other margarine substitute)
> ½ cup ground sunflower seed butter

Add:

> ½ cup white sugar
> ½ cup brown sugar

Add:

> 3 tablespoons water
> 1 teaspoon pure vanilla extract
> 2½ tablespoons rice milk or other non-dairy milk substitute
>
> ¼ cup gluten-free/dairy-free chocolate chips

Beat well. Add dry ingredients to wet ingredients. Shape by teaspoon into balls. Roll in sugar and place on an ungreased baking sheet. Make a small indentation in the center of the cookie before baking. Bake for 8 to 9 minutes. Remove from oven and place a few gluten-free/dairy-free chocolate chips in the center of the cookie. Return to the oven and bake for 2 to 3 minutes. Gluten-free/dairy-free chocolate chips can be found from the Enjoy Life Foods Company (see Appendix or Special Ingredient Section). These cookies freeze well.

Hershey's® "Perfectly Chocolate" Chocolate Frosting

This recipe comes from the back of a Hershey's® Cocoa Powder can, and with minor changes it becomes a useful recipe to us.

1 stick (½ cup) margarine or acceptable substitute
⅔ cup Hershey's® cocoa
3 cups powdered sugar
⅓ cup acceptable milk substitute
1 teaspoon pure vanilla extract

The directions on the cocoa powder said to melt margarine and stir in cocoa. Then alternately add powdered sugar and milk substitute, beating until spreading consistency. I found that just mixing it all in an electric mixer was sufficient without melting the margarine. Add an additional tablespoon of water if necessary to get the proper frosting consistency. Makes about 2 cups.

Homemade Marshmallows

If you can eat corn, store-bought marshmallows are much easier than making your own. If you cannot tolerate corn, you may find that a product called "Suzanne's Ricemellow Crème" is preferable to making your own. Suzanne's Ricemellow Crème is made with brown rice syrup, soy protein, natural gums and natural flavors, so it may not work for you either. I made marshmallows very few times after finding other alternatives that my children could tolerate.

> 2 tablespoons gelatin
> ¼ cup cold water
> ¾ cup boiling water
> 2 cups sugar
> ⅛ teaspoon salt
> 1 teaspoon pure vanilla extract
> Confectioners' sugar (see page 322 about how to make
>   your own confectioners' sugar)

In a medium bowl soak the gelatin in the cold water until all of the water has been absorbed by the gelatin. Boil the sugar and water in a medium saucepan until it reaches the soft-ball stage which is about 238°. Add pure vanilla and salt to your gelatin mixture. Pour the sugar and water syrup over the gelatin slowly beating the gelatin constantly with a fork or wire whisk until it is cool and thick. Grease a shallow baking pan and then lightly dust with confectioners' sugar. Turn the marshmallow mixture into the prepared baking pan and smooth out the top. Dust the top with confectioners' sugar. Let sit overnight. Cut the marshmallows into squares the next morning and dust with confectioners' sugar. If you can't use confectioners' sugar due to the corn or cornstarch, you can make your own. The recipe for confectioners' sugar is on page 322.

Corn-Free Confectioners' Sugar

The reason some people cannot tolerate confectioners' sugar is because corn or cornstarch is frequently added to prevent caking. While making confectioners' sugar from scratch is not difficult, it is not something that I enjoyed or did often. To make confectioners' sugar at home you simply use cane or beet sugar in granular form and whirl it in a blender until it is powdered.

½ cup light raw sugar or white sugar (or beet sugar)

Whirl in a blender until powdered.

Molasses Cookies

This is a soft molasses cookie that is not only gluten-free and milk/casein-free, but free of soy, rice and corn. These keep well in an airtight container and freeze well.
Preheat oven to 350°.

2 tablespoons olive oil (or other acceptable oil)
⅔ cup sugar
½ cup molasses
4 tablespoons hot water mixed with
5 teaspoons Egg Replacer™
1¼ cups tapioca flour (full cups)
¾ cup potato starch (full ¾ cup)
1 teaspoon baking soda
1 teaspoon xanthan gum
½ teaspoon salt
½ teaspoon ground ginger

Mix together oil and sugar. Then add molasses and mix well. Add the remaining ingredients and mix well. This dough will <u>not</u> appear as if there is enough liquid when you start mixing it. Don't panic; continue to mix by hand until dough comes together. Form small balls and place on an <u>ungreased</u> cookie sheet. Slightly flatten the balls and top with white sugar. Bake about 7 to 9 minutes depending upon the size cookie you have made. Over baking will give you hard cookies which are not nearly as nice as the soft ones. This recipe makes about 26 to 30 cookies of a smaller size.

Best Banana Chocolate Chip Cookies

My grandmother Holcombe used to make these excellent banana oatmeal chocolate chip cookies, which contained gluten. I think she'd be surprised at how similar this conversion is to her original recipe. We use puffed millet in place of the oatmeal. These cookies freeze well.

Preheat oven to 350°.

> 1 cup white or brown sugar (or ½ cup of each)
> 1 cup shortening or other margarine
> 4 tablespoons hot water mixed with
> 5 teaspoons Egg Replacer™
> 3 mashed bananas
> ½ teaspoon salt
> ¾ teaspoon ground cloves
> 1 teaspoon ground cinnamon
> 1 teaspoon pure vanilla extract
> 1 teaspoon baking soda
> 2 cups gluten-free flour mix (full cups)
> 2 cups puffed millet (full cups)
> 1 cup gluten-free chocolate chips
> 2 teaspoons xanthan gum

Cream together shortening and sugar. Add Egg Replacer™ and bananas. Then add in dry ingredients and pure vanilla extract and mix well. You may need to add a bit more flour if your cookies flatten out too much. Drop onto greased cookie sheets and bake 7 to 9 minutes depending upon the size of your cookies. These should be a soft cookie, not crispy or crunchy. This is an excellent way to use up old bananas.

Soft & Chewy Chocolate Chip Cookies
Preheat oven to 350°.

2½ cups gluten-free flour blend (bland flours make the best cookie)
½ cup gluten-free baby rice cereal
1 cup white sugar
1 cup brown sugar, firmly packed
1 cup acceptable margarine, softened
4 tablespoons hot water mixed with
1½ tablespoons Egg Replacer™ (or 2 eggs)
1½ teaspoons pure vanilla extract
1 teaspoon baking soda
1 teaspoon salt
1 teaspoon xanthan gum
5 to 10 ounces acceptable chocolate chips

Make sure your margarine is at room temperature. If you can use eggs, use two and delete the 4 tablespoons of hot water. Place all ingredients except for the chocolate chips into a mixing bowl. With your mixer, blend at the lowest speed until the dough begins to incorporate. Then gradually increase the speed of your mixer, and beat on high for about 3 or so minutes. You can also mix this by hand although it is more difficult. Refrigerate the cookie dough for at least 1 to 2 hours (a must for the best cookies). Also, make sure to use an oven thermometer to ensure that your oven is 350° and _not_ higher (lower your oven temperature accordingly if your oven runs hot).

Spoon the cold dough onto ungreased baking sheets and bake for 8 to 10 minutes, but no more than that. If your cookies flatten like pancakes, check your oven temperature because it is probably off. One other thing you can try if your cookies flatten is adding more flour to your dough, refrigerate and try again. These will be just like the "mall" cookies that contain all those no-no ingredients. They will be nice and chewy and soft. If they are crunchy, you over baked them or your oven temperature is too high.

Lemon Bars

This is a recipe from my mom, which has been converted to be gluten-free. If you can tolerate eggs, I would use them for the topping.

Preheat oven to 350°.

Crust:

> **2 cups gluten-free flour mix (lighter flours work best in this recipe; rice, tapioca, cornstarch, or potato)**
> **½ cup sugar**
> **1 cup acceptable margarine**

Combine above and pat into a greased 9" x 13" pan. Bake for 20 to 25 minutes (more or less depending on your true oven temperature). While this is baking, mix up the following:

Topping:

> **1 cup hot water mixed with**
> **7 tablespoons Egg Replacer™ (see note below)**
> **5 tablespoons lemon juice**
> **2 cups sugar**
> **1 tablespoon gluten-free flour**

When the pan comes out of the oven, pour the Egg Replacer™ mixture over the crust immediately. Return to the oven and bake for 15 to 20 minutes. Bake until the edges start to brown lightly. Remove from the oven and sift confectioners' sugar over the top while the pan is *HOT!*

Note: If you can tolerate eggs, then use 4 eggs in the topping and delete the 1 cup water and the 7 tablespoons Egg Replacer™.

Ultimate Chocolate Chip Cookies (Double Batch)

Just about everyone will enjoy these chocolate chip cookies!

Preheat oven to 375°.

- 1½ cups butter flavor shortening or other shortening
- 2½ cups brown sugar, firmly packed
- 4 tablespoons non-dairy milk substitute
- 2 tablespoons pure vanilla extract
- 6 tablespoons hot water with
- 7 teaspoons Egg Replacer™ (or 2 eggs)
- 3½ cups gluten-free flour
- 2 teaspoons xanthan gum
- 1½ teaspoons baking soda
- 2 teaspoons salt
- 2 cups gluten-free chocolate chips

Cream together shortening and brown sugar until smooth. Add milk and pure vanilla extract and mix well. Add Egg Replacer™ and mix until smooth. In a large bowl, mix flour, baking soda, xanthan gum and salt together. Add to wet ingredients. Stir in chocolate chips. Refrigerate cookie dough for at least an hour or two or until well-chilled. On an ungreased cookie sheet, bake 8 to 10 minutes for chewy cookies, 11 to 13 minutes for crisp cookies. Makes about 6 dozen 3-inch cookies.

Super Sugar Cookie Cut-Outs

Bland gluten-free flours will provide a better flavor than some of the stronger flours.

Preheat oven to 375°.

1¼ cups white sugar
1 cup shortening or margarine, softened
6 tablespoons hot water mixed with
5 teaspoons Egg Replacer™ (or 2 eggs)
¼ cup light corn syrup or brown rice syrup
1 tablespoon pure vanilla extract
3 cups gluten-free flour
2½ teaspoons xanthan gum
1½ teaspoons baking powder
1 teaspoon baking soda
½ teaspoon salt

Cream the sugar and shortening in a mixing bowl and beat until creamy. In a separate bowl, mix the hot water and dry powdered Egg Replacer™ stirring to remove lumps, and adding it to the sugar and shortening mixture. Add the pure vanilla extract and syrup. Combine the remaining dry ingredients and add to the shortening/sugar mixture gradually. Divide the dough into 4 pieces. Wrap each piece in waxed paper and refrigerate for at least 1 hour (or place in the freezer for 15 to 20 minutes). Roll out between 2 sheets of waxed paper that have been dusted with a light coating of gluten-free flour. Cut out your favorite cookie shapes with floured cookie cutters. You can sprinkle decorator sugars on the cookies before baking if you do not intend to frost the cookies. Bake on an ungreased baking sheet. The baking time will depend completely on the size of the cutout AND how thick you roll the dough! The larger and thicker the cookie, the longer the baking time. The time will vary from 4 to 9 minutes. Whatever you do, do *not* over bake! Cool cookies on a cooling rack. You may then frost as desired. This recipe makes 3 to 4 dozen cookies, depending on the cookie size.

Chocolate Pudding

2 cups non-dairy milk
¼ cup sugar
2 tablespoons cocoa powder
Dash of salt

To thicken:

3 tablespoons gluten-free flour mixed with
½ cup non-dairy milk

In a saucepan, heat the 2 cups non-dairy milk, sugar, cocoa and salt until the sugar is melted and all the ingredients are well combined. In a separate measuring cup or bowl, mix the flour and ½ cup of non-dairy milk until well blended. Add the non-dairy milk and flour mixture to the saucepan and cook until the pudding is thick and creamy stirring constantly. It will thicken just a bit as it cools. If you desire pudding that is firmer, you can increase the flour by 1 tablespoon or more. Makes five ½ cup servings.

Black Bottom Cupcakes

This is a favorite recipe that I converted to be gluten-free, dairy-free and egg-free. The original recipe came from Pat Laudeman, a dear friend. If you make these in mini-muffin pans, they make adorable sweet treats suitable for any party or festive gathering. *Preheat oven to 350°.*

Line mini-muffin pans with baking papers and set aside. You will also need some mini-chocolate chips for this recipe.

Batter One:

> **One 8 ounce container Tofutti Brand non-dairy cream cheese (or regular cream cheese)**
> **⅓ cup sugar**
> **2 tablespoons hot water combined with**
> **3 teaspoons Egg Replacer™ (or 1 egg)**
> **⅛ teaspoon salt**

Beat Batter One ingredients together until well combined and set aside.

Batter Two:

> **1½ cups gluten-free flour**
> **1 cup sugar**
> **⅓ cup cocoa powder**
> **1 teaspoon baking soda**
> **1 teaspoon xanthan gum**
> **½ teaspoon salt**

In a separate bowl, sift Batter Two ingredients together.

Add to Batter Two:

> **1 cup boiling water**
> **½ cup oil**
> **1 teaspoon vinegar**
> **1 teaspoon pure vanilla extract**

Beat Batter Two ingredients together until well combined. Fill mini-muffin baking pans ½ full with Batter Two. Top each muffin with ½ to 1 teaspoon of Batter One. Then top each muffin with 6 to 8 mini-chocolate chips (gluten-free, milk-free ones like Enjoy Life™ Natural Brands Chocolate chips) if desired. Bake for about 20 to 25 minutes or until done. Makes about 48 mini-size cupcakes.

Sunflower Cookies
(a.k.a. Mock Peanut Butter Cookies)

This is a family recipe for peanut butter cookies converted to be FREE of peanut butter, gluten, dairy, and eggs. They could easily pass for peanut butter cookies. We use ground sunflower seeds butter in this recipe, which looks and tastes very much like peanut butter. It contains no nuts or peanuts and is allergy friendly..

Preheat oven to 350°

> 1¼ cups gluten-free flour
> 1 teaspoon baking powder
> ½ cup margarine or solid shortening
> ½ cup white sugar
> ½ cup brown sugar, packed
> 2 tablespoons hot water mixed with
> 3 teaspoons Egg Replacer™ (or 1 egg slightly beaten)
> 1¼ teaspoons xanthan gum
> ½ cup ground sunflower seed butter

Sift dry ingredients together twice. In a large bowl cream margarine and both sugars until soft and blended, but not fluffy. Add Egg Replacer™ (or egg) and ground sunflower seed butter and mix well. Add dry ingredients and mix well. Make balls of dough the size of a walnut or so and roll the balls of dough in sugar. Place on an ungreased baking sheet and then press the ball of dough with a fork twice to make a crisscross pattern on top of the cookie. Bake for 12 or so minutes. Do not over bake. These cookies do not brown. Makes about 3 dozen cookies depending upon the size of the cookie.

Non-Dairy Cheesecake

This makes a great cheesecake for those of us who do not eat dairy. You can make it with or without a crust. A crumb crust recipe is provided, however you can make it without the crust. This recipe is best made in a spring form pan designed for cheesecakes so that you can remove the cheesecake from the pan easily. If you don't have a spring form pan, you can simply cut slices from your baking pan and remove the slices from the pan individually. It is best not to store the cheesecake in the pan. This recipe is to be used with an 8" or 9" spring form cheesecake pan with a removable bottom.

Preheat oven to 350°.

Crumb crust:

> 1½ cups gluten-free cereal crushed into crumbs either by hand or with a food processor
> 2 teaspoons xanthan gum
> ⅓ cup sugar
> 6 tablespoons acceptable oil (or solid shortening*)
> 1 to 2 teaspoons ground cinnamon

If you can use a solid shortening or margarine in the crust, you will get a better result. If using a solid shortening or margarine, use just ¼ cup. Mix crumb crust ingredients together well, and press firmly into your spring form or baking pan. Use either a rolling pin or the bottom of another baking pan, plate, or other hard, flat surface to mash the crumbs together. The crumbs should be pressed very well together. If they are not, your crust will fall apart and be crumbly. Bake in a 350° oven for 10 to 12 minutes. Do not over bake. You do not need to brown the crust. After removing the crust from the oven, increase the heat to 375°.

Cheesecake First Layer:

16 ounces Tofutti Brand™ non-dairy cream cheese
¾ cup sugar
½ teaspoon pure vanilla extract
¼ teaspoon xanthan gum
½ teaspoon salt

Mix all first layer cheesecake ingredients listed above until creamy. Place on top of crumb crust if you are using one, or directly in your cheesecake baking pan or other 8" or 9" square baking dish if you are not. Bake in a **375° oven** for 45 minutes (note higher temperature). While this is baking, mix up the second layer.

Cheesecake Second Layer:

One 12 ounce container Tofutti Brand ™ non-dairy
  sour cream
4 tablespoons sugar
½ teaspoon pure vanilla extract
⅛ teaspoon salt
¼ teaspoon xanthan gum

Mix second layer ingredients well and pour on top of the cheesecake after it is done baking. Return the cheesecake to the oven and **increase the oven temperature to 425°.** Bake for 30 minutes. Allow to cool and then refrigerate overnight before serving.

Bakery Frosting

Yes, you can get frosting at home that is very much like what you would get from a bakery! I highly recommend that you consider taking a Wilton® Cake Decorating Class if you are going to be baking for a gluten-free, dairy-free family member. Through the Wilton® Cake Decorating Classes, you can learn to decorate any cake that you make and have it look just like it came from a bakery! The Wilton® Cake Decorating Classes are typically offered at crafting stores where their products are sold. For this recipe I have deleted the Wilton Butter Flavoring because it is not the most natural product.

2 pounds confectioners' sugar (10 X or powdered sugar)
1 cup shortening or solid fat* (white, if possible)
2 teaspoons pure vanilla extract
Dash of salt (⅛ teaspoon)
8 tablespoons water (see details in directions)

Place powdered sugar in the mixing bowl of an electric mixer. Cut up the fat or shortening into small chunks and place on top of the powdered sugar. Add the dash of salt, and pure vanilla. Add the water 1 tablespoon at a time evenly around the powdered sugar.

**In the Wilton® Cake Decorating Classes you are taught the proper consistency for frostings and decorative icings.

Gently start and stop your mixer to blend the powdered sugar, shortening and water until it is well combined. Then gradually turn up your mixer speed and mix for 2 to 3 minutes until the frosting is light and fluffy.

White Frosting or Filling

¼ cup shortening
1 teaspoon milk substitute
4 tablespoons gluten-free flour
1 teaspoon pure vanilla extract
4 tablespoons hot water
5 teaspoons Egg Replacer™
1- 16 ounce box powdered or confectioner's sugar

Combine the hot water and Egg Replacer™ and mix well. Then add the shortening, milk substitute, flour, pure vanilla and mix well. Then add the powdered sugar and beat well.

Confectioners' Icing or Glaze

This is the recipe that we use for the Danish recipes included in this book. It is fast and easy. We make it in smaller batches so it is fresh.

2 cups powdered or confectioners' sugar
1 teaspoon pure vanilla extract
2 tablespoons pure drinking water
Pinch of salt

Optional:

1 to 2 teaspoons of margarine

Mix all ingredients and stir until smooth and creamy. This makes about 1 cup of icing or glaze. You can add a few drops of water to make your icing thinner. If you add too much water and your icing becomes too runny, simply add more powdered sugar one tablespoon at a time. To apply icing or glaze to Danish, place icing in a plastic ziplock bag with one corner cut off on a diagonal. Cut off a tiny diagonal as you can always increase the size of the whole in the bag. Pipe the icing over your Danish or other treat in a swirling or zigzag pattern.

Hard Candy or Lollipops

It is not difficult to make your own hard candy, but you do need a candy thermometer. Candy thermometers are sold at the craft stores in the Wilton® Baking section or at better cooking stores. You will also need flavoring for your candy. We special ordered ours on-line, however you can get candy flavors at craft stores and specialty kitchen stores.

There are now natural colorings that you can use instead of the traditional food colorings. The natural food colorings are made from foods that are rich in color like beets and blueberries. These do not add flavor to your candy. I recommend that you have hard candy molds which are sold on-line and in craft and baking stores. There are two different kinds of candy molds. One is for melted chocolate only and the other can be used for melted chocolate OR hard candy. The molds used for hard candy are made of a different material to withstand the heat of the hot candy when you first mold it. The candy molds suitable for melted chocolate only are not to be used with making hard candy.

1 cup pure drinking water
2 cups organic sugar
¾ cup light corn syrup
1 tablespoon oil
1 teaspoon candy flavoring

Optional:

Natural food coloring

All hard candies become sticky unless individually wrapped. Instead, we place our finished candy in a hard plastic storage container separated in layers by waxed paper. This has worked very well. Grease your candy molds and set aside. This candy recipe made a fair amount of candy. It made more than 12 lollipops (4 to 6 of which were very large), and many smaller candies. If you run out of molds you can pour a small amount of the candy onto an oiled cutting board. Cut the candy on the cutting board into squares or pieces with a knife or scissors and roll into balls.

Boil 1 cup of water in a large heavy pan. Remove from heat. Add sugar, light corn syrup and oil and stir until dissolved. Return pan to heat and bring to a boil. Cover the pan for about 3 minutes so that the steam washes down any crystals from the pan. Remove the lid from the pan and insert the candy thermometer. Cook the sugar mixture to what is called the "hard-crack" stage, about 300°.

Remove from heat and cool to about 160°. If you are using food coloring, add it now. Add candy flavoring now. Suggested flavors include ¼ teaspoon oil of peppermint or cinnamon, 1 teaspoon of oil of orange, lime or wintergreen, or other flavor of your choice. We have used bubblegum and cotton candy flavors too. Pour the candy into the candy molds or shape as directed above.

Chocolate Lollipops

We've had a great deal of fun making chocolate lollipops and they are very simple. Just as simple as melting chocolate chips in the microwave and putting the chocolate into lollipop molds. The lollipop molds are sold at baking stores, craft stores like Jo-Ann's and Michael's and usually where Wilton® baking products are sold.

For the chocolate chips, we use Enjoy Life semi-sweet chocolate chips. The ingredients listed on their package <u>at the time of this publication</u> are evaporated cane juice, chocolate liquor, non-dairy cocoa butter. The package is also labeled dairy, soy and gluten-free made in a dedicated nut and gluten-free kitchen.

To make the lollipops, place your chocolate chips or other chocolate in a microwave and cook for 30 seconds. Remove from microwave and stir. It may not look like it's melted, but it will begin to melt. If the chocolate chips are not melted, return to microwave for another 15 to 20 seconds. When melted, pour into the lollipop molds which you have prepared with a lollipop stick. If the chocolate is not melted, then return to the microwave and cook until melted.

Once you have filled each lollipop or candy mold, place in the refrigerator to cool. Once cooled, the lollipops should not be hard to remove from the mold. Simply bend the mold slightly and pop the chocolate lollipop from the mold. These have a short shelf life and are best made on the day they will be eaten. Otherwise the chocolate will whiten as it ages and it loses a lot. Storing the lollipops in the refrigerator helps lengthen the shelf life.

Whoopie Pies or Moon Pies

Who can resist two chocolate cookies with a white creamy filling? These cookies freeze well. We typically freeze them without the filling, but you can do it either way.

Preheat oven to 350°.

> 1 cup shortening or margarine
> 2 cups sugar
> 6 tablespoons hot water mixed with
> 2 tablespoons Egg Replacer™
> 1 cup milk substitute "soured": add 2 teaspoons baking soda to 1 cup non-dairy milk substitute
> 1 cup hot water
> 1 teaspoon baking powder
> 4 cups gluten-free flour
> 1 cup cocoa
> 3½ teaspoons xanthan gum

Mix above ingredients in order as listed. Drop by teaspoonful onto a baking sheet. Bake for 10 minutes. When cool, use white frosting in between two cookies. You can use one of the frosting recipes in this cookbook, or you can use any frosting recipe that you like. This recipe makes a lot of whoopie pies, so you may want to cut the recipe in half until you are sure that you like them! These do freeze fairly well.

Marshmallow Cups & Sunflower Cups

These are too cute and very exciting for children and for those adults who remember the days of Reese's® Peanut Butter Cups and Mallow Cups which are now taboo due to allergies! I served little Sunflower cups at our Valentine's Day party and our guests thought they tasted just like the real (peanut butter) thing! These are excellent for children who want to fit in, but can't have dairy, peanut butter, soy or other ingredients.

You can either purchase a special mold or you can use regular or mini-sized muffin tins. I like using the mini-muffin tins lined with mini baking papers.

1⅓ to 1½ cups of acceptable chocolate chips
2 to 3 tablespoons of filling, either ground sunflower seed butter or marshmallow creme or Suzanne's™ Ricemellow Crème

This recipe will make 24 mini-sized marshmallow or ground sunflower seed butter candy cups. Line 24 mini-muffin tins with baking papers and set aside. Place ½ cup of chocolate chips in a small glass bowl and microwave for 25 seconds. Remove and stir well. They may not look like they're melted but they will have begun to melt. Return them to the microwave for another 15 seconds to finish melting the chocolate. Place ½ teaspoon of chocolate in each muffin tin. Use the back of a spoon or rubber spatula to press the chocolate up the sides of the baking papers or mold. Once chocolate is uniformly pressed against the sides with a thin layer on the bottom, repeat with next muffin tin.

When you run out of chocolate, place another ½ cup in the glass bowl and repeat the above process to melt the chocolate chips. Once the chocolate cups are formed, place the chocolate in the freezer for 5 to 7 minutes to mold. Remove from freezer and fill with filling. Then top with final layer of chocolate to complete the candy.

For Marshmallow Cups:
Fill center with ¼ to ½ teaspoon of marshmallow creme or Suzanne's™ Ricemellow Crème if you can't tolerate corn. Melting marshmallows does not work well to fill these candy cups because the marshmallow is too sticky to get into the cups before it cools and becomes unmanageable again. Top with a final layer of melted chocolate. Place in the refrigerator until chocolate is hardened. These store best in the refrigerator.

For Sunflower Cups:
Fill center with ¼ to ½ teaspoon of ground sunflower seed butter. Top with a final layer of melted chocolate across the top. Place in the refrigerator until chocolate is hardened. These store best in the refrigerator.

Old Fashioned Caramel Corn

This recipe calls for 6 quarts of popcorn. While 6 quarts is a lot of popcorn, let me assure you that this caramel corn will be popular with everyone and will disappear FAST! I make most recipes in bulk so that I only have to make them once a month or so. This recipe will make approximately 10 to 12 cups. The directions for this recipe are long; however it really is a very easy recipe!

Old Fashioned Caramel Corn begins with popping the popcorn from scratch (or use an air popper if you would prefer).

Popcorn recipe:

> **3 tablespoons corn oil**
> **⅓ cup popcorn kernels**

Grease two 9" x 13" baking pans and set aside. Place the corn oil in a large skillet that has a secure or tight-fitting lid. The larger the skillet, the better the results because you have a larger surface area for popping and that decreases the likelihood of the popcorn burning. Place the skillet with the oil over medium heat and place 3 popcorn kernels in the pan. Cover immediately. Listen quietly for the 3 kernels to pop. Once the 3 kernels have popped, lift the lid and quickly add the ⅓ cup of kernels to the hot oil. Cover. Keep skillet or pan on the burner until the popping has slowed a great deal, but make sure to remove it from the heat before all the popping has stopped or you may end up with burned kernels.

Pour popcorn from the pan into a greased 9" x 13" baking pan. Pick out any unpopped kernels. To obtain the 6 quarts of popcorn for this recipe, repeat this procedure two more times as each batch makes approximately 2 quarts. When the popcorn is all popped, you will have enough to fill two 9" x 13" pans. Be sure to grease the pans!

Caramel recipe:
Preheat oven to 250°.

1 cup (2 sticks) margarine or acceptable substitute
2 cups brown sugar firmly packed (or other sugar
**   substitute)**
½ cup light or dark brown corn syrup
1 teaspoon salt

Immediately after cooking add:

½ teaspoon baking soda
1 teaspoon pure vanilla extract

Make the popcorn and place in two greased 9" x 13" pans before starting the caramel recipe. In a saucepan, slowly melt the margarine or margarine substitute. Once melted, add the brown sugar, salt, and corn syrup. Bring to a boil, stirring constantly. Then boil for 5 minutes without stirring. Remove from heat and add all at once the 1 teaspoon of pure vanilla extract, and the ½ teaspoon of baking soda. As soon as you add the baking soda and pure vanilla extract, the caramel mixture will begin to foam up and become much lighter in color (unless of course your baking soda is bad). Stir quickly, but well and then pour ½ of mixture over one pan and ½ of the mixture over the second pan. Working quickly, toss the popped corn and caramel mixture to coat the popcorn well. Repeat with second pan.

Place both pans in the oven and bake for 45 minutes, stirring every 15 minutes. Allow to cool, and break apart and place in storage container. Other nuts or seeds may be added to this caramel popcorn recipe.

Grandma Jo's Perfect Pie Crust

This is adapted from my grandmother's pie crust recipe. It works every time.

Preheat oven to 450° (if baking ahead of time)

3 cups sifted gluten-free flour mix
1¼ cups shortening
4 tablespoons hot water mixed with
5 teaspoons Egg Replacer™
1 teaspoon vinegar
1 teaspoon salt
5 tablespoons cold water (Must be cold!)
2 teaspoons xanthan gum

Add the xanthan gum to the flour mix. Add salt. Cut shortening or lard into the flour mixture until crumbly. In a separate bowl, beat Egg Replacer™ and water. Add vinegar and salt to the Egg Replacer™ mixture. Then add to flour mixture. Add cold water and form dough. Roll out between 2 sheets of waxed paper. Makes 2 double pie crusts.

To bake an unfilled shell, prick before baking. Place in the oven for 10 to 12 minutes or until lightly browned. You can protect the edges from over-browning by covering them with aluminum foil strips or commercially available pie crust rings.

Savory Quinoa Crust for Pot Pies & Quiche

Preheat oven to 450° (if baking ahead of time)

1½ cups quinoa flour or other flour
1½ cups corn starch, tapioca flour, potato flour or rice flour
1 cup shortening or lard
2 teaspoons xanthan gum
1 teaspoon onion powder
2½ teaspoons garlic powder
1 teaspoon vinegar
4 teaspoons Egg Replacer™ mixed well with
4 tablespoons hot water

5 tablespoons cold water

Add the xanthan gum to the flour mix. Add salt. Cut shortening or lard into the flour mixture until crumbly. In a separate bowl, beat Egg Replacer™ and water. Add vinegar and salt to the Egg Replacer™ mixture. Then add to flour mixture. Add cold water and form dough. Roll out between 2 sheets of waxed paper. Makes 2 double pie crusts. Follow pot pie (see page 245) or quiche (see page 265) recipes for baking directions.

To bake an unfilled shell, prick before baking. Place in a preheated 450° oven for 10 to 12 minutes or until lightly browned. You can protect the edges from over-browning by covering them with aluminum foil strips or commercially available pie crust rings.

Apple Crisp
Preheat oven to 375°

Crisp mixture:

 1½ teaspoons ground cinnamon
 ½ cup tapioca flour
 1 cup garfava flour
 ¾ cup brown sugar, packed
 ¾ teaspoon xanthan gum

 6 tablespoons acceptable oil
 or
 ¼ cup acceptable solid shortening

Mix the above dry ingredients and then add 6 tablespoons oil. If you can tolerate a solid shortening of any kind, use ¼ cup or more of that cut into the flour mixture instead of the oil. Set the mixture aside while you prepare the apples.

 5 cups peeled, sliced apples
 3 tablespoons lemon juice

Mix the apples with the lemon juice. Place the apples in a glass pie plate. Top with crisp mixture. Bake for 30 minutes. Remove from oven and add 1½ cups of pure water. Stir apple crisp to mix well and return to the oven for 15 more minutes. This may be served hot or cold.

Cherry Pie

This is a great beginner recipe if you are teaching your children to bake. It is simple and assuming that you've helped them out with the crust, it's a real winner. My mom taught me to make cherry pie and once you've done it, you are struck by how easy it is.

Preheat oven to 450°.

One 16 ounce can sour cherries (water packed sour cherries; NOT canned cherry pie filling)
3 tablespoons cornstarch (or other thickening agent)
1 cup sugar
Pinch of salt
1 tablespoon lemon juice
Dash of lemon extract (optional)
Dash of natural food coloring
1 gluten-free pie crust – topping is optional

Drain cherries and place the cherry juice in a medium size saucepan. Add sugar, cornstarch, salt, and lemon juice as well as optional ingredients. Increase heat to medium high stirring at all times. Once the cherry juice is thickened, add cherries to saucepan. Place filling into pie shell and bake. You can top your cherry pie with a crust topping, make lattice topping (strips of pie crust dough woven together and used for a topping), or leave your pie without a topping. Place pie in a 450° oven for 10 minutes. Reduce heat to 350° and bake for 40 minutes or until golden brown.

A recipe for pie shells is provided in this cookbook on page 342.

Strawberry Pie

Once we started getting strawberries from our local organic farmer came the question what would we do with all of the strawberries? Strawberry pie and strawberry ice cream are two great answers to that question.

2 quarts fresh strawberries, tops removed
1 cup sugar
3 tablespoons cornstarch or other flour for thickening
½ cup water
Pinch of salt
1 tablespoon oil
1 tablespoon lemon juice
1 gluten-free pie crust, baked and cooled

Bake a single gluten-free pie crust for 10 to 12 minutes or until lightly golden and set aside to cool (see page 342). In a medium saucepan dissolve the cornstarch in the water and set aside. Then sort the berries into excellent and less than excellent condition setting aside the strawberries in mint condition. Mash up the secondary strawberries and place in the saucepan with the cornstarch. Add the sugar, salt, oil and lemon juice. Cook over medium heat stirring constantly until mixture is thick. Remove from heat and allow to cool. In the meantime, cut the best strawberries in half. When the saucepan mixture is cold, stir in the remaining strawberries. Place in the baked pie shell and chill before serving.

Non-Dairy Ice Creams

Easiest Ever All Natural Banana Soft Serve Ice Cream

After years and years, and then more years of making non-dairy ice cream the "traditional" way by mixing up non-dairy beverages, adding sugar, and other ingredients, I almost fell off my chair when I saw a demonstration of how to make ice cream using a Champion Juicer. Christine Schaefer and Bernard Gosset, two friends of ours, had my husband and I and another couple over for a raw foods dinner. They topped off the most delicious raw foods dinner with fresh made, soft serve ice cream. There is no excuse not to have fresh made ice cream now. And for those people watching their sugar and fat intake, this ice cream has none of that. This recipe works extremely well with Champion Juicers. I am not familiar enough with other juicers to know how they would compare. But for the ice cream application alone, it was well worth the price of the juicer.

8 whole bananas

Peel bananas <u>before</u> they start to turn brown. Place peeled banana on a sheet of waxed paper on a metal cooking sheet and place in the freezer. When bananas are frozen solid, remove from freezer. Place frozen bananas in juicer with no mesh attachment and turn on your juicer. You will have to plunge the frozen banana into the machine with the plunger attachment. Out will come creamy soft serve ice cream. One banana equals ½ cup serving. This recipe yields 4 one cup servings or 8 one-half cup servings. This soft serve ice cream can be frozen and eaten as regular ice cream instead of the soft serve.

All Fruit All Natural Soft Serve Ice Cream
Following the previous banana soft serve or regular ice cream recipe, we tried using frozen strawberries to see what that would produce. It worked exactly like the banana ice cream recipe above however I feel that most people, me included, would find the soft serve produced by the frozen strawberries to be too tart. We added a small amount of sugar, which made it acceptable to our palates.

2 cups frozen strawberries = ¾ cup soft serve ice cream

If sugar is a problem for you allergy wise or blood sugar wise, you could try adding a pinch of stevia as a sweetener as that is a root plant and does not have the same effect on your body as sugar or other sweeteners.

Banana Strawberry Swirl Ice Cream
Using a heavy-duty juicer in combination with bananas and strawberries will produce a nice ice cream that needs no sugar!

1 whole banana, frozen (peel before freezing)
4 to 5 whole strawberries, frozen

Put half of the banana though the juicer followed by 2 frozen strawberries. Repeat the process with remaining banana and strawberries. Makes 2 one-half cup servings or one cup.

Non-Dairy Vanilla Ice Cream

This recipe requires the use of an automatic ice cream maker. Be careful when mixing the DariFree™, as it can "explode" easily if mixed in a container with a tight lid.

16 ounces hot water
⅔ heaping cup DariFree™ powder

Mix well, then add the following:

½ cup sugar
1 tablespoon Egg Replacer™ dry powder
1 tablespoon acceptable oil (e.g. olive or safflower)
½ teaspoon pure vanilla extract (use only if making
    vanilla ice cream)
Pinch of salt

Carefully mix hot water and DariFree™ in a blender. Add sugar, Egg Replacer™ dry powder, oil, and pure vanilla and blend to mix well. Transfer the liquid into a refrigerator container and refrigerate until well chilled. You could also place it in the freezer for 30 minutes or so. Once the mixture is very cold, pour it in the frozen ice cream canister and begin machine. The ice cream will get to the stage of soft custard and then it is done, which will take about 12-15 minutes depending upon your ice cream maker. Place soft custard in a plastic container and freeze. Remove ice cream about 5 minutes prior to serving so it can soften just a little, but do not leave out too long.

Raspberry Ice Cream

Follow the preceding recipe omitting the pure vanilla extract and adding 1 teaspoon of raspberry extract and 1 to 1½ cups fresh or frozen raspberries (that have been thawed) to the liquid ingredients. Follow remaining directions.

Chocolate Ice Cream

Add ⅓ cup chocolate syrup to the liquid ingredients. Follow preceding recipe directions.

Chocolate Chocolate Chip Ice Cream

Add ⅓ cup chocolate syrup to the liquid ingredients. Follow preceding recipe directions, adding ½ cup to ¾ cup acceptable crushed or chopped chocolate chips to the soft custard ice cream after it comes out of the ice cream maker and before it goes into the freezer.

Gourmet Chocolate Ice Cream

Add ⅓ cup chocolate syrup to the liquid ingredients, and in place of the pure vanilla extract, use 1 teaspoon of cherry extract. This will give your chocolate ice cream some pizzazz and a bit of mystery.

Mint Chocolate Chip Ice Cream

Delete the pure vanilla extract and use 1 teaspoon of mint extract. You can use a few drops of natural food coloring to give your ice cream that store-bought look if desired. Add ½ to ¾ cup crushed or chopped chocolate chip pieces to the ice cream once it comes out of the ice cream maker, stirring well before freezing.

Cookie Dough Ice Cream

Add chunks of unbaked cookie dough to your ice cream after it is a soft custard and before it is frozen in the freezer. You will use about 1 cup of cookie dough, which should be added in teaspoons to your soft custard. This is delicious!

Rice or Soy Ice Cream

This recipe requires the use of an automatic ice cream maker.

24 to 28 ounces rice milk or soy milk
½ cup sugar or other sweetener
1 tablespoon Egg Replacer™ dry powder
1 tablespoon oil
½ teaspoon pure vanilla extract
Pinch of salt

Place all ingredients into a blender and mix well. Transfer to a container and store in the refrigerator until very cold, about 2 hours. You can also place in the freezer for 30 or more minutes. Once it is very cold, pour it into your automatic ice cream maker.

Chocolate Ice Cream
Add ⅓ cup chocolate syrup to the liquid ingredients. Follow above directions.

Mint Chocolate Chip Ice Cream
Follow above recipe deleting the pure vanilla and adding instead 1 teaspoon of mint extract, and several drops of natural food coloring if desired. After the ice cream is nearly done, add ½ to ¾ cup crushed or chopped chocolate chip pieces.

Chocolate Chocolate Chip Ice Cream
Use base recipe omitting the pure vanilla extract and adding ⅓ cup chocolate syrup to the mixture instead. Follow recipe instructions above adding ½ to ¾ cup chopped or crushed chocolate chips at the end of the ice cream making session.

Gourmet Chocolate Ice Cream
Add ⅓ cup chocolate syrup to the liquid ingredients, and in place of the pure vanilla extract, use 1 teaspoon of cherry extract. This will give your chocolate ice cream some pizzazz and a bit of mystery.

Raspberry Ice Cream
Omit pure vanilla extract and use 1 teaspoon of raspberry extract or flavoring instead. Add 1 to 1 ½ cups of fresh or frozen raspberries and follow above directions.

Cookie Dough Ice Cream
Add chunks of unbaked cookie dough to your ice cream after it is a soft custard and before it is frozen in the freezer. You will use about 1 cup of cookie dough, which should be added in teaspoons to your soft custard. This is delicious!

Sweet Sorbets

Here are the basics for making a nice sorbet.

The foundation for sorbet is a simple syrup which is just white sugar and water. Heat equal parts sugar and water in a saucepan and heat until the sugar is completely dissolved and the syrup is clear with no sugar crystals. Let the simple syrup cool. Then add your fruit or flavoring to the simple syrup and mix in an ice cream maker.

Raspberry Sorbet

¾ cup water
¾ cup sugar
2 cups raspberries (fresh or frozen)

Mix water and sugar in a saucepan. Heat to make a simple syrup as above and cool. Strain the seeds from the raspberries by mashing them through a fine mesh strainer. Mix the raspberries and simple syrup and place in ice cream maker. You can vary the strength of the taste by the quantity of simple syrup you use and the quantity of fruit.

Strawberry Sorbet

¾ cup water
¾ cup sugar
2 cups strawberries (fresh or frozen)

Mix water and sugar in a saucepan. Heat to make a simple syrup as above and cool. Strain the seeds from the strawberries. Mix the strawberries and simple syrup and place in ice cream maker. You can vary the strength of the taste by the quantity of simple syrup you use and the quantity of fruit.

Flavored Ices

Flavored ices only require the use of a freezer. They can be made with less sugar and as a result are not as creamy as ice creams or sorbets. They must be scraped out of a container with the tines of a fork or other scraping tool. The more sugar in the flavored ice, the easier it will be to get out of the container and serve.

Lemon Ice

This is one of my children's favorites. It is a treat on a hot summer day. You can use another acceptable sweetener than sugar if needed.

1 cup sugar or other sweetener
2 cups pure drinking water
Dash of salt
2 teaspoons fresh lemon zest (children may not like
   this ingredient)
½ cup lemon juice

Place the sugar and water in a medium saucepan and heat over medium heat until it comes to a light boil. Reduce heat and cook for 2 minutes. Remove from heat and allow to cool completely. Add the salt, fresh lemon zest and lemon juice. Stir well, and place in a container in the freezer for several hours. Because this is an ice, you will need to use a scraper, tines of a fork, or sharp blade to scrape the ice out to serve.

Lime Ice

This has significantly less sugar than the Lemon Ice recipe. It is harder to scrape out of the container, yet it is very refreshing on a hot day!

4 tablespoons lime juice
4 tablespoons sugar or other sweetener
1½ cups pure drinking water

Mix ingredients well and freeze. Stir after the lime ice has been in the freezer for two or so hours and then re-freeze. Because this is an ice, you will need to use a scraper, tines of a fork, or sharp blade to scrape the ice out to serve.

Cranberry Ice

8 ounces of pure cranberry juice*
8 ounces of pure drinking water
4 tablespoons sugar or other sweetener

*This recipe adds sugar because pure cranberry juice is very tart. If you are using diluted or sweetened cranberry juice, then you can decrease or eliminate the sugar in the recipe. Mix all ingredients well. Place into a container and freeze. After the cranberry ice has been in the freezer for two hours, remove and stir well. Place back into the freezer until frozen. Because this is an ice it will require a scraper, tines of a fork, or sharp blade to scrape the ice out for serving.

Watermelon Ice

¼ or ⅛ of a watermelon

Optional:

Sugar or other sweetener

Seed watermelon and cut into chunks. Process the watermelon in either a food processor or a blender until mushy. Sugar is not required or necessary; however you can add a small amount of sugar if desired. Place the liquid watermelon into a freezer container and freeze. Use the tines of a fork, or other sharp blade to scrape out servings of the watermelon ice.

Beverages

Homemade Rice Milk

The reason that I am including a rice milk recipe is because for a while there were no commercial rice milks available that my daughter could tolerate. Most commercially made rice milks contain oil and added vitamins for nutrition. This particular recipe is a bit thicker than commercially made rice milks. If you like thinner rice milk, simply increase the water in the recipe by 1 to 2 cups or until desired consistency.

2 cups cooked rice, cooled
2 cups pure drinking water
¼ teaspoon salt
Sweetener, if desired (to taste)
Oil, if desired (to taste or for added calories)

Blend the water and rice in a blender until smooth and creamy. Add salt, sweetener and oil if using. My children's tastes dictated a small amount of sweetener was necessary. You can add oil for nutrition, if desired, but be forewarned that it will separate unless you add a blending/binding ingredient like xanthan gum. We do not add oil. Use within 5 to 7 days. Store in the refrigerator. This recipe yields approximately 2½ cups. If you thin the rice milk out more, you will obviously increase the recipe yield.

Homemade Sunflower Milk

1½ cups pure drinking water
¾ cup raw, organic sunflower seeds
¼ teaspoon sea salt

Soak the above in a bowl for 24 hours.

2 tablespoons maple syrup
½ teaspoon salt
1 quart or more of pure drinking water

After soaking, drain the sunflower seeds and place in a blender. Add maple syrup and salt and half of the water. Blend until smooth and creamy. Add remaining water and blend again. This can be a beverage to drink or it can be used for making ice cream or for cooking. This sunflower milk will thicken substantially as it stands, so you will have to add water to get it to the desired consistency that you like. Use in 5 to 7 days. Makes 1- 1 ½ quarts.

Non-Dairy Milk Shake

There is nothing like a milk shake on a hot day. Non-dairy milk shakes are just as refreshing. You can make them ahead and freeze the milk shake to have a cool frozen treat.

½ cup non-dairy milk your choice
⅓ to ½ cup non-dairy ice cream of your choice
1 teaspoon sugar or other sweetener
1 teaspoon chocolate sauce or syrup (see page 365)

Optional:

Vitamins, minerals or supplements

Blend until creamy. Makes one serving.

Vitamin Shake

12 ounces rice milk or other non-dairy milk
2 tablespoons cranberry juice*
2 tablespoons honey or other sweetener
Vitamins: as indicated

*Pure unsweetened cranberry juice is used in this recipe. If you are using a diluted, sweetened cranberry juice then you will probably want to decrease or eliminate the honey for this recipe. Blend all ingredients with 5 or 6 ice cubes.

Vitamin Water

My son Noah saw "vitamin water" in the health food store and wanted to make some at home! I thought this was a fabulous idea. Noah went right to work and created this recipe. We saved some empty 12-ounce glass bottles that had organic lemon juice in them and they made the perfect vitamin water bottles.

½ cup pure cranberry juice (or other juice)
½ cup pure drinking water
4 teaspoons sugar or other sweetener
Vitamins and minerals of your choice

Mix all ingredients well. Makes 1 cup. I can say with certainty that this is one great way to get vitamins and minerals into your children. You can use any other kind of juice with water. The sugar or other sweetener is only necessary if you use pure cranberry juice because it will be too tart otherwise.

Noah's Organic Cranberry Grape Juice

Noah invented this recipe at about age seven. We had pure organic cranberry juice on hand, and he did not like the taste. Too tart for most of us!

4 ounces organic cranberry juice
4 ounces organic grape juice
8 ounces pure drinking water
3 tablespoons sugar

Mix well. Makes 16 ounces juice.

Fresh Squeezed Lemonade

I never thought about making fresh squeezed or homemade lemonade until Sister Helen Sharkey from Saint Elizabeth's parish in Whitehall, Pennsylvania taught me. This recipe is helpful when you have a child who cannot tolerate preservatives and additives. I've listed sugar as an ingredient, however you can use any other sweetening agent if you cannot tolerate cane sugar or if you are doing a rotation diet and use a different sweetener on your lemon day. Besides using fresh squeezed lemon juice, you may also use bottled organic lemon juice. You can use more or less sugar depending upon your tolerance for tartness.

Ingredient	Single Serving	One Quart	Half Gallon
pure water	¾ cup	3¼ cups	6½ cups
lemon juice	2 tablespoons	½ cup	1 cup
sugar	2 tablespoons	½ cup	1 cup

As a reference, 1 large lemon equals about 3 tablespoons of lemon juice.

Green Smoothies

We were introduced to green smoothies by Christine Schaefer, a friend who advocates and lives on the raw foods diet. The basic idea is to combine fresh greens like kale or spinach with fresh fruits and water to make a tasty beverage rich in nutrition. My husband and I were a bit doubtful, but we were quite easily won over by the good taste of the green smoothies. You really, really don't need a recipe to make a green smoothie, but I wrote down two of ours for those of you who would otherwise be too timid to try it! This is an outstanding way to get fruits and vegetables into your children!

One thing that you can do with the smoothies is to add vitamins or the flavored cod liver oil. I would only use the flavored cod liver oil if you are not allergic to fish. Cod liver oil is one of the best oils for you if your allergies allow for it.

Apple-Raspberry Smoothie

> 1 cup pure drinking water
> 2 apples, cored and sliced
> ½ cup raspberries, either fresh or frozen
> 3 fresh kale leaves

Mix the water, apples and raspberries in the blender and purée until smooth. Then add the kale leaves and blend until smooth and creamy. You may add more water if necessary. This makes 2 servings or a little more than 2 cups.

Banana-Blueberry Smoothie

2 bananas
½ cup blueberries (fresh or frozen)
⅓ cup pure drinking water
2 fresh kale leaves or 2 handfuls of spinach

Mix the bananas, water, and blueberries in a blender until creamy and smooth. Add the 2 fresh kale leaves and blend until the kale is puréed and smooth. Add more water if necessary. This makes 2 cups or 16 ounces.

Banana-Raspberry Smoothie

This is a great way to get vitamins into yourself or your children.

1 banana
1 cup raspberry ice cream (recipe in this cookbook)
2 cups non-dairy milk
2 tablespoons sugar or other sweetener, if desired

Optional:

Vitamins and minerals

Blend all ingredients in a blender until well mixed. Makes over 2 cups.

Non-Dairy Hot Chocolate Mix

With this recipe you can have instant and portable hot chocolate. This is a powdered, non-dairy hot chocolate mix that uses DariFree™ as a base. You could use other non-dairy powdered milk substitutes and adjust the sugar if needed. If you love hot chocolate, you may want to double this recipe! We limit chocolate in our house, so this is a real treat!

2 cups DariFree™ Milk Substitute powder
⅓ heaping cup Hershey's® Cocoa powder
¾ cup sugar
Dash of salt

Mix above and store in an airtight container. To make hot chocolate, spoon 3 tablespoons of the mix into a mug. Add a little boiling water (1 to 2 tablespoons) and mix well. Then fill mug with hot water.

Non-Dairy Hot Chocolate

If you have acceptable chocolate syrup on hand, you can have hot chocolate or chocolate milk anytime!

1 to 2 tablespoons chocolate syrup (see page 365)
8 ounces non-dairy milk substitute

Mix chocolate syrup and non-dairy milk substitute in a saucepan and heat until boiling. Remove from heat immediately and serve.

Chocolate Syrup (Corn-Free)

Single Batch	Double Batch
1 cup sugar	2 cups sugar
½ cup cocoa powder	1 cup cocoa powder
Dash of salt	2 dashes of salt
1 cup water	2 cups of water
Optional:	
1 teaspoon of pure vanilla extract	1 teaspoon of pure vanilla extract

Mix the sugar, cocoa, and salt in a saucepan. Add the water and mix well. Bring to a boil stirring constantly, then reduce the heat and simmer for 2 or 3 minutes. Be careful not to burn. Chocolate scorches easily so don't leave this unattended. Remove from heat and add pure vanilla extract if using it. Once the syrup is cool, store in the refrigerator. This can be used to make chocolate milk, milkshakes, or poured over ice cream. A single batch makes about 1 cup. Syrup can be made thicker by reducing the amount of water used.

Heavenly Kahlúa®

This is a recipe that was given to me by Barbara Hornak some years ago. This is an excellent recipe that fooled even some astute bartenders in my hometown. This is for adults only!

> **2 cups vodka (80 proof)**
> **2 cups pure drinking water**
> **1¼ cups sugar**
> **1½ tablespoons pure vanilla extract**
> **1½ tablespoons instant coffee**

Place the water and sugar in a saucepan and bring to a boil. Boil for about 5 minutes and then remove from heat and add pure vanilla extract and instant coffee. Allow to cool and then add the vodka. Serve on the rocks and share with a friend!

Miscellaneous Recipes

Special Seasoning Salt

1 tablespoon salt
½ teaspoon white pepper
1 teaspoon garlic powder
½ teaspoon sweet basil
1 teaspoon onion salt
½ teaspoon crushed rosemary
½ teaspoon thyme
1 tablespoon chopped dried onion
½ teaspoon dried mustard
½ teaspoon oregano
1 tablespoon parsley
1 tablespoon sugar
Dash of turmeric
Dash of paprika

Optional:

Dash of cayenne pepper
To taste: fresh ground pepper

Mix all together and store in a airtight container. This can be used on French fries, mashed or sliced potatoes, on meats or vegetables. It is an ingredient in the dry soup base in this cookbook.

Cream of Amaranth Cereal

This is an easy breakfast cereal to make. You can top your cereal off with fresh fruit if desired.

⅓ cup amaranth grain
1 cup water
To taste: sweetener

Bring the water and amaranth grain to a boil and then reduce heat to low and simmer until the water is absorbed by the amaranth grain. Sweeten with maple syrup, honey, sugar or other sweetener as desired.

Turkey Giblet Broth

This is what to do with the turkey or chicken neck and giblets that you get with a full bird. Most people throw the giblets and neck out simply for lack of knowing what to do with the bird parts. Once you have this broth, you can use it in soups, to cook pasta with and anywhere broth is required.

4 cups pure drinking water (you will need to add about
   2 cups of water to the broth as it cooks down
1 turkey neck, raw
   giblets from bag in turkey
1 onion, peeled and cut in quarters
2 cloves of garlic, peeled, whole
To taste: salt and pepper

Place neck and giblets in water with onion and garlic. Boil for 25 minutes making sure to "skim the scum" while cooking. Reduce heat to a rolling simmer and cook for another 30 minutes. This is a great use for those parts that you don't typically use.

Annie's Mock Butter

½ cup olive oil
1 tablespoon DariFree™ dry powder
½ cup lard
1 tablespoon water
¼ teaspoon salt (more to taste)
¼ teaspoon xanthan gum

Mix the above in a blender. This will be a creamy white color. You may add coloring to give it more of a "butter" look either with food coloring or by using a dash of a natural spice like turmeric. This recipe is a modified version of the Better Butter recipe from Laurel's Kitchen.

Taco Seasoning Mix

6 teaspoons chili powder
4½ teaspoons cumin
5 teaspoons paprika
3 teaspoons onion powder
2½ teaspoons   garlic powder
⅛ teaspoon cayenne pepper

Mix ingredients together and store in an airtight container. This is twice as strong as the store-bought packets and has none of the preservatives, so use one-half the amount or sparingly.

Note: We've found this to be a great item to mix and have on hand for when we are making quesadillas or tacos, etc.

Lisa's Creamy Dry Soup Base

I created this recipe so that we could have chicken divan and other recipes that call for a cream of celery-type soup. You can use it to make soup with or to make a white cream sauce. It is flavorful.

½ cup DariFree™ dry powder
½ cup potato starch (or rice flour or other acceptable flour substitute)
1 tablespoon salt
½ teaspoon white pepper
1 teaspoon garlic powder
½ teaspoon sweet basil
1 teaspoon onion salt
½ teaspoon crushed rosemary
½ teaspoon thyme
1 tablespoon chopped dried onion
½ teaspoon dried mustard
½ teaspoon oregano
1 tablespoon parsley
1 tablespoon sugar
Dash of turmeric
Dash of paprika

Optional:

Dash of cayenne pepper

Mix above and store in an airtight container. To use, mix about 4 tablespoons of dry soup base with about 8 ounces of water. It can also be used in your own recipes that call for a condensed cream soup. This will thicken as it cooks.

Allergy-Free Baking Powder

If you are really restricted because of your allergies, you may need to make your own baking powder. At least we did for a few years. This recipe is one that you make in small quantities as it does not store well.

½ teaspoon cream of tartar
¼ teaspoon baking soda
¼ teaspoon potato starch or tapioca flour

This will equal one teaspoon of regular baking powder. You can use cornstarch for the potato starch or tapioca, but the recipe above is corn-free for those restricted in their corn use.

Gluten-Free Play Dough

This is our family play dough recipe converted to be gluten-free.

1½ cups gluten-free flour
¾ cup salt
3 teaspoons cream of tartar
1½ cups cool water
1½ tablespoons oil
natural food coloring

Mix dry ingredients together in a large pot. Add all of the liquids and mix well. Cook over a medium heat, stirring constantly. Remove from heat when the dough pulls away from the sides of the pot and can be pinched without sticking. Turn onto a board or counter and knead until smooth. Professional decorating pastes (used in frostings) can be used to color the dough instead of food coloring. This recipe makes about 3 cans of play dough. You can double the recipe, however it does work best to have the coloring added during cooking instead of trying to add it after the dough is made.

Baking Soda Play Clay

This is an easy recipe which children will enjoy. This play clay can be allowed to air dry if your children make items that they want preserved.

2 cups baking soda
1 cup cornstarch
1¼ cups water

Optional:

Natural food coloring or non-toxic paints

Place the baking soda, cornstarch and water in a medium saucepan and mix well. Over low heat, cook mixture, stirring continuously until the dough becomes a consistency of mashed potatoes. This will take up to 15 or so minutes. Remove from heat and separate into 3 or 4 bowls if you are adding food coloring. Add a different food coloring to each and enjoy! If you don't want to use natural food coloring, you can use candy coloring or the cake frosting coloring to the play clay. This will air dry in about 12 hours. The play clay pieces can also be painted with non-toxic or acrylic paints. As with all play dough or play clays, you can use cookie cutters, a garlic press, and other kitchen tools to style and shape your clay figures. This makes about 3 cups of play clay.

Finger Paints

This is an old recipe for homemade finger paints. The finished product is not nearly as nice as store-bought finger paints. However, for children who react to some ingredients in commercially made finger paints, this at least provides an alternative.

4 tablespoons sugar
½ cup cornstarch
2 cups cold water
natural food coloring

In a medium saucepan, mix the sugar and cornstarch together. Add the cold water and then cook over medium heat until the mixture thickens. This will thicken a bit more once it is cooled. Divide the mixture into three or four bowls or containers and add a different food coloring to each. Naturally made food colorings can be found at some health food stores or on-line. These naturally made food colorings are made from colorful foods like beets, turmeric, and blueberries.

Homemade Stickers

Can you believe it? Stickers made at home. And wait until you see how easy they are to make! Start with this small batch. A little bit goes a long way! This is the perfect way to recycle old gift wrap. This is a great activity to do with children and adults.

Small Batch Size: (Enough for 3 or 4 children to use)
  2 tablespoons white, washable, non-toxic glue
  2 tablespoons white vinegar

Large Batch Size: (Enough for a large group)
  ¼ cup white, washable, non-toxic glue
  ¼ cup white vinegar

The following are needed for all batch sizes:

  **Collection decorative papers or scraps of old recycled
    gift wrap or cut out pictures from magazines.
  1 paint brush for each child or adult
  Several cookie sheets (for sticker paper to air dry on)**

Mix equal parts of glue and vinegar in a small mixing bowl. Using a paint brush, quickly paint the white liquid on the back of decorative papers, scraps of old gift wrap, and/or pictures from magazines. Allow to air dry. We found it best to work on a surface of scrap paper and to then move the wet papers to a cookie sheet to dry.

Once the papers are dry, apply a second coat of the white glue mixture to the back of the papers and allow to air dry again. The sticker paper is now ready to use. You can use decorative paper punches to punch out shapes, or you can cut out your own shapes. To moisten the sticker for use, wet a paper towel or sponge and dab the back of the sticker.

Laundry Soap

If you have trouble with allergies, it may be wise to consider some hypoallergenic laundry supplies. We have found the following works very well for regular laundry loads. Baking soda and vinegar can be purchased in large quantities in discount warehouse-type stores rather inexpensively. This mixture would not be cost effective if you are not purchasing the baking soda and vinegar at a warehouse supply store.

For an Extra Large Load:
   ½ cup baking soda
   1 cup white vinegar

Start your laundry on hot water and add the baking soda right away so it begins to dissolve. The reason for this is that baking soda dissolves better in hot water than in any other temperature we have found. You can swish the water around to speed up the process. Add ⅓ of the vinegar to the washtub, ⅓ to the bleach cup, and ⅓ to the fabric softener cup or dispenser. Then turn your wash load to the temperature that you plan on using like warm or cold, and add your laundry. For smaller loads, use less.

For Extra Dirty Loads or Bleaching Effect:
Use the same ingredients above, and add:
   ¼ cup Borax
   ¼ cup Arm & Hammer Washing Soda

Dissolve these ingredients in the washer tub, add you laundry and wash as usual. We find that these two products work well to brighten white loads or to add extra washing power to dirty loads.

Toilet Bowl Cleaner

Baking soda and white vinegar work well to clean your toilet bowl. Simply add a few tablespoons of baking soda and ½ cup vinegar to the toilet bowl, and scrub as usual.

Bathtub Cleaner

To scrub your bathtub, you can use good old baking soda and white vinegar. We sprinkle the baking soda all over the tub, and scrub with a scrub brush dipped in white vinegar.

Appendix A

Cooking Measures

Many years ago I purchased a refrigerator magnet that had cooking measures printed on it. I would have to say that this is one of my most valued items. If I lost the magnet, I would have to replace it, or at least the information on it. It is so valuable that I am going to include the measurements here with the idea that you could copy this page and cut out the measurements and keep them handy in your kitchen.

1 cup = 8 fl. oz.	= 16 Tbsp	= 48 tsp	= 237 ml
¾ cup = 6 fl. oz.	= 12 Tbsp	= 36 tsp	= 177 ml
⅔ cup = 5⅓ fl. oz.	= 10⅔ Tbsp	= 32 tsp	= 158 ml
½ cup = 4 fl. oz.	= 8 Tbsp	= 24 tsp	= 118 ml
⅓ cup = 2⅔ fl. oz.	= 5⅓ Tbsp	= 16 tsp	= 79 ml
¼ cup = 2 fl. oz.	= 4 Tbsp	= 12 tsp	= 59 ml
⅛ cup = 1 fl. oz.	= 2 Tbsp	= 6 tsp	= 30 ml
½ fl. oz.	= 1 Tbsp	= 3 tsp	= 15 ml

Appendix B

Organizations and Resources

Allergy Companies & Resources

Allergy Buyers Club
AllergyBuyersClub.com
486 Totten Pond Road, 3rd Floor
Waltham, MA 02451-1917
1-888-252-3148
This company sells air cleaners, HEPA vacuum cleaners, dehumidifiers and other allergy related products.

Austin Air Systems, Limited
C/o Customer Service
500 Elk Street
Buffalo, NY 14210
Toll-Free: 1-800-724-8403
www.austinair.com
Air purifiers for allergy consumers,

Blueair
Blueair Inc.
17 N. State, Suite 1830
Chicago, IL 60602
Toll-Free: 1-888-258-3247 (1-888-BLUEAIR) FAX: (312) 727-1153
www.blueair.com
Air purifiers for allergy consumers.

Food Allergy & Anaphylaxis Network, The (FAAN)
11781 Lee Jackson Highway, Suite 160
Fairfax, VA 22033-3309
Toll-Free 1-800-929-4040 FAX: (703) 691-2713
faan@foodallergy.org or *www.foodallergy.org*
Food allergy non-profit organization.

Autism Organizations

Autism One
www.autismone.org
Edmund Arranga - Executive Director, 714-680-0792
Offers the most comprehensive conference on autism as well as a social networking site, radio programs and many other resources.

Autism Research Institute
4182 Adams Avenue
San Diego, CA 92116
FAX: (619) 563-6840
www.autismwebsite.com
One of the first autism organizations formed by Bernard Rimland, Ph.D. (1928-2006), who is considered to be the father of autism and pioneer in autism research.

Autism Society of America
7910 Woodmont Avenue, Suite 300
Bethesda, Maryland 20814-3067 USA
(301) 657-0881
Toll-Free: 1-800-328-8476
www.autism-society.org
Autism non-profit organization.

Autism Speaks
2 Park Avenue
11th Floor
New York, New York 10016
(212) 252-8584
FAX: (212) 252-8676
www.autismspeaks.org
Autism non-profit organization;   NAAR (National Alliance for Autism Research has merged with Autism Speaks).

Generation Rescue
info@generationrescue.org
www.generationrescue.org
Autism non-profit organization.

National Alliance for Autism Research (NAAR)
NAAR has merged with Autism Speaks; see previous listing for
Autism Speaks (*www.autismspeaks.org*).

National Autism Association
1330 W. Schatz Lane
Nixa, MO 65714
Toll-Free 1-877-622-2884
naa@nationalautism.org
www.nationalautismassociation.org
Autism non-profit organization.

Safe Minds
Sensible Action for Ending Mercury-Induced Neurological
Disorders
254 Trickum Creek Road
Tyrone, GA 30290
(404) 934-0777
eksafeminds@gmail.com
www.safeminds.org
Autism non-profit organization.

Celiac Organizations

Celiac Disease Foundation
13251 Ventura Blvd. #1
Studio, CA 91606
(818) 990-2354
www.celiac.org

Celiac Sprue Association USA
PO BOX 31700
Omaha, NE 68131-0700
(402) 558-0600
www.csaceliacs.org

Gluten Intolerance Group (GIG®)
31214 124th Avenue SE
Auburn, WA 98092
(253) 833-6655
FAX: (253) 833-6675
www.gluten.net
E-mail: *info@gluten.net*

Dietary Intervention Organizations

Feingold® Association of the United States, The
554 East Main Street, Suite 301
Riverhead, NY 11901
(631) 369-9340, FAX (631) 369-2988
E-mail: *fausmem@yahoo.com*
Website: *www.feingold.org*
This organization offers support for parents and consumers looking at dietary intervention for a wide range of symptoms and behaviors. Their website has a good selection of medical references to support the positive impact of changing your diet.

GFCF Diet Support Group
www.gfcfdiet.com
PO BOX 1692
Palm Harbor, FL 34683

Gluten-Free & Specialty Food Companies

In addition to the companies that are listed in this section, there are many other manufacturers that make gluten-free products, flours and mixes. Due the fact that we limit our rice, potato, corn and soy intake and that we have to avoid other foods, we do not use baking mixes and other commercially made gluten-free foods. Commercial mixes are expensive, and I found many did not work well with egg substitutes. You can find additional manufacturers of gluten-free foods online that may suit your needs.

Authentic Foods
1850 W. 169th Street, Suite B
Gardena, CA 90247
(310) 366-7612
www.authenticfoods.com
Gluten-free products sold through retail stores, online Internet businesses and through their own online supermarket: *www.glutenfree-supermarket.com*

Barkat
Gluten-Free Foods, LTD (U.K.)
www.glutenfree-foods.co.uk
This is a United Kingdom company that manufacturers a variety of gluten-free foods that are often dairy-free and nut-free. These products can be purchased through a variety of online sources and in some specialty stores.
We particularly like the Barkat Organic Porridge Flakes, and in the past have used their gluten-free, dairy-free ice cream cones. Look for their products at the Gluten-Free Mall and your favorite gluten-free outlet.

Bob's Red Mill
5209 SE International Way
Milwaukee, OR 87222
1-800-349-2173
www.bobsredmill.com
Sells both gluten-free *and* gluten flours and other specialty baking ingredients.

Dakota Lakes Products
1305 6th Avenue, NW
Jamestown, ND 58401-2105
(701) 952-2611
www.dakota-lakes.com
Makes an outstanding gourmet coating mix that is gluten-free and dairy-free that can be used for meats, poultry, potatoes and vegetables!

Ener-G Foods, Inc.
5960 First Avenue South
PO BOX 84487
Seattle, WA 98124-5787
1-800-331-5222
www.ener-g.com
An established manufacturer of gluten-free flours, Egg Replacer™, gluten-free pasta, pretzels and other gluten-free / dairy-free items.

Enjoy Life Foods
3810 River Road
Schiller Park, IL 60176-2307
1-888-503-6579
(847) 260-0300
FAX: (847) 260-0306
www.enjoylifefoods.com
Markets gluten-free, dairy-free specialty food items like chocolate chips that don't contain gluten, dairy, soy or nuts!

GLUTANO
Gluten-Free Foods, LTD (U.K.)
www.glutenfree-foods.co.uk
This is a United Kingdom company that manufacturers a variety of gluten-free foods that are often dairy-free and nut-free. These products can be purchased through a variety of online sources and in some specialty stores.

We particularly like the GLUTANO Ice Cream Cones and pasta. Look for their products at the Gluten-Free Mall and your favorite gluten-free outlet. Their products are out if you have a corn allergy as they most often contain a high amount of maize flour (corn flour) and maize starch (corn starch).

Gluten-Free Mall, The
4927 Sonoma Highway, Suite C1
Santa Rosa, CA 95409
Toll-Free 1-866-575-3720 or (707) 509-4528
FAX: (707) 324-6060
www.glutenfreemall.com
Online business selling gluten-free and allergy friendly foods.

Gluten-Free Trading Company, LLC
3116 S. Chase Avenue
Milwaukee, WI 53207
(414) 747-8700
FAX: (414) 747-8747
info@food4celiacs.com
www.gluten-free.net
Online business selling gluten-free products.

Gluten Solutions
www.glutensolutions.com
Online business selling gluten-free products.

Mrs. Leeper's Pasta
World Finer Foods Inc.
300 Broadacres Drive
Bloomfield, NJ 0700
(973) 338-0300
www.mrsleepers.com
Gluten-free pasta made from rice and corn.

Nu World Amaranth
922 S. Charles Avenue
Naperville, IL 60540
(630) 369-6819
www.nuworldfoods.com
Makes a nice selection of amaranth grain based products
including cereals, flours, flatbreads as well as flours and other
snack items. These items are gluten-free, and many are also
dairy-free and nut-free.

Perky's™
1-888-4-PERKYS
www.perkysnaturalfoods.com
Five outstanding gluten-free, dairy-free and nut-free cereals,
which you can purchase at select stores in the U.S. and Canada, or
online through the Gluten-Free Mall (*www.glutenfreemall.com*).

Special Foods!
9207 Shotgun Court
Springfield, VA 22153
(703) 644-0991
www.specialfoods.com
They offer a unique line of gluten-free, and gluten flours and
special dietary items that may be of interest to highly sensitive
individual. Not all items are gluten-free.

Squirrel's Nest
One North Broad Street
Middletown, DE 19709
(302) 378-1033
www.squirrels-nest.com
They offer natural food colorings and other products. Not all products are free of milk or other allergens, so buyer beware.

Suzanne's Specialties, Inc.
421 Jersey Avenue, Suite B
New Brunswick, NJ 08901
Toll-Free: 1-800-762-2135
(732) 828-8500
FAX: (732) 828-8563
info@suzannes-specialties.com
www.suzannes-specialties.com
Ricemellow Crème, a non-dairy, gluten-free, vegan alternative to traditional marshmallow crème. Does contain soy.

Tinkyada Rice Pasta
A proud product of Food Directions, Inc.
120 Melford Drive, Unit 8
Scarborough, Ontario, Canada M1B 2X5
(416) 609-0016
FAX: (416) 609-1316
Rice pasta in different forms; available in many health food stores and other food outlets.

Tofutti Brands, Inc.
50 Jackson Drive
Cranford, NJ 07016
(908) 272-2400
info@tofutti.com
www.tofutti.com
Non-dairy sour cream, non-dairy cream cheese, and non-dairy rice cheese, and other non-dairy products. Some items contain gluten, so please read the labels.

Vance's Foods
PO BOX 627
Gilmer, TX 75644
Toll-Free 1-800-497-4834
info@vancesfoods.com
www.vancesfoods.com
Non-fat, non-dairy milk substitute and other non-dairy items.

Miscellaneous Organizations and Companies

Alliance for Natural Health (ANH-USA)
1350 Connecticut Ave NW, 5th Floor
Washington, DC 20036
1-800-230-2762
FAX: 202-315-5837
Website: *www.anh-usa.org*
E-mail: *office@anh-usa.org*
From their website: *"Since 1992, we have worked to shift the medical paradigm from an exclusive focus on surgery, drugs and other conventional techniques to an "integrative" approach incorporating food, dietary supplements and lifestyle changes."*

Beyond Pesticides
701 E Street, SE, Suite 200
Washington, DC 20003
Office Hours: 9 AM-5 PM EST STD
Phone: 202-543-5450
FAX: 202-543-4791
E-mail: *info@beyondpesticides.org*
Excellent information on the impact of pesticides on you and your family.

Environmental Working Group
Washington DC Headquarters
1436 U Street NW, Suite 100
Washington, DC 20009
Phone: 202-667-6982
FAX: 202-232-2592

California Office
1904 Franklin # 703
Oakland, CA 94612
Phone: 510-444-0973
FAX: 510-444-0982
Website: *www.ewg.org*
Excellent organization devoted to the environment and human health

Great Plains Laboratory, Inc., The
11813 West 77th Street
Lenexa, KS 66214
(913) 341-8949, FAX (913) 341-6207
E-mail: *gpl4u@aol.com*
Website: *www.greatplainslaboratory.com*
This laboratory carries a wide array of test kits to help children, adults and families reach their potential.

Index